America's Great Illustrators

America's Great Illustrators

Susan E. Meyer

Galahad Books · New York

Editor: EDITH M. PAVESE
Designer: JOHN S. LYNCH

Copyright © 1978 by Harry N. Abrams B.V., The Netherlands

Published in 1982 by
GALAHAD BOOKS
95 Madison Avenue
New York, NY 10016

Published by arrangement with Harry N. Abrams, Inc., New York
Printed and bound in Japan
10 9 8 7 6 5 4 3 2 1

Library of Congress Catalog Card Number: 82-82721
ISBN 0-88365-645-0

Contents

For My Mother

Acknowledgments

*E*ach of the ten illustrators selected for this volume achieved a considerable degree of fame in his lifetime, yet surprisingly little research has been done on several of them. Where material was absent or inaccessible I was obliged to turn for considerable assistance to several people, friends and associates who gave freely of their time to help. I could not have written this book without them.

Two chapters in particular required major assistance: J. C. Leyendecker and Howard Chandler Christy. For the former I am most sincerely indebted to the author of the only book ever published on this very private artist, Michael Schau, who so graciously provided the material needed to illustrate the chapter. With Howard Chandler Christy—about whom virtually nothing has been written—I was very fortunate indeed. Just at the time I was beginning my research I learned that the Allentown Art Museum in Allentown, Pennsylvania, was preparing the first major exhibition of work by Howard Chandler Christy. The curator of this exhibition, Mimi Miley, her mother Jane Conneen, and her uncle Robert Conneen were invaluable to me in assembling the material for the chapter on Christy, admitting me to Christy's studio for photography, and providing me with essential research data on this too-neglected artist. Without their assistance this chapter could not have been written. Judy Goffman was also of great assistance to me with Christy, and my thanks go also to Norris Schneider of Zanesville, Ohio, for providing me with the only written account of Christy's life in Ohio.

My difficulties with research were greatly eased by the able assistance of Faith Stern, who located the essential dusty volumes and periodicals, and to Tom Bloom of Argosy Book Store, who came through with some crucial reference material when I had just about given up hope. Gene Harris of the Brandywine River Museum went far beyond the call of duty in assembling the pictures and obtaining the permissions for the chapters on Pyle, Wyeth, and Parrish. Thanks also to Lonnie Scheps for his patience and enthusiasm.

I am also indebted to Jean Parrish for her careful reading of the chapter on her father, to Walt Reed for his assistance with the material on John Held Jr., to Mary Ann Crowe for her handling of several important details, to Tony Musak of Studio Nine who performed miracles with the camera, and to Marcy Shain who did as much with the typewriter.

There are no greater aficionados of illustration than those who have been illustrators themselves, a special and wonderful breed of enthusiasts. I am grateful that two of the most impassioned examples of this breed are good friends of mine—Everett Raymond Kinstler and Murray Tinkelman—both of whom have fired me with their enthusiasm for the subject and encouraged me to write about it. The knowledge and understanding of illustration that they have generously shared with me has been a great gift, one for which I will always be most appreciative.

And to Bobbie my eternal gratitude for her consistent patience through the weekends.

Introduction

1. Howard Pyle

For nearly seven centuries all artists in the Western hemisphere were employed to display the wealth and power of their patrons. In the nineteenth century, however, a change occurred and the publishing industry—replacing all traditional patrons—emerged as the chief employer of artists. The publications succeeded both church and court as the great showcase for artists, and illustration, a creation of the Industrial Revolution, became a significant avenue for the artist.

At the end of the nineteenth century and during the early decades of the twentieth, books and periodicals provided the major source of public entertainment. Consequently, the contributors appearing in those pages—the writers and the illustrators—assumed an importance of unprecedented proportions. Now that publishing has surrendered its exclusive power, overshadowed by the more pervasive presence of television, it is not easy for the contemporary reader to imagine the extent of the artists' influence on the public mind. Yet the ten American illustrators represented here were far more than mere picture-makers: they presided over the public and had a crucial role in governing the cultural appetites of the day. No American of that period could possibly remain unaffected by the millions of pictures circulated each week.

The artists of this period were part of an era now called The Golden Age of Illustration. Their part in shaping the American character as we know it today is inextricably linked to the development of an industry whose main purpose is to embrace the aspirations of an entire nation, to create an American Dream.

2. N. C. Wyeth. The Delaware Art Museum, Wilmington

3. Maxfield Parrish

THE SETTING

The years between 1865 and 1917 represent publishing's most exciting and dramatic time of expansion, a period in which the industry evolved from a collection of small enterprises into a great American business institution. Immediately after the Civil War, hundreds of new publications were launched. (While only seven hundred periodicals existed in 1865, for example, by 1900 nearly five thousand more had come into being, a staggering number indeed!) Those publications that survived the nineteenth century became significantly larger and more powerful in the first decades of the twentieth century. It should come as no surprise that the expansion of publishing during these years corresponded directly to the growth of all American industries during the same period. After all, the ingredients needed for the success of publishing were the same as those required for the expansion of any industry: a sufficiently large market, an economical method of manufacture, and an efficient means of distribution. All three of these components fell neatly into place for publishing after the Civil War.

The War Between the States had nationalized the country. The Union Pacific Railroad joined East and West; farmlands in the Midwest grew almost as rapidly as industry in the North, and the American people were becoming homogeneous.

The explosion of books and periodicals produced was a direct result of America's growing demand for reading matter that had increased substantially after the Civil War. The widespread

4

5

introduction of public education throughout the nation had greatly reduced illiteracy, and more Americans than ever now possessed reading skills. Public libraries—another great American institution that expanded substantially after the Civil War as a result of legislation and private philanthropy—provided ready access to reading matter. (In 1876, for example, the United States Commission of Education published the first general statistics on libraries: 12,000,000 volumes were contained in 2500 libraries. By 1896, this number had increased to 33,000,000 in 4000 libraries!) If an appetite for reading had been created by public schools and libraries, private industry had also given Americans the increased time and income needed for reading. Reader consumerism was a direct outgrowth of the Industrial Revolution.

The success of publishing periodicals depends not only on readers, however, but on advertisers as well. The expansion of industry after the Civil War meant new wares to be sold, and periodicals provided the vehicles for manufacturers to hawk their merchandise, competing against their rivals in these pages for a greater share of the market. Starting with the first magazine to carry pages of advertising (*Scribner's* in 1887), this source of income grew increasingly important with the years.

While the market had developed, so had the means of distribution. The growing network of railroads provided an economical and rapid method of carriage across the nation. A new postal law in 1885 reduced the rate for second-class matter to a cent a pound and a rural free delivery system was instituted in 1897. Newsstand distribution became its own kind of business, beginning with the founding of the American News Company in the 1860s, and later replaced by the monopoly created when the Railroad News Company merged with the Union News Company. With this merger the principal retail and the primary wholesale periodical businesses in the nation were united.

Because of the greater dependence on advertising for income, the emphasis was increasingly placed on acquiring more readers at any cost. Sophisticated methods of expanding circulation were instituted—such as premiums—and it became less important to distribute magazines economically, but mandatory to reach more and more readers to attract larger advertising revenues. A circulation of 100,000 may have been considerable in 1890, but relatively insignificant by 1910. Every literate American was reading published material.

Technological improvement had as great an impact on the publishing industry as it had on other industries. Toward the end of the nineteenth century, the rotary press was introduced, a machine that enabled publishers to produce larger editions more rapidly and at lower cost. Of all the technological advances, however, none was more important to the American illustrator than the improvements made in pictorial reproduction. The significance of this advancement is worthy of greater elaboration here, since it was the single most important factor in making it possible for artists to expand their creative powers, liberated from the limitations formerly imposed upon them. This freedom hastened the development of illustration as popular art.

Until the 1880s all reproduction was accomplished by means of wood engraving. The task of preparing the art was arduous and restrictive. On boxwood imported from Syria, the art would be prepared for printing. Boxwood is finely grained, ideal for engraving, but small in size because of the relatively small torso of boxwood trees.

6

4. The Leyendecker brothers: Frank (left) and Joe, in their rooms in Paris, 1896. Courtesy Michael Schau

5. J. C. Leyendecker. Arrow Collar advertisement, 1912. Courtesy The Arrow Company

6. Frederic Remington

11

Introduction

A large illustration might require a composite of several blocks. (As many as thirty-six such blocks, for example, might be used to accommodate an illustration of 16 × 22 inches.) After the block was sliced "type high"—about one-inch thick to conform to the depth of the type—its surface was highly polished and whitened to accept pencil or pen lines. First the artist would draw a rough sketch on paper exactly the size of the single or composite wood blocks. From this, a tracing was made and rubbed, in reverse, onto the block. After tracing, the artist—using a pencil or pen, or brush and India ink—would lay in the main broad shadows. The composite block would then be taken apart and the artist would draw the details of the picture with pencil, pen, or brush, carefully attending to margins and merging tones.

As the blocks were completed in this way, they were sent off to the engraver who would begin the task of cutting out the wood not covered with marks. In other words, the engraver would cut between the lines to create the white areas in the printed form. These engravers sat at high tables to which the blocks were securely fastened. Wearing eye shades as they worked under clear light, and aided by large magnifying glasses, they would make their cuttings with the triangular point of their short-handled gravers. Their work was extremely difficult when shading was required and when lines required cutting at the interstices of the crossings. One inaccurate stroke and an artist's intention could be thoroughly altered. It would take an expert engraver ten or twelve hours to complete a wood engraving 4 × 5 inches in size. A full-page illustration would normally require one week to engrave. When the engraver had completed his work, the blocks were reassembled—bolted together along the back sides—and sent to the press room. During the Civil War and later, when big news events had to be covered rapidly in order to meet imminent deadlines, artists and engravers would sometimes work steadily for as long as thirty-six hours.

The only way to shorten the engraving time was to assign each section of a composite block to a different engraver. For consistency, the engravers were required to have similar styles and skills. Where the sections would meet, the engravers would leave a strip of about ⅛ to ³/₁₆ inch untouched. When the engravers had finished their work, bolts were run through the sections, and the sections joined for a close fit. Then the master engraver tooled across the unfinished strips where the sections joined, bringing together the lines on both sides of the joint.

When the block was inked, only the parts untouched by the graver received the ink, while the recessed portions removed by the tools remained white. A drawing made with sharp pen strokes was obviously the easiest to engrave. On pictures presenting tonal areas the various shades of gray would have to be translated onto a block with delicate, thread-like lines in order to leave sufficient space between to receive the ink. Translating this effect to the tiny network of lines demanded skill and taste on the part of the engraver.

In the 1870s one small technical advance improved the results for those artists preferring to create tonal works: the black-line was substituted by a white-line engraving. In the black-line engraving forms had been defined by areas of wood in high relief that carried the ink. With the white-line method the reverse was true, and the engraver was able to use flecks, dots, or lines to describe tones on the surface of the block. Frederic Remington took advantage of this minor technical advancement, preferring to work realistically whenever possible.

Introduction

7. Norman Rockwell at 25

8. Charles Dana Gibson

Traditional pen-and-ink artists, such as Howard Pyle and A. B. Frost, however, continued to work with black-line engraving.

Artists found it difficult to accept the fact that their drawings were only one step in a complex sequence of operations. (In many instances the engraver actually shared the credit for the illustration by signing his name alongside that of the artist.) The artist was beholden to the engraver, knowing full well that his reproduced illustration was only as good as the craftsman translating the work onto the block. An artist whose style was individual was particularly susceptible to mistranslation. In the hands of a mediocre craftsman his work could be destroyed. It is no wonder that bitterness and animosity often arose between artists and engravers.

Engraving improved greatly throughout the nineteenth century, primarily because of the great number of European craftsmen to enter this country, but the cost of reproduction was extremely high. An average engraver received from $25.00 to $50.00 a week (some even higher), and the House of Harper claimed that it ultimately cost about $500 to engrave an average full-page block.

When photography was introduced into the printing process all this was to ultimately change. The photo-mechanical operation of translating the image to the plate by means of creating a photographic negative permitted the reduction or enlargement of the original design for reproduction. By using the electrotype process (known since 1839), a metal relief plate could be created mechanically from the photographic image, eliminating the need for wood engravers to perform comparable operations by hand. While the engraving of line drawings could be accomplished with relative ease, tonal work required

Introduction

9. Howard Chandler Christy. Courtesy Robert F. Conneen   10. James Montgomery Flagg, 1918

a system of breaking up the continual tones into separate printing elements in order to simulate the middle (or half) tones between black and white. The so-called "halftone process" of photo-engraving provided this solution. With this method, the art was photographed with a large camera through a sheet of glass on which a series of cross lines had been finely and expertly drawn. This photograph would result in a screen negative, the lines of the glass breaking up the tones of the original art into a series of dots, larger or smaller, densely or sparsely populated, depending on the nature of the tones in the original subject. These dots could then be etched into the plate chemically so that the image would be translated onto the final printing surface mechanically in the form suitable for reproduction.

As in most inventions, the credit for the discovery of the halftone process of photo-engraving cannot be attributed to any one inventor, although Frederic Ives is traditionally (if erroneously) credited for the process as a result of his 1881 version of the cross-line screen. During the 1880s the publications experimented extensively with the halftone method of photo-engraving. After the first commercial application of the screen process appeared in the New York *Daily Graphic* (a picture entitled "Shantytown"), other halftones were seen more and more frequently. These early examples tended to be flat and muddy, and engravers were still employed to improve upon the plates produced by the process. But by 1900 halftone reproduction—and the results obtained on the clay-coated papers created specially for the new process—had advanced so greatly that staff artists and engraving departments could be dispensed with altogether. No longer could the engraver be blamed for a poor illustration. No longer could poor

14

Introduction

draftsmanship be concealed with slapdash techniques. The new process recorded everything: it could display the best qualities of an expert illustrator, and expose the deficiencies of the less qualified.

The newly developed screen halftone process created a preference for realistic pictures, fully modeled, and a new school of illustrators emerged to meet this popular demand. By 1900 additional experiments with printing had improved the process sufficiently to permit the printing of color halftones. A work in full color could now be photographed four times through filters (to eliminate all but the desired color each time), in order to separate the four colors—blue, black, yellow, and red—that composed the work. Each color was screened in the same manner as used for a black-and-white halftone, then etched into a metal plate. After the appropriate color ink had been applied to each plate, the four colors could be printed successively onto a sheet of paper, thereby reconstituting the original appearance of the art. Color printing, though it remained costly, became one of the chief attractions in the publishing of books and periodicals, and contemporary illustration advanced greatly as improved technology made possible the reproduction of more ambitious work.

Because of these technological, social, and economic developments hundreds of publishing companies naturally emerged to produce a vast array of books and periodicals. It became a vigorous and aggressive industry that far outrivaled European counterparts. From this large field, only a few companies actually constituted the arena in which appeared America's favorite illustrators. Yet these few publications —and the few illustrators whose work appeared in them—represented a force in American cultural life that is almost unimaginable today. These publications had a major impact on the taste, humor, morals, and buying habits of the public. The aspirations of an entire American civilization, in fact, tended to be influenced by the material printed in these pages! A brief survey of the giants who led their industry through its most colorful period (by and large gentlemen of taste, and generally quite eccentric) provides a rich assortment of personalities as diverse and idiosyncratic as the publications they produced.

11. John Held Jr. Courtesy Mrs. John Held Jr.

THE PUBLICATIONS

Until the War Between the States, the richest pictorial illustration appeared in English books and periodicals. Even the American book publishers tended to rely primarily upon English sources for their material. The British magazines, particularly *Punch* and *The Illustrated London News,* were imported to the States, and the early American illustrators—Howard Pyle, Edwin Abbey, A. B. Frost, for example—were greatly inspired by the English artists whose work they followed regularly. Charles Keene, Arthur Boyd Houghton, John Tenniel, John Leech were among those whose art they admired, as well as the artists who worked only temporarily as illustrators before moving on to their careers as fine artists, such as James McNeill Whistler, Edward Burne-Jones, John Millais, and Dante Gabriel Rossetti.

The publishing arena shifted from England to the United States during the 1860s as the American news weeklies directed their efforts to supplying their readers with written and pictorial reports of the Civil War. The two great American news weeklies of the day were *Frank Leslie's Illustrated Newspaper* and *Harper's Weekly,* each publication

Introduction

12. *Leslie's Illustrated Weekly,* December 14, 1916

13. *Harper's Weekly,* Christmas edition

sending forth its own reporters to provide eyewitness accounts. As a result of this intensive campaign, these publications evolved into mature news magazines, no longer poor imitations of their English counterparts.

Frank Leslie, who had migrated from England and launched his weekly in 1855, originally patterned his publication after *The Illustrated London News* and spared no expense in surpassing its American circulation. Sending as many as a dozen correspondents to the field, Leslie insisted on thorough coverage of the War. At the end of 1864 he boasted, "We have had since the commencement of the present war, over eight artists engaged in making sketches for our paper, and have published nearly three thousand pictures of battles, sieges, bombardments, and other scenes incidental to war." The publication flourished under his direction and under the modified name, *Leslie's Weekly,* providing colorful and lively pictorial representation of the news, reaching its peak during World War I, when the circulation mounted to 400,000.

Nineteenth-century publishing tended to be somewhat of a gentleman's industry, adopting many of the characteristics of an exclusive club. The most eminent member of the club was The House of Harper, a publishing firm founded by the four Harper brothers in the second decade of the 1800s. Known primarily as book publishers of fiction, nonfiction, and textbooks, the Harpers launched their first magazine in 1850, calling it *Harper's New Monthly Magazine,* and using it primarily as an aid to selling their books. Seven years later they began their *Harper's Weekly,* which was described as a "family newspaper" to distinguish it from the more literary *Monthly.* The Civil War guaranteed its success and it competed vigorously against Leslie's publication. While Frank Leslie assigned his staff artist William Waud to the Confederates to report on the campaign against Fort Sumter, for example, *Harper's* commissioned drawings of the battle from several of the officers *within* the fort! Winslow Homer, who had contributed his illustrations regularly to *Harper's* since 1857, has since become the best-known artist to draw the Civil War pictures for *Harper's Weekly.* His scenes of the War tended to be those of everyday life in the camps, and they did much to enhance the prestige of the magazine.

The House of Harper was, for many years, the reigning dynasty of the publishing kingdom. After the successes of both their *Monthly* and *Weekly,* Harper's launched a magazine for women in 1867 which they called *Harper's Bazar* (the second *a* was added to *Bazaar* in 1929, after William Randolph Hearst had purchased the publication). *Harper's Young People,* a monthly magazine established in 1879, rounded out their program to include readers of all ages. The Harpers' headquarters, located on Franklin Square in New York City, became a mecca for the contemporary artists, and every young hopeful dreamed of the time when he, too, might climb the great spiral staircase to triumph at the House of Harper.

Harper's reputation for visual excellence can be attributed to the good taste and keen eye of their art editor, Charles Parsons, who served as Harper's art editor for twenty-six years after succeeding John Chapin in 1863. He was a man "distinctly American in appearance," wrote Howard Pyle, "not the lanky, cadaverous American cast, though. He has a bald forehead, and gray hair, which he brushes back, a gray beard, and wears glasses. He is kind, cordial, and in every way encouraging.... He is a gentleman, and a gentleman of refined tastes."

Introduction

14. *Harper's Monthly,* November, 1908

15. *Harper's Bazar,* June, 1914

16. *Harper's Young People,* March, 1895

Parsons was the most respected art editor of his day, having discovered dozens of artists who were to become eminent in later years. (Remington referred to himself as "Parsons' discovery" and Pyle, another Parsons find, claimed that the art editor was, without doubt, the best art critic in the United States.) Parsons' gift lay in his ability to detect potential in an unformed young artist and to direct the untapped artistic resources toward an authentic form of self-expression. He also directed what was regarded as the finest group of wood engravers of the time. Consequently, the art to burst forth from Harper's during the Parsons tenure was distinguished above all by its singularity, devoid of the imitative qualities frequently seen in other publications.

The success of *Harper's Weekly* and *Monthly* induced other book publishers to launch their own periodicals designed to extend their book publishing programs by featuring the books they were publishing and by serializing their novels to promote the sales of the hardcover editions. Ticknor & Fields purchased the two-year-old *Atlantic Monthly* in 1859, Putnam's operated *Putnam's Monthly Magazine* for four years, and *Scribner's* became the most prestigious publication, attracting some of the best writers of the day and distinguished by its handsome appearance. "To be reproduced in *Scribner's* in 1904," wrote James Montgomery Flagg, "was the same thing to an illustrator as being hung in the Paris Salon was to a painter." Its outstanding visual appearance was the handiwork of Theodore Low DeVinne (a leading reproducer of wood engravings and a distinguished typographer), who was in charge of printing the magazine from 1874 to 1914. Meanwhile Joseph Hawley Chapin, *Scribner's* art editor, was attracting the finest artists of the day. "Joe Chapin," Flagg observed, "because of his friendly ways, his natural dignity, and a thorough knowledge of his profession, was the beau ideal of art editors to us artists."

A dispute within *Scribner's* resulted in a new magazine. In 1881 *Scribner's* ceased publishing its periodical and *The Century Illustrated*

17. *Scribner's* poster. Library of Congress

18. *The Century*

19. *Ladies' Home Journal*

Monthly Magazine was introduced in its place. After five years, *Scribner's* resumed publishing and the two magazines, *Scribner's* and *The Century,* were published simultaneously. *The Century* became a leading literary magazine until its demise in 1930, and *Scribner's* managed to acquire a circulation of about 200,000 by 1910 and advertising that ran more than one hundred pages per month. (Its decline began in 1912 and it finally ceased publication altogether in 1939.)

None of these periodicals, however, could compete successfully with the magazines that emerged toward the end of the nineteenth century. The growing American middle class of the nineties was less high-brow than their predecessors, but they were eager to spend money for good reading matter. The rotary press now made it possible to reach this wider market. The publications to emerge in the 1890s, therefore, lavished large amounts on cultivating this new mass market, attracting the more popular novelists and illustrators with enormous fees, and spending a great deal of money on building circulation to attract bigger advertising revenues. To the American illustrators, the most important of this new breed of so-called "family magazines" included *Ladies' Home Journal, Saturday Evening Post, Collier's, Cosmopolitan,* and *McClure's.*

Cyrus H. K. Curtis—a mild-mannered, white-whiskered gentleman—was one of the first great businessmen in the publishing industry. Unlike his rivals, Curtis did not regard himself as an editor, preferring instead to hire the appropriate person for a particular publication and granting virtual autonomy to the editor of his choice. In his ability to select the ideal man for the position lay Curtis' genius as a publisher. The two most successful magazines in America—*Ladies' Home Journal* and *Saturday Evening Post*—were the creations of Cyrus H. K. Curtis, and in each resided the complete authority of two very gifted editors.

Curtis began his publishing empire on a modest scale in 1883 when he separated the women's supplement from his newspaper, *The Tribune and Farmer,* calling the new publication *Ladies' Home Journal.* The *Journal* began as a small pamphlet of dress patterns designed by his wife, who was a talented dressmaker, and as the pamphlet grew in popularity, stories, recipes, and other features were added until the publication blossomed into a full-fledged magazine. The circulation of the *Journal* began at 20,000, and using his uncanny talent for building lists, Curtis managed to expand it to twice this size in six months. By 1886 the circulation had reached 270,000; by 1889, 400,000. His wife continued as editor until she retired to spend more time with her children, and Curtis set about looking for an editor to replace her. His choice of Edward William Bok seemed an odd selection: Bok was a bachelor who showed no particular interest in the fair sex and had very little magazine background. (Bok was known to be an egocentric, often referring to himself in the third person; true to character, he entitled his autobiography *The Americanization of Edward Bok.*) But Curtis' instinct about the editor was correct. Under Bok's direction, the *Ladies' Home Journal* reached heights unprecedented for any magazine in America. Bok was equally brilliant in boosting circulation as he was in acquiring the best foreign and domestic writers of the day. By 1903 the circulation reached the million mark, and by 1919 it mounted to two million.

Curtis was even more successful with the *Saturday Evening Post.* He purchased this struggling Philadelphia family magazine in 1897, acquiring not much more than its name and that of its founder

Introduction

20. Norman Rockwell. *On the Top of the World* (Illustration for *Ladies' Home Journal* cover, April 1928). Oil on canvas, 33 x 25"

21. *Saturday Evening Post*, August 19, 1911

22. *The Arithmetic Lesson* (Published in *Collier's*, September 30, 1911). Graphite under oil on stretched paper, 22½ x 16½". Collection Achenbach Foundation for Graphic Arts, California Palace of the Legion of Honor, San Francisco

(Benjamin Franklin), a few cases of type, and a circulation of less than 2000. The circulation sagged even more immediately after the acquisition, and Curtis set about looking for the right editor to rescue the ailing property. His selection for the *Post* was even more unlikely than the editor he had hired for the *Journal:* George Horace Lorimer. Not only did Lorimer lack a literary background (he had never even graduated from college), but he also had very little magazine experience, having been only a newspaper reporter in Boston. Eager to prove his worth, Lorimer instantly reorganized the magazine and secured for himself the confidence of Curtis and the position of editor for more than thirty-nine years.

"George Horace Lorimer was an impressive man," wrote Norman Rockwell about his famous employer. "His long, massive head was crowned with an unruly shock of sandy hair shot through with steel gray. He had a strong, square jaw, piercing eyes, and a nose which was large, straight and angular. He wore dark, double-breasted suits and continually paced the floor, his heels thudding on the green carpet which stretched from wall to wall in his office." Lorimer's success was based on a simple formula: he directed the *Post* to every American citizen—regardless of class or regional origin—building what Rockwell described as a "high class Horatio Alger magazine." He created the image of a middle-class America through these pages, a reassuring and light-hearted vision of the ideal American life, one that could be accessible to all Americans. Curtis believed in Lorimer completely and gave him full support through all his years. "I take some of the profits," said Curtis, "but the *Post* really belongs to Lorimer. I would no more think of telling him how to run it, what to print and what not to print, than I would think of telling Commodore Bennett how to run the *New York Herald*." Curtis could not have trusted a more dedicated editor. "He ran the *Post* with an iron hand," Rockwell observed. "It was his magazine, his alone. He made the final decision on every story, okayed every cover, approved every article assignment. And he thought the *Post* was the greatest magazine ever published." The success story of the *Saturday Evening Post* needs no re-telling. It became America's most successful magazine, an American institution, in fact, just as the *Post's* illustrations by Norman Rockwell became the visual record of the American dream George Horace Lorimer had created.

Another great leader of the publishing industry emerging from the 1890s was P. F. (Pat) Collier. He made his start by publishing Bibles and other books in the public domain, then selling library sets of standard authors on the installment plan by mail. Using the names he had accumulated from his mail order business, Collier launched a magazine with a ready base of subscribers in 1888. He called the magazine *Once a Week,* then changed its name to *Collier's Weekly* in 1895. When he died, Pat Collier passed the torch on to the even more capable hands of his son, Robert Collier, who had already engineered a very successful series, *Dr. Eliot's Five Foot Shelf of Classics*. Bob Collier, a bon vivant who liked to hobnob with American and European socialites, surrounded himself with an able staff and gave his employees free rein. (His brilliant business manager, Condé Nast, later started his own publishing company.) Collier and staff transformed the family magazine from an amorphous review to a popular home weekly, fresh and experimental, attracting the foremost writers and artists of the day with irresistible contracts. Maxfield Parrish signed an exclusive contract with them, as

Introduction

did Frederic Remington, but the most extravagant contract was offered to Charles Dana Gibson: one hundred pen-and-ink drawings at the rate of $1000 per drawing, a staggering figure for the year 1903!

Cosmopolitan was one of the most significant ten-cent magazines to enter the field of publishing. Launched in 1886 and edited ably by E. D. Walker, its circulation reached 300,000 by 1898. Losing interest in the magazine, Walker sold it to William Randolph Hearst in 1905, and it became the second of Hearst's acquisitions in the magazine field. Hearst hired Perriton Maxwell as editor and William C. "Pop" Gibson as art editor, promoting the magazine as "the very best at any price." Under the new ownership *Cosmopolitan* soon became a more sensational magazine, known for its aggressive series of muckraking articles, then abruptly it turned entirely to fiction in 1912. James Montgomery Flagg was one of *Cosmo's* favorite illustrators, and the sharp-tongued artist enjoyed bantering with the art editor: "Pop Gibson was a great favorite of the artists," Flagg recollected in his autobiography. "His fierce truculence awed some of the younger artists. But so far as I was concerned his manner was only a subject of open derision between us, and we had lots of phony battles; cussing each other out, which signified nothing at all but a bit of vocal sparring. Instead of saying goodbye at the end of a phone conversation he invariably ended with a Bronx cheer. We had fun."

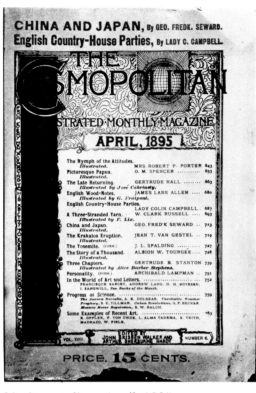

23. *Cosmopolitan,* April, 1895

Still another giant to emerge from the 1890s was S. S. McClure, a publishing genius who analyzed the industry to determine what part he would take for himself. An eccentric and dynamic Irish immigrant, McClure was the first publisher to institute the syndicated novel—a concept based on the syndicated news story—and who launched another important ten-cent magazine, *McClure's,* in 1893. In his autobiography McClure described his thoughts about the new magazine: "The success of *Ladies' Home Journal* at ten cents in this country made me think that a cheap popular magazine would be possible in the United States. The development of photo-engraving made such a publication then more possible. The impregnability of the older magazines, such as *The Century* and *Harper's,* was largely due to the costliness of wood engraving. Only an established publication with a large working capital could afford illustrations made by that process. *The Century Magazine* used, when I was working for it, to spend something like five thousand dollars a month on its engraving alone. Not only was the new process vastly cheaper in itself, but it enabled a publisher to make pictures directly from photographs which were cheap, instead of from drawings which were expensive." With his vitality and vigor, and his natural flair for business and magazine-making, S. S. McClure developed his publication into one of the most sensational of the day. It contained a remarkable assortment of popular fiction writers, excellent reporting on the scientific discoveries of the day, and its coverage of the Spanish-American War—based entirely on eyewitness accounts—was about the best of its day. It became the best known of the muckraking journals. By 1900 *McClure's* had a circulation of 370,000 and by 1907 close to 500,000.

24. *McClure's Magazine,* March, 1900

While the mass circulation family magazines—*Ladies' Home Journal, Saturday Evening Post, Collier's, Cosmopolitan,* and *McClure's*—represented important periodicals for the illustrators of the day, they did not provide the only important sources for work. Two other great magazine institutions were also significant showcases for the illustrators:

Introduction

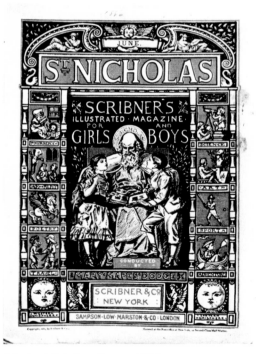

25. *Youth's Companion*, May 4, 1911

26. *St. Nicholas*, June, 1880

children's magazines and humor magazines.

Before the advent of radio and television, magazines for younger readers represented a major enterprise for publishing. *Harper's Young People* was the oldest and most enduring of the children's magazines and *Youth's Companion* the most successful. The latter was founded in 1827 and published until 1929, coming into full blossom immediately after the Civil War. The content of the magazine stressed action, adventure, humor, and the activities of young people, with emphasis on moral instruction as well. An outgrowth of a Boston Congregational paper, the *Companion* was founded with the self-proclaimed intent to "warn against the ways of transgression, error and ruin, and allure to those of virtue and piety." Using highly innovative methods of building subscriptions (it was the first magazine to institute premiums for new subscribers), the circulation of the magazine passed the half million mark in 1898.

The best of the children's magazines was *St. Nicholas.* Unlike the *Companion, St. Nicholas* was described simply by its editor as the "child's playground." A warm magazine, beautiful to look at and inviting to read, *St. Nicholas* introduced children to Little Lord Fauntleroy and Rudyard Kipling's *The Jungle Book.* When its great editor Mary Mapes Dodge (who herself had created the character of Hans Brinker) passed away in 1905, the magazine declined, yet did not expire altogether until the 1940s.

Americans took themselves very seriously as they set about establishing their new nation. It was not until after the Civil War that the American public seemed to want a form of harmless relaxation, welcoming the self-indulgence of laughter and self-mockery. Toward the close of the War, and for some years after, there appeared in Frank Leslie's *Weekly* a number of cartoons signed only with the initial *N* (thought to be the work of William Newman). At the same time the great satirist Thomas Nast joined the staff of *Harper's Weekly* and provided material for this publication for several years.

Magazines devoted entirely to humorous material seemed doomed, however. Roughly twenty-five attempts had been made to launch humor magazines in the 1870s, with no success. In his *History of Journalism,* written in 1873, critic Frederic Hudson rationalized this failure: "Our people don't want their wit on a separate dish. Wit cannot be measured off like tape, or kept on hand for a week; it would spoil in that time.... No one can wait a week for a laugh; it must come in daily with our coffee." Shortly after this writing, Hudson was proved wrong in his assessment. Three humor magazines appeared, survived, and enjoyed success into the next century: *Puck, Judge,* and *Life.*

Begun as a German-language comic magazine—the creation of a Viennese artist named Joseph eppler—*Puck* was launched in 1877, and survived until 1918. *Judge,* originally founded by a dissident group from *Puck* in 1881, surpassed its rival (in 1912 its circulation had reached 100,000), surviving until the 1930s.

Life was the most successful of these humor magazines. Against the advice of authorities in the publishing business, a thirty-seven-year-old New York cartoonist named John Ames Mitchell decided to create a new humor magazine with the $10,000 he had received from a relative. The new satirical weekly ("of high artistic and literary merit," as it was described) was launched in Mitchell's Broadway studio in 1883 and fought an uphill battle for six months as it established readership. The

Introduction

27. *Puck,* October, 1901 28. *Judge,* June 1, 1912 29. *Life,* June 2, 1921

magazine was an extension of its founder, impulsive, warm-hearted, featuring crusades against whatever issues Mitchell found of personal importance: to favor sanitation over serum treatments, to decry the use of vivisection on dogs, to express his aversion to "Trusts." *Life*'s standards for drawings were higher than those of its rivals, and Mitchell discovered many young talents who were to develop into the major artists of their time. The most illustrious of his discoveries was Charles Dana Gibson.

The 1890s were lively and fashionable and *Life* presented itself as America's tastemaker, providing in its text and drawings hints as to dress and conduct. This was the "genteel school of humor." In their drawings Palmer Cox paraded his Brownies through its pages; W. H. Hyde and Harry V. McVickar satirized society; and E. W. Kemble became known for his satirical drawings of black folk. The social drawings of Charles Dana Gibson were followed by those of James Montgomery Flagg and John Held Jr. By 1916 the magazine had reached 150,000 circulation.

The comic magazines were victims of the postwar years of World War I. The tastes and needs of the American public had changed drastically. Into this void walked the brilliant editor Harold Ross, founder of *The New Yorker,* who caught the tide and far outdistanced his rivals with the journalistic slant readers were then demanding. Gone were the leisurely, contemplative days. First-rate reporting and up-to-the-minute comment, not only for newspapers but in magazines, were the essential things. *The New Yorker* combined the humorous nature of the old magazines with the journalistic quality of the two other outstanding magazine successes of the period, *Time* and *Fortune.*

Ross' theory behind *The New Yorker* was based on his study of the other humor and sophistication magazines. He deliberately avoided their tendency to provide national editorial content, preferring to attract local New York City advertising instead. He also agreed with Alexander King who, in an article for *Vanity Fair,* had analyzed the

30. *New Yorker,* August 14, 1926. Drawing by Ilonka Karasz; © 1926, 1954 *The New Yorker* Magazine, Inc.

Introduction

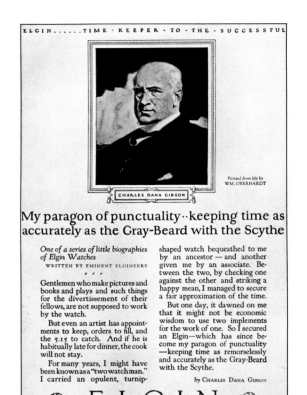

31. Charles Dana Gibson testimonial for Elgin National Watch Company, 1925

32. Howard Chandler Christy testimonial for Waterman's left-handed pen, 1934

failure of the humor magazines: "They became arrogant, conservative, and stuffy, and losing complete sight of their prime functions as humorous weeklies, they standardized their material until it lost all contact with the turbulent life and reality about them." By contrast, Ross' humor was designed to appeal to the sophisticated set only and could therefore afford to indulge in more controversial and timely issues.

Ross felt that the humor in *Life* and *Judge* had gone stale because the editors could not get it to their readers rapidly enough. The other magazines—because they were national—were unable to print timely material that would still be of interest when it reached the reader's doorstep. Ross' calculations were correct and his magazine replaced the other humor magazines entirely. *Judge* petered out in the thirties and *Life* was acquired by *Time* in 1936. Under the new ownership, only the name was retained, and the publication was converted into a photo news magazine.

TEN AMERICAN ILLUSTRATORS AND HOW THEY LIVED

The tremendous activity in publishing—the proliferation of adult and children's books, family magazines, youth magazines, and humor magazines—inevitably produced a diverse group of illustrators to serve the varied functions being demanded. Illustration, which until this point had been a field limited in potential by the restrictions of production technology and the small numbers of publishers, was now open to all possibilities. The outlets for artists were vast and lucrative.

There were, in fact, more opportunities than there were artists, and every editor and publisher faced an increased budget to compete for the limited supply of fine illustrators available to them. With their extravagant expenditures on art and their vast circulations, magazines constructed the most spectacular—if not the most enduring—showcase for illustrators. Radio, motion pictures, and television would later eclipse the printed word and picture as the greatest source of public entertainment, but until their arrival the magazine captured the exclusive attention of millions of Americans and, like the newer arrivals, represented in their day a particular form of show business.

The illustrators were treated like any other product. Their names were synonymous with fashion and they were used to endorse products (watches and fountain pens, perhaps), to attract readers, to aggrandize the writers whose work they illustrated. (Leyendecker's Arrow Collar man received 17,000 love letters one month, even more than Rudolph Valentino received at the peak of his career!) Billed as heroes by their magazines, the artists became celebrities, adored and idolized by the public, much as movie stars are revered today. Their names were uttered with passion by all those who devoured the publications. Their amorous activities were reported in gossip columns; their social activities announced in society columns; their personal views featured in newspapers and magazines throughout the nation. Even the way they signed their names was unforgettable. Their deliberately idiosyncratic signatures, attached to the creations sent forth from their celebrated studios, represented their personal trademarks. Although some of these signatures may seem like illegible scrawls today, they elicited immediate recognition of the entire American public at the time.

The ten illustrators selected for this volume represent the spectrum of personalities, subjects, styles, and attitudes shared by the American illustrators of the day. These ten were America's beloved illustrators, a composite of the Golden Age of Illustration. In their work they offered what was wanted by the publishers, and displayed the diversity and range of the industry they served: the public wanted to be entertained by romantic tales of adventure, chivalry, and valor that demanded the services of narrative, historical illustrators (Pyle, Remington, and Wyeth); a fashionable audience wanted to pattern its appearance and behavior on pictures of society and urban activity, and so required the drawings and paintings of social illustrators (Gibson, Flagg, Christy); businessmen insisted on strong decorative poster artists to sell their products and to augment newsstand and bookstore sales (Parrish and Leyendecker); light-hearted popular fiction required the touch of the humorous illustrator (Gibson, Flagg, Christy, Held, Rockwell); dramatic news events were documented by reportage artists (Remington and Christy); and Americans welcomed the reassurance of gazing upon good-natured, loving families in the pages of their home publications (Rockwell). These enterprising, industrious illustrators satisfied an entire American public for several decades with their diverse talents. A few generalizations about them—their similarities and differences— may help to explain their extraordinary part in shaping American cultural history.

First, and above all, they were American—by temperament *and* by birth. (J. C. Leyendecker is the single exception, having emigrated from Germany with his family when he was a boy. Not surprisingly, his work and his personality tended to be the least "American" of the ten.) These artists represented, therefore, prototypes of the white Anglo-Saxon American middle class. Some of their families were better off financially than others (Parrish and Flagg both came from rather well-to-do parents, for example), but all were middle-class Americans. All embodied the Puritan values of hard work and self-reliance, so characteristic of their Protestant upbringing. (Held was raised as a Mormon, Parrish and Pyle as Quakers, the remainder in other Protestant denominations.) All came from literate parents who had been reared on a steady diet of American and English books and periodicals, a fact which inevitably affected their own taste in art and literature.

Originating from distinctly American backgrounds meant that these artists had a natural affinity for the American ideals of the Victorian and Edwardian eras and that these views were expressed in their work and in their personal philosophies. The pages of the magazines were shared equally by those artists depicting urban areas (Pyle, Wyeth, Christy) and those describing rural environments (Gibson, Flagg, Rockwell). They provided the American public with its first total image of a diverse country blending into a single nation. While Pyle, Remington, and Wyeth celebrated American history, Parrish and Rockwell romanticized rural life, and Gibson, Christy, Leyendecker, Flagg, and Held depicted the growing urbanization of their country. All readers could confirm their American identity through these artists, and the thousands of immigrants pouring into the country each day would find here a common image of the ideal American type, patterning themselves after this model.

In varying degrees, each of these illustrators shared a common conviction that America must be freed of the shackles imposed by

33. Their signatures were their trademarks

25

Introduction

European traditions and values. Gibson was a fierce opponent of the Anglomania so prevalent in his day, and Remington's only interest in traveling to Europe lay in his desire to canoe down the Volga. Each of the artists received his earliest training in America—at the Art Students League in New York, at Drexel Institute in Philadelphia, at Howard Pyle's school of illustration, in Wilmington, Delaware, and Chadds Ford, Pennsylvania, at Chicago's Art Institute—and only a few bothered attending the hallowed Académie Julian or Colarossi's in Paris that were considered sacred to the fine artists of the day. Gibson, Flagg, Leyendecker, and Parrish adopted what they pleased from their limited European training, but never altogether imitated the fashionable artists so widely seen in France and England at the time. All believed that American art should be liberated from European domination, and all were convinced that one day it would be considered equal if not superior to that seen in Europe. Maxfield Parrish wrote from England in 1895, "I firmly believe now that America will in time outclass any on this side of the water; it will take a long time to be sure, but she has not as much to contend against as England and France, though she has much more to learn."

Howard Pyle dedicated himself to building a group of American "picture-makers" that would be unrivaled by European counterparts. Wyeth was reluctant to visit Europe at all, fearing that such a voyage would fragment his vision, that he would invite "the profound risk of being adulterated by others." As he wrote, "A man can only paint that which he knows even more than intimately; he has got to know it spiritually. And to do that he has got to live around it, and be a part of it!" (Wyeth never did cross the Atlantic.) Flagg traveled abroad frequently but never took his experiences seriously: Europe was his playground and he merely laughed at the Americans who insisted on measuring themselves against the standards of an old culture that was basically out of step with the American character.

Without exception, the American illustrators were patriots all. Christy, for example, made a ritual of raising and lowering the American flag each day at his Ohio home, and it is reported that his eyes would fill with tears upon hearing the *Star Spangled Banner*. The illustrators displayed their devotion to America with the multitude of posters they created for both World Wars and for a variety of other American crusades and they rendered these services without remuneration. (Flagg stalked out of a meeting in disgust when a few illustrators dared to request payment for their government posters.) Charles Dana Gibson assumed leadership of the Division of Pictorial Publicity during World War I, and Christy, Flagg, and Leyendecker produced posters that were circulated by the millions, continuing to serve their government in other causes even after the war was over. Wyeth was saddened when he discovered that he would be unable to join the other American artists who ventured to the front lines to record incidents of combat. And Rockwell's illustrations based on war themes—particularly those of World War II—have become classic scenes of the simple ways in which human lives are disrupted by political events beyond their control.

While all the artists here took great pride in their American roots, there was less agreement among them about the value of illustration itself. The cleavage between fine art and illustration has widened over the years, the prejudices between the two having magnified greatly

34. Howard Chandler Christy alongside the model and painting for a patriotic cause. Courtesy Robert F. Conneen

since the nineteenth century. In his time, however, Howard Pyle saw no distinction between them, feeling that fine art was simply a term designating quality and that the best in illustration would certainly qualify as fine art. Norman Rockwell did not recall any distinction made between the illustration classes at the Art Students League and the portrait or landscape classes. "To us illustration was an ennobling profession," Rockwell recalled. "That's part of the reason I went into illustration. It was a profession with a great tradition, a profession I could be proud of."

During Rockwell's student days, illustration was still associated with the very finest writing, when the best literature of the day was interpreted in pictures by the best artists. As Rockwell noted, "Illustration was in the main stream of the arts, was vitalized by contact with fine writing." This was to change, of course, as illustration became associated with the commercial interests of publishing, with big business, when reaching a mass audience was given higher priority than providing the best in pictures and words. "The people who bought the mass magazines, the best-selling books, didn't particularly care about fine illustration," Rockwell observed. While this expansion tended to attract artists to illustration for practical—rather than idealistic—motives, it also meant that magazines demanded greater conformity from the illustrator because of the higher financial stakes now in force. Far greater limitations were placed on the magazine illustrator by editor and art director. An increasing conservatism in the magazines, combined with the illustrators' more commercial motives for entering

27

Introduction

the field, caused illustration to diminish in stature after 1920. The
feeling toward the "ennobling profession" is expressed by the ten
illustrators here by their differing attitudes toward their profession and
toward their ultimate self-worth as artists. In spite of their
overwhelming success, three of the artists here would have preferred
recognition as fine artists rather than as illustrators: Wyeth, Remington,
and Christy.

N. C. Wyeth was particularly bitter about illustration. "To read the
lives of the masters," he wrote, "from Angelo down, confirms me—and
to listen to the writings and talkings of our best men confirms me—the
underlying quality of every great work is truth, and the magazines
of today, with their commercial spirit, their limitations of picture
production, and their price limitations make it impossible for a man to
paint pictures for them. The same love, the same enthusiasm that goes
to make illustration goes to make painting—the one is born into the
world under limitations that choke and distort and soon die—the other
is born full and free as the air; if it ripens it will stand as a perfect
expression of those loves and will last forever."

For years Wyeth was plagued by self-doubt and intense remorse
about his career. "It undoubtedly seems strange to you," he wrote to his
mother, "to hear me say that the very source of my livelihood (and a
good one it is too) is the very thing that is standing in my way. All that I
have done in the past, all that I could do in the future (in illustration)
would be utterly forgotten in a preciously few years except by a few
friends and relatives perhaps. It is my purpose to create pictures that
will last, like the works of men like Michelangelo, Raphael, Millet, and
scores of others." With the years Wyeth's frustration intensified rather
than diminished, particularly after he witnessed the early efforts and
success enjoyed by his son Andrew as a fine artist. N. C. Wyeth turned
more toward personal work in later years, but contrary to his

28

Introduction

36. N. C. Wyeth. *Blind Pew.* 1911 (From *Treasure Island* by Robert Louis Stevenson, Scribner's). Oil on canvas.
Collection Mr. and Mrs. Andrew Wyeth

predictions, Wyeth's commercial creations have endured longer, no doubt because the illustrations were simply far more compelling than his easel paintings.

After fifteen years as an illustrator, Remington abandoned commercial work entirely, turning exclusively to sculpture and easel painting. Here, however, the change was less influenced by his prejudice against illustration than it was by his disillusionment in the West, the primary source of his subject matter. "Shall never come to the West again," he wrote in 1900. "It is all brick buildings—derby hats and blue overhauls—it spoils my early illusions—and they are *my* capital." Finding these changes contemptible, he became increasingly disinterested in documenting the West as a reportage artist. Instead, he gradually turned toward a more lyrical and impressionistic interpretation of the West's unchanging qualities—the land and light—and to a more romantic depiction of the earlier days when the region was still a worthwhile subject.

Howard Chandler Christy launched his career as an illustrator on a decidedly defensive note: his teacher and great mentor William Merritt Chase was infuriated upon hearing of Christy's decision to sell his work for publication, and the student was obliged to drop out of Chase's class. He continued to work as an illustrator, but out of necessity not choice, because "it was a question of food and shelter." Finally, in 1921, Christy was able to retire from illustration to become a portrait painter in the tradition of John Singer Sargent, a more laudable profession in his eyes.

While Wyeth, Remington, and Christy may have held greater respect for fine art, James Montgomery Flagg was most decidedly opposed to what he regarded as a false set of values. "The only difference between a fine artist and an illustrator," he said, "is that the latter can draw, eats three square meals a day, and can afford to pay for them." When one of Flagg's paintings was selected to hang in the Paris Salon of 1900—a great honor for a fine artist—Flagg was altogether indifferent. And he had only the greatest contempt for the illustrator-turned-portrait-painter. Without mentioning Christy's name in particular, Flagg lambasted all so-called "society portrait painters": "It was nauseating to watch their venal plans and traps and downright bootlicking, their insincere flattery, their cringing compliances to the vulgar rich and to stupid dowagers whom they inveigled into sittings for 50 × 60 canvases, ugly old mammas—most of them harridans—sitting down strutting in ropes of pearls and diamonds and expensive wrappings."

Like Flagg, Leyendecker spurned any but his illustration assignments. Gibson, who became an easel painter late in life, did so not because he was dubious of the value of illustration. He simply yearned to replace pen and ink with oil paints and he regarded landscapes and portraits as a natural outgrowth of this change in medium.

Typically, Rockwell was balanced in his appraisal of fine art and illustration, although there is a suggestion that he thought that perhaps illustration is actually the more demanding. "A fine arts painter has to satisfy only himself. No outside restrictions are imposed upon his work. The situation is very different in commercial art. The illustrator must satisfy his client as well as himself. He must express a specific idea so that a large number of people will understand it; and there must be no mistake as to what he is trying to convey. Then there are deadlines, taboos as to subject matter;...the proportions of the picture must

Introduction

conform to the proportions of the magazine. Most fine arts painters feel that these restrictions constitute pure slavery. An artist friend once said to me, 'If the average person likes a painting of mine I'd destroy it.' A young art student remarked once, 'I think I'll take up fine arts. Commercial art is too difficult.' Which was a silly thing to say, because obviously the requirements of fine arts are as exacting as those of commercial art. But they are self-imposed. Fine arts painters, working entirely out of their own instincts and feelings, refuse to allow any restrictions to be superimposed on their paintings by others."

Held, Parrish, and Flagg saw no conflict in turning out an occasional easel painting or sculpture purely for pleasure, although Parrish was just as likely to command a high price for a landscape as he was an illustration. While many illustrators had little regard for the original art once it was reproduced, Parrish was a notable exception. Accurately dubbed "a businessman with a brush," Parrish sold only the reproduction rights of his work to publishers, retaining the originals for sale elsewhere.

Talent in the art of business was not a prerequisite for a high income, however. Any artist who was employed as steadily as these illustrators (particularly those working after Pyle's time) could anticipate a very handsome income indeed. The magazines paid extremely well for the major artists of the day, often competing fiercely for exclusive contracts. *Collier's* was the most aggressive, paying $1000 to Remington for one painting per month, $1250 to Parrish for an oil painting per month, and to Gibson $1000 each for one hundred pen-and-ink drawings! Additionally, royalties on books and prints, to say nothing of the income earned from advertising art, meant that each would make an average annual income of $60,000 or $75,000, some even more, staggering sums for the early decades of this century!

Rockwell recalled his student days when such earnings would have seemed shameful: "Art Young, Charley Kuntz, and I signed our names in blood, swearing never to prostitute our art, never to do advertising jobs, never to make more than fifty dollars a week. That sounds like something only fine-arts students would do, but all three of us were dead set on being illustrators. (That oath has long since been broken. But it signifies nothing. At the time I was like a little boy who vowed he would never grow up to be a man—I just didn't know myself.)"

Lavish incomes signified sumptuous living. Among the rural illustrators, Pyle and Parrish managed to live quietly refined lives, in spite of the restraint they each exercised in spending, a result no doubt of their Quaker upbringing. (Parrish's elegant home in Cornish, New Hampshire—a dwelling of his own design—was the subject of several articles in architectural journals.) Wyeth, too, felt self-conscious about his wealth—he had one beautiful home in Pennsylvania and another in Maine—and was uneasy at not having adopted the austere life recommended by Thoreau. ("I am living too well, too luxuriantly for the proper disciplining of my nature," Wyeth lamented.)

The urban illustrators had no such difficulty in accepting a high-toned way of life, actively spending and investing their money throughout their careers. Several New York illustrators chose to live in the suburbs. John Held Jr. bought nearly two hundred acres of land in nearby Westport, Connecticut, and brought into his farm a full menagerie of dogs, horses, servants, a team of mules, his own golf pro, and a Chinese cook. New Rochelle, a New York suburb, attracted a

37

Thank You Very Much, Mr. James Montgomery Flagg

38

39

great number of the city's successful artists, including Frederic Remington and Norman Rockwell. In the same community, J. C. Leyendecker ordered a fourteen-room palatial home built in the style of a French chateau. (The residence has since been converted into a children's day school and is still elaborately landscaped.) Commuting to his luxurious New York studio, Leyendecker was driven to the train station each day in a chauffered limousine.

Gibson and Christy entered society with their new wealth, attending the operas, formal dinner parties, and cotillions of the fashionable aristocracy. Meanwhile, Mr. Flagg—who didn't give a hoot about the social register—spent his money on whatever he jolly well pleased, on women, on motor cars, on first-class travel abroad, and was to become one of the city's favorite bohemians. He hobnobbed with New York writers, actors, and illustrators, and continually shocked the public with outrageous observations on sacred American institutions. He was a rogue, and savored every opportunity to display this aspect of his character.

When Christy and Gibson were not attending their fashionable social affairs, they were most likely with Flagg, joining the festivities at the New York clubs—the Dutch Treat Club, the Lambs Club, the Society of Illustrators, the Artists and Writers Club, the Players Club—frequently seen with their wives or paramours at costume balls, raising their glasses in boisterous toasts, and performing in the annual club shows.

Gibson, Flagg, and Christy did more than participate personally in these New York activities. They used their favorite pastimes as material for their illustrations of urban life. While Pyle, Wyeth, and Parrish, from their pastoral settings, portrayed gnomes, knights, and pirates, Gibson, Flagg, and Christy produced vivid scenes of urbanites who visited the zoo, attended sports and operatic events, served on juries, commuted in buses and trains. While Remington galloped off to dusty horizons, Gibson, Flagg, and Christy invited their readers to view the elegant dinner parties, to muse at the familiar bores, bullies, and lovelies populating the dance floor. Every summer the New York maiden traveled to gai Paris for an education in the sophisticated art of living, or to the beach where she met her romance but must sadly bid adieu to him at the end of the holiday. Gibson, Flagg, and Christy were always nearby observing her.

So closely associated were these three illustrators, in fact, that they were frequently confused with one another. Flagg tells a favorite story of an old lady who edged her way up to him, autograph book in hand, and inquired, " 'Tell me, Mr. Flagg, aren't you really the originator of the Gibson Girl?' I gagged and looked to see if she were serious—she sure was. I solemnly told her, 'No, Ma'am, thank you for the compliment, but it was Howard Chandler Christy!' She retired happily with her new-found misinformation." Because Gibson was the oldest, the most established and (Flagg would be the first to agree) the most gifted in his medium, the others were often labeled as imitators. Flagg's retort to this accusation: "Charles Dana Gibson is the Papa of the Gibson Girl. Howard Chandler Christy and James Montgomery Flagg were not that good. Let this end that stupidity!"

The question of imitation should not be dismissed altogether, however, since it does play a part in the evolution of American illustration as we know it today. The artist propelled into stardom by his

40

37. James Montgomery Flagg. *Charles Dana Gibson*

38. James Montgomery Flagg's statement about Charles Dana Gibson imitators

39. News clipping featuring the participants at the annual costume ball of the Society of Illustrators in New York. From left to right: Mr. and Mrs. James Montgomery Flagg; Miss Hayden Harris and Charles Dana Gibson; Miss Nancy Palmer and Howard Chandler Christy. (From *Illustrated Current News*, January 31, 1916, New Haven, Connecticut)

40. James Montgomery Flagg. *Howard Chandler Christy*. Collection Robert F. Conneen

Introduction

41. Howard Pyle and his students. N. C. Wyeth stands second from the right. The Delaware Art Museum, Wilmington

42. Howard Pyle students, Chadds Ford, Pennsylvania. The Delaware Art Museum, Wilmington

magazines represented a dazzling example for a young hopeful to follow, hero worship being a natural phenomenon in any field where only a few ever rise to the top. (Magazines have also encouraged imitation, moreover, by purchasing less expensive versions of the same "look," hoping to lure their readers with the illusion of prestige.) The greatness of the illustrators represented here does not mean that their work was unique from the outset. They each borrowed the best from their predecessors, adapting these qualities into a unique form of expression. Gibson's earliest work is reminiscent of George DuMaurier; early Rockwell bears a striking resemblance to Leyendecker; Wyeth's early creations were much like those of Pyle—yet all these artists developed individual approaches. The artists who remained permanently under the spell of their heroes were inevitably forgotten with time, their work blurred by the greater achievements of their predecessors. The outstanding artists vitalized their creations with their own personality, transcending a mechanical translation of what had already been created.

Each artist here began his studies with similar raw materials and each reconstituted those materials into an entirely individual form. All ten submitted to some kind of formal education in art, if only briefly (Remington and Held had very minimal training), and in retrospect all tended to be skeptical of such preparation. They would agree that most formal education amounted to little more than mechanical repetition, and that developing technical skills alone would never produce great art. "Art cannot be taught. Artists are born that way," asserted Flagg. While Wyeth was critical of schools in general ("Every mother's son of us is born with that supreme gift of individual perception, but the sheeplike tendency of human society soon makes inroads on a child's unsophistications, and then popular education completes the dastardly work with its systematic formulas, and away goes the individual, hurtling through space into that hateful oblivion of mediocrity."), he was most distressed by the teaching in art schools: "I have watched with keen interest what such men as Garber, Lathrop, Rose, Hawthorne, Henri and others are transmitting to students, and 'tis the same old story. No attempt to cultivate the powers of individual conception, but merely the handing out on a platter the regular stock of tricks and stunts that tickles the palate of the aspiring boy and which in the end leaves him marooned and starving on Garber's Island or Rose's Reef."

Yet in spite of their convictions about art schools and teaching, the ten artists here were not tempted to remedy the ills of art education. Only one made a major contribution in this field (Howard Pyle), forming his own school to provide a better training ground for artists, and only one other bothered to teach even on a modified scale (Wyeth). The others, of course, influenced younger artists indirectly—through their widely reproduced work—but displayed no interest whatsoever in instructing them directly.

The fact that these artists tended to be wary of too much emphasis on technique did not mean that they were negligent of this aspect of their own work. They all labored assiduously at their craft, perfecting their technical skills much as a concert pianist returns to the scales even after mastering the most complex compositions. They worked from direct observation—not from their imagination—and were painstaking in their concern for details, employing models, props, and sets to assure accuracy, and possessing an uncanny ability to render the visual truth

34

Introduction

43. Frederic Remington transported numerous artifacts from the West, using them as props for his paintings

44. James Montgomery Flagg working from a live model in his studio, 1910. Courtesy Everett Raymond Kinstler

45. Maxfield Parrish in his machine shop, Cornish, New Hampshire

with precision. Drawing was, for them, the basis of their craft and even the most painterly of these illustrators could draw exceedingly well.

On the question of technique, only one subject would have been the source of contention between them: the camera. While they were grateful for the improved quality of reproduction made possible by the camera at the printer, they would have argued bitterly over the place of photography in the artist's studio. Remington used the camera to supplement his sketchbooks on his expeditions to the West. He would record the movements of animals and document important details for reference after returning to his studio in the East. Parrish used the camera even more extensively, employing innovative methods of photographing himself and his models with a large plate camera, and inventing a system of projecting his photographs onto a drawing surface over which he would trace the image. To the other artists, however, the camera was like a harlot whose place was in the streets, not in the studio. Flagg, for example, was convinced that only an artist who was unable to draw would turn to the photograph to conceal his handicap, a shameful gimmick unworthy of the trade. The artist most in conflict over this issue was Norman Rockwell, acutely sensitive to the moral implications of the camera's presence in the studio. Urged by his art director to incorporate new angles and poses into his work, Rockwell saw no alternative but to resort to the camera, the only means by which he could record more complex positions from unorthodox viewpoints. But the transition wasn't easy. "It was quite a wrench, I felt like a traitor to my profession, but I set my teeth and plunged in. At first I used photographs only occasionally, trying to hang onto at least the shreds of my self-respect. But it was like taking a touch of morphine now and then. Pretty soon, before I knew it, I was an addict. A guilty, shamefaced addict, but an addict nevertheless." Rockwell was a symbol of the changing times. Before long, nearly all illustrators became addicts.

Regardless of their tools, these ten artists worked from some visual reference—from photographs or models—not "out of their head," as Flagg called it. They differed in their selection of material—not in their reliance on observation—and in the way they reshaped visual reality to serve their ends. Leyendecker and Parrish, the most stylized of the artists in this group, were more concerned with the formal arrangements of shapes and colors and so were less intent on achieving realism, subordinating their imagery to an effective design instead. Both Pyle and Wyeth believed that the visual truth was vital to convincing work. ("A thing done right," asserted Wyeth, "is done with the authority of knowledge.") They studied nature closely, with an honest attempt at truthful representation, placing their subject in an imaginary, romantic world made plausible by its realism. Gibson, Flagg, Christy, and Held drew upon their own everyday lives, their personal experiences in the city, for their material, capturing what they knew most intimately.

Environment, of course, greatly influenced the artists' choice of subject and their methods of handling it. Pyle and Wyeth both saw the advantages of living away from the competitive urban centers. ("The city is no place for any artist to work, young or old," wrote Wyeth. "I do not refer to the men who dissipate or to dissipation, but simply to the too-close contact of sensitive personality, which is bound to breed dislikes and disrespect, and which is often the underlying impulse that

36

Introduction

44

brings out a man's inferior qualities unless he holds himself in severe check.") Pyle and Wyeth were free to contemplate the unchanging qualities in nature, the universal elements surrounding them. Their illustrations of history, adventure, and classics did not rely upon contemporary fashions (a fact that explains why their work has not dated with time), and their intimacy with their pastoral environment provided an endless source of inspiration for the subjects they depicted. Sherwood Forest was, after all, at their very doorstep.

Unlike Wyeth, Rockwell suspected that too much intimacy with an environment could be undesirable. The strangeness of a subject, the mystery that ignites the imagination, was more stimulating to him. He compared himself, in this respect, to Remington: "Frederic Remington painted the romantic glamorous aspects of the West—cowboys sitting around a campfire, an attack on a stage coach. Any old-timer can tell you that the West was a lot more than that—that life in the wild West was at times pretty drab. But Remington, who was born and raised in upstate New York and traveled in the West as a tourist, didn't experience that drudgery and boredom. Just as I missed the dullness of farm life. I doubt that I would have idealized the country if I had grown up as a farm boy."

The many ways in which these artists may have differed should not obscure the single thing they had in common: a passion for work. They painted as long as the sun cast its gentle north light on their canvases, even after age had weakened their faculties and hurt their pride. Work was their joy, their pain, their sustenance. They could not survive without it. Wyeth summed it up when he wrote: "There's only one kind of work that counts, and that is constant, sustained effort. Drive, drive, drive in the one direction—painting. Without a break. It is the only way any man ever accomplished anything worthwhile."

45

37

Introduction

Chronology

YEAR	Pyle	Wyeth	Remington	Parrish	Leyendecker
1850–1870	1853: Born in Wilmington, Del. 1869–1871: Studies at Van der Weilen School		1861: Born in Canton, New York		
1870–1890	1876: First illustration is published; moves to New York 1879: Returns to Wilmington 1881: Marries Anne Poole 1883: *Robin Hood* 1885: *Within Capes* 1888: *Otto of Silver Hand*	1882: Born in Needham, Mass.	1876–1878: Attends Highland Military Academy 1878–1880: Yale School of Fine Arts 1881: First trip to West 1882: Comes into inheritance; buys ranch in Kansas 1884: Marries Eva Caten 1884–1886: Lives in Kansas City 1886: Moves to New York; sells first drawings to *Harper's Weekly, St. Nicholas, Outing* 1889: Silver Medal at Paris Exposition	1870: Born in Philadelphia 1884–1886: Travels to Europe with parents 1888–1891: Attends Haverford College	1874: Born in Germany 1882: Family emigrates to America 1889: Apprenticeship to J. Manz Engraving 1889–1894: Attends Art Institute of Chicago
1890–1910	1894: Begins teaching at Drexel 1898: First summer classes, Chadds Ford, Pa. 1900: Resigns from Drexel to begin school 1903: Terminates school 1904: Lectures Art Students League 1905: Art Editor at *McClure's* 1905–1910: Paints murals	1902: Arrives at Howard Pyle School 1904: Trip to West 1906: Marries Carolyn Bockius 1907: Henriette born 1909: Carolyn born	1896: Cuba for *Hearst, New York Journal* 1898: First sculpture. Travels continually to West 1903: Exclusive contract with *Collier's* 1904: Turns to fine art 1908: Moves from New Rochelle to Connecticut 1909: Dies in Connecticut	1892–1894: Attends Pennsylvania Academy of the Fine Arts 1895: First cover design published; marries Lydia Austin; travels to Europe 1898: Moves to Cornish, N.H. 1900: Honorable Mention at Paris Exposition 1903: *Italian Villas and their Gardens*	1896: Wins first prize *Century* cover contest 1896–1897: Studies in Paris 1899: First *Post* cover 1900: Moves to New York 1901: Meets Charles Beach 1905: First Arrow Collar ad
1910–1930	1910: Leaves for Italy 1911: Dies in Florence, Italy	1911: Nathaniel born; *Treasure Island* 1913: *Kidnapped* 1915: Ann born 1917: Andrew born; *Robin Hood* 1919: *Last of the Mohicans* 1920: *Robinson Crusoe* 1921–1923: Lives in Needham, Mass. 1924: Peter Hurd comes to study 1925: *Deerslayer*		1920: *Garden of Allah* 1922: *Daybreak*	1910: Moves to New Rochelle 1914: Mt. Tom Mansion complete 1920: Gives up New York studio 1924: brother Frank dies
1930–1950		1934: John McCoy comes to study 1939: *The Yearling* 1945: Dies Chadds Ford, Pa.		1934: Begins painting for Brown & Bigelow	1943: Last *Post* cover
1950–				1953: wife dies 1966: Dies in Cornish, N.H.	1951: Dies in New Rochelle, New York

Rockwell	Gibson	Christy	Flagg	Held	OTHER EVENTS
	1867: Born in Flushing, New York				1850: *Harper's Monthly* launched 1855: *Frank Leslie's Newspaper* launched 1857: *Harper's Weekly* launched 1860–1865: Civil War 1867: *Harper's Bazar* launched
	1883–1885: Attends Art Students League 1886: Sells first drawing to *Life* 1889: First trip to Europe 1890: Gibson Girl first appears	1873: Born in Zanesville, Ohio 1889: Attends Art Students League in New York	1877: Born Pelham Manor, New York 1889: Sold first illustration to *St. Nicholas*	1889: Born in Salt Lake City	1870: *Scribner's* launched 1873: *St. Nicholas* 1877: *Puck* 1879: *Harper's Young People* 1881: Ives invents screen halftone process; *Judge* begins; *Scribner's* replaced by *The Century* 1883: *Life, Ladies' Home Journal, Saturday Evening Post* launched 1887: New *Scribner's*
1894: Born in New York City 1909: Attends National Academy	1895: Marries Irene Langhorne 1898: Mr. Pipp appears 1903: Famous contract with *Collier's*, 100 drawings at $1000 each 1905–1907: Leaves illustration to paint in Europe	1892–1895: Studies with William Merritt Chase 1895: Sells first illustration 1898: Spanish-American War: goes to Cuba 1899: *Men of the Army and Navy;* marries Maybell Thompson 1905: *Drawings by H. C. Christy* 1906: *The Christy Girl* 1907: *Our Girls* 1908: *The Christy Book of Drawings* 1909: Separates from wife 1908–1914: Returns to live in Ohio	1894–1898: Attends Art Students League 1898–1899: Studies in England 1899: Marries Nellie McCormick 1900: Studies in Paris; painting hangs in exposition: *Yankee Girls Abroad* 1904–1908: Four books of limericks 1909: *City People*	1898: Sells first illustration for $9.00 1904: Sells first drawing to *Life* 1905–1910: Works on *Salt Lake City Tribune*	1893: *McClure's* 1897: Curtis buys *Saturday Evening Post* 1898: Sinking of the Maine; end of *Harper's Young People* 1900: End of *Harper's Weekly* 1901: Society of Illustrators formed 1907: Hearst buys *Cosmopolitan*
1910–1912: Attends Art Students League 1911: *Tell Me Why Stories* 1913: Art Editor *Boy's Life* 1916: First *Post* cover; marries Irene O'Connor 1917–1918: Serves in Navy 1923: Trip to Paris; divorces wife	1917–1918: Director of Division of Pictorial Publicity 1918: Art Editor of *Life* 1920: Becomes owner of *Life*	1912: *Liberty Belles* 1915: Returns to live in New York 1919: Marries Nancy Palmer 1921: Leaves illustration to paint portraits 1927: Portrait of Mussolini	1912: *Kitty Cobb* 1914: *The Well Knowns; I Should Say* 1916: *Mystery of the Hated Man* 1917–1919: Designed War posters 1917–1920: Wrote 24 silent films 1923: Wife dies 1924: Marries Dorothy Wadman 1925: *Boulevards All The Way—Maybe*	1910: Marries Myrtle Jennings 1912: Moves to New York City 1916: Work appears in *Vanity Fair* signed Myrtle Held 1918–1919: Serves Naval Intelligence 1918: Marries Ada Johnny Johnson	1911: Dutch Treat Club formed 1913: *Harper's Bazar* sold to Hearst 1917–1919: World War I 1918: Editor of *Life* dies; end of *Puck* 1920: *Life* under new ownership 1921: First Miss America contest 1925: *The New Yorker* launched 1929: Hearst changes to *Harper's Bazaar;* End of *Youth's Companion*
1930: Marries Mary Barstow 1932: Extended trip to Europe 1935: *Tom Sawyer* and *Huck Finn* 1939: Moves to Vermont 1943: Fire in Vermont destroys much work	1932: Resigns from *Life*; resumes oil painting 1944: Dies in New York City	1934: Dedication of Christy Room at Café des Artistes, New York 1940: Paints *Signing of the Constitution*	1946: Autobiography *Roses and Buckshot*	1931: Has nervous breakdown 1932: "Miss New Orleans" books 1937: Tops Variety Radio Show 1938: Designed sets for *Hellzapoppin'* 1940: Artist in Residence, Harvard 1942: Marries Margaret James	1930: End of *The Century* 1936: *Life* bought by *Time* 1939: *Scribner's* ends
1953: Moves to Stockbridge, Mass. 1960: Autobiography 1961: Marries Molly Punderson 1963: Last *Post* cover 1976: Last magazine cover		1952: Dies in New York City	1960: Dies in New York City	1958: Dies Belmar, New Jersey	

Howard Pyle

2

1. *The Mermaid* 1910. Oil on canvas, 57 x 39″. The Delaware Art Museum, Wilmington

2. *Sir Lamorack Herds the Swine of Sir Nabon* (Illustration for *The Story of the Champions of the Round Table*, Charles Scribner's Sons, 1905)

3. *Robin Hood Slayeth Guy of Gisbourne* (Illustration for *The Merry Adventures of Robin Hood*, Charles Scribner's Sons, 1883)

4. *The Stout Bout Between Little John and Arthur a Bland* (Illustration for *The Merry Adventures of Robin Hood*, Charles Scribner's Sons, 1883)

5. *Robin and The Tinker at the Blue Boar Inn* (Illustration for *The Merry Adventures of Robin Hood*, Charles Scribner's Sons, 1883)

6. Illustration for *The Story of the Champions of the Round Table*, Charles Scribner's Sons, 1905

6

*H*oward Pyle occupies a unique position in the history of American illustration. His creative output alone would have qualified him as a great artistic pioneer. But his legacy was far greater than the hundreds of books and articles he wrote and illustrated at the turn of the century. He was a natural teacher, the major force in what later came to be known as the Brandywine School. A compelling and vital man, Pyle was possessed with the idea of training—both spiritually and artistically—a younger generation of artists to conquer new, unexplored frontiers. If any one person could be called the Father of American Illustration, it would be Howard Pyle, for no other American artist has left such a personal and enduring influence on its development during the twentieth century.

No doubt such exalted words would have embarrassed Pyle, whose Puritanism discouraged lavish praise. Pyle himself was more restrained and such flourishes would have seemed indulgent. Howard Pyle was born on March 5, 1853, the eldest of four children in an established Quaker family. At the time, his birthplace—Wilmington, Delaware—was still a small town just beginning to develop into a city. From his earliest years, young Howard was an avid reader, his imagination fired by the books he devoured: *Grimm's German Fairy Tales, A Midsummer Night's Dream, The Arabian Nights* were only a few of the romantic tales he read regularly in front of the open fireplace or out in the countryside. Even from these early days the printed word and picture occupied a vital association in his world of imaginary heroes and villains. Years later, in an article about his boyhood that he wrote for *Woman's Home Companion,* Pyle observed: "We—my mother and I—liked the pictures in the books the best of all. I may say to you in confidence that even to this very day I still like the pictures you can find in books better than wall pictures...my mother taught me to like books and pictures, and I cannot remember a time when I did not like them; so that that time, perhaps, was the beginning of that taste that led me to do the work that I am now doing." These hours spent reading, combined with the Quaker's recognition of the need for reflection and contemplation, formed the substance of his inner life on which he drew in later years. His imagination was nourished by his surroundings as well. The countryside was a source of comfort and stimulated his curiosity regularly as he tramped the fields, hills, and meadows around Wilmington.

43

H· Pyle.

7. Heading for *The Story of King Arthur and His Knights* (Published in *St. Nicholas,* November, 1902 to October, 1903)

Throughout his entire life this region was his haven, and would later be home to several other artists who would venture to the area just for the chance to be associated with him.

During Pyle's boyhood years the Civil War raged nearby. Although Wilmington was not in the battle zone, the conflict seemed especially close because Delaware was the entry and exit from the south. Regularly through Wilmington came troops and supply trains, railroad cars carrying injured soldiers and Confederate prisoners. War never felt far away.

If the War was nearby geographically, it was also the main topic of discussion in the newspapers and magazines that circulated everywhere. Through these accounts of the War, young Pyle came into his first contact with the kind of immediacy and vitality only periodicals could provide. In the early days of the War, the reporting of the battles tended to be theatrical and inaccurate, but during the later years, pictorial reporting matured, developing from outbursts of Victorian sentimentality to factual accounts of the real bitterness and sufferings of war.

Pyle devoured all the publications he could find. Among American periodicals, he regularly read *Harper's Weekly* and *Frank Leslie's Illustrated Newspaper.* But the finest in publishing came from England, not from America. The British family magazines and the children's papers had far exceeded comparable American efforts, which tended to be imitative and commonplace by comparison. The illustrations in such British publications as *Punch,* the *Illustrated London News,* and others were superior in quality and abundance. Here Pyle discovered the splendid drawings of Arthur Boyd Houghton and Charles Keene, and the humorous illustrations of John Leech and John Tenniel. Other English illustrators Pyle discovered were to become eminent painters years later: Dante Gabriel Rossetti, Edward Burne-Jones, John Millais, among others. From these artists Pyle developed his earliest ideas about successful picture-making, resolving that literary ideas could be depicted convincingly if two elements were present: a total surrender to the world of imagination on the one hand, and a firm commitment to realism on the other. The two—romance and reality—were vital to every successful picture.

In spite of the boy's obvious intelligence, his parents observed that his performance in

H. Pyle.

school was mediocre at best. He tended to be a daydreamer, sketching idly, roaming the countryside, and writing on imaginary subjects that had little relationship to his studies. Abandoning any hopes that he might go to college, the Pyles sent their sixteen-year-old son to the nearest art school, Van der Weilen's school in Philadelphia, where Howard's performance as a student improved remarkably. For nearly three years he commuted daily to Philadelphia and acquired the technical training which was assumed necessary for an artist who hoped to make his way in the world. By neglecting the faculty of the imagination, however, Van der Weilen was a disappointment to Pyle. Convinced that it takes more than mechanical skill to be a creative artist, Pyle was to become a very different kind of instructor than his first had been.

Pyle was determined to experiment with his drawing, no longer interested in the mechanical copying he had endured at art school. As he observed years later: "The hardest thing for a student to do after leaving an art school is to adapt the knowledge there gained to practical use—to do creative work, for the work in art school is imitative.... When I left art school I discovered, like many others, that I could not easily train myself to creative work, which was the only practical way of earning a livelihood in art."

And so Pyle returned home: "Being offered a position by my father in his leather business in Wilmington I availed myself of it and during my spare time created illustrations, stimulated my imagination, and worked assiduously on drawings I never submitted. My work was idle for several years while I experimented."

During this period he read voluminously and applied himself to his writing and drawing. Finally, in 1876, he sent an offering to *Scribner's Monthly*, which was accepted. Shortly afterward another acceptance came from *St. Nicholas*, the most enterprising children's magazine of the day. Elated with these triumphs and encouraged by the compliments of *Scribner's* editor, Howard Pyle embarked for New York City to make his way as an artist. He was twenty-three years old.

His decision to leave the protective environment of Wilmington to embark on a career in New York City was a true act of courage. The city was a ruthless and impatient judge of new talent, and only a young man with tremendous determination could withstand the anonymity and isolation thrust upon him in his foreign setting. For every triumph the young artist encountered a reversal, some disappointment that would shake his confidence until the next triumph restored it. By the end of his first year, he had sold a group of drawings to *St. Nicholas*, and made the rounds of the other publishers. Finally, he received a favorable response from Charles Parsons, the editor at the largest publishing company in the country, the House of Harper. In addition to being aggressive book publishers, Harper also published the periodicals *Harper's Monthly, Harper's Weekly, Young People*, and later *Harper's Bazar*. Pyle's relationship with the House of Harper was continually challenging, and he continued this association with the company for years to come. Although Pyle was not a salaried staff member, he could watch the publishing process from original manuscript and drawing to the printed bound copy, and he could meet some of the finest artists in the business. The art department at the House of Harper formed a nucleus that represented the beginnings of professionalism in illustration, with a staff equipped to adapt to a changing and dynamic new publishing industry.

Here Pyle acquired a basic understanding of printing technology that would be indispensable to him in preparing his work for the best possible results on the printed page. At the time of Pyle's residence in New York, wood engraving was the only feasible method for production in periodicals. It was a slow and tedious method in which an engraver translated the artist's drawing onto a block of wood with a burin, or small chisel. The engraved lines in the wood would hold the ink. A small drawing made in simple black line was relatively easy to execute, but tonal pictures in oil or watercolor meant interpreting simple gray tones with an intricate network of dots and threadlike lines engraved into the wood.

Wood engraving was a highly skilled craft, and there were only a few fine engravers in the field. (Harper had the best of them.) After all, the artist's work was only as good as the wood engraver's translation of it onto the block. Pyle witnessed the frustrations of his colleagues when they worked with the wood engravers. On one hand, the artist would argue that the

8. *How Two Went into Partnership* (Heading for *The Wonder Clock*, Harper and Brothers, 1886)

engraver had destroyed the original drawing; on the other hand, the engraver complained that the artist was disinterested in the technical limitations and had unrealistic expectations of an engraver's ability to resolve the mechanical problems. This was Pyle's first exposure to the practical aspects of illustration, and these lessons were well learned. As technology improved, Pyle was quick to adapt, and was innovative in his exploitation of new developments in production. Pyle understood that only as technology improved could an artist expand his powers of expression. In his lifetime, Howard Pyle was to witness these important technological developments in the printing industry, and along with it the increasing sophistication of the art it was capable of reproducing. Until 1887 all of Pyle's work was in line form—pen and ink—so that the engravers could reproduce his art effectively. When photo-mechanical halftones were introduced, Pyle would also add tonal work to his artistic repertoire as well.

Pyle continued to live in New York for three years, an apprenticeship that established him as a professional. Always gregarious, Pyle had a large circle of friends, a close association with such notable artists as Edwin Abbey, Arthur B. Frost, William Merritt Chase, Julian Weir, Frederick Church, among others. Pyle was a professional among professionals. He was also developing a following among his readers as well. He returned to writing occasionally, illustrated several of his own stories, and found no lack of opportunity to draw or write.

In 1879 his group of friends began to disperse—Frost returning to Philadelphia, Abbey to England—and Pyle decided to return to Wilmington. From that point on, Pyle's life continued in a direct and even course; he rarely left Wilmington again.

Pyle's return to Wilmington brought him back in touch with his earliest associations: the Civil War, his Quaker heritage, the gentle landscape, and the literature he had devoured as a boy. Leaving the urban stimulation of New York, returning to his childhood home, Pyle rediscovered his roots. Throughout the rest of his career as an illustrator, he would draw from these rich associations and he would stress their significance to his students. He wrote and illustrated stories that described colonial life in his region during the next few years. Between magazine assignments he worked on a book of his own—*The Merry Adventures of Robin Hood*—which was to be published finally in 1883 by Scribner's. So devoted was he to this project that he worked many long hours on the text and on the pen-and-ink drawings and went to great lengths to supervise the design and production of the book. Nearly a century later his *Robin Hood* is still in print.

The success of *Robin Hood* was followed by several others—*Within the Capes, Pepper and Salt, The Wonder Clock, The Rose of Paradise, Otto of the Silver Hand.* Six books, in fact, appeared between 1883 and 1888, four of them children's books (most of which are still in print today), and two adult novels of piracy and adventure.

While Howard Pyle's books focused primarily on the romance and daring of imaginary heroes and villains from Europe, Africa, and the Caribbean, Pyle's magazine stories and illustrations concentrated almost exclusively on the American scene. And so he expressed the two, equally passionate, sides of his character—one deeply tied to his American roots, the other bound by his devotion to the legends and fables, romance and valor connected with his boyhood readings.

If his subject matter indicated two entirely divergent tendencies, so did his style as an illustrator reveal the marked influence of two very different trends: a traditional, decorative approach on the one hand, and an Impressionist's fascination with the transitory effects of movement and light on the other. Nowhere is this more evident than in his pen-and-ink illustrations, where he did the greatest amount of experimentation. Henry C. Pitz, in his excellent 1975 book, *Howard Pyle: Writer, Illustrator, Founder of the Brandywine School,* has described this aspect of Pyle's work in the following terms: "Pyle was a multiple person and an ambivalent artist. Opposites met in him, but in the main they excited and enriched both his pictorial and writing talents. Study of his varied pen styles reveals many of his deepest characteristics.... The *Robin Hood* drawings represented an important milestone in the development of his decorative style, but it had been in formation for years, reaching back to

46

9. *The Prince Aids the Old Woman* (Illustration for *Pepper and Salt,* Harper and Brothers, 1886)

10. *Two Knights Do Battle Before Camilard* (From *The Story of King Arthur and His Knights* by Howard Pyle. Published in *St. Nicholas*, March, 1903) Ink, 9⅛ x 6⅛". The Delaware Art Museum, Wilmington

childhood and his first awareness of picture books and magazines. His impressionistic style had more recent roots, from the time of his apprenticeship in New York City." At one extreme Pyle's pen drawings show the influence of Albrecht Dürer—whose work Pyle very much admired; yet other drawings reveal the influence of the contemporary Spanish pen artist—then very much in vogue—Daniel Vierge. Pitz continues, "We can now scan the pageant of Pyle's pen art in either reproduction or original and it is the story of growth and expansion. It clearly shows two dominant styles: an urgent decorative sense that liked to deal in large impressive forms and to indulge in pattern, and an equally powerful urge to capture the fleeting effects of nature's light, to establish a sense of atmosphere and aerial recession, and to report the world with a realist's eye."

Such extremes in other artists might have created unnerving conflicts, but for Pyle these contradictions could be reconciled. No doubt this was possible because of his expansive character, an intensity and energy that permitted him to put forth all aspects of his abundant and complex character without confusion. He had, for example, an extraordinary capacity for intense concentration so that his productivity never faltered, despite the varied nature of his commitments. Even after he married, became a devoted father of six, and a dedicated teacher as well, Pyle continued to be an inexhaustible artist and writer. One of his students— Thornton Oakley—was astonished to observe this scene on entering the Pyle house one summer day: "On the stairway landing I found my teacher at his easel, working on a canvas for his series 'Travels of the Soul,' his young children cavorting about his knees, a model posed nearby in costume to give him some detail of texture, Mrs. Pyle sitting beside him reading aloud proofs from King Arthur for his correction, he making comments for her notation." It became well known that Pyle was able to paint and dictate a text to his secretary at the same time. Rumor had it that Pyle's mind worked in separated compartments which did not interfere with each other.

Nowhere was Pyle's extraordinary personality more evident than in his brilliant achievements as a teacher. Just when Pyle decided to teach is not altogether certain. As early as

H. Pyle.

1872 an item in Wilmington's evening newspaper announced that Howard Pyle was prepared to give lessons in drawing, sketching, and painting in oils. There is, however, no indication that he ever received any students as a result of this notice or that he had, at that time, any real commitment to teaching other than desiring an added source of income during his early period as an unpublished artist. It was not until 1894—twenty-two years later—that he actually taught his first class. By that time, Pyle had already become well known, author and illustrator of numerous books and magazine articles, and secure in his field. He still had enough energy and ambition within him to make a most significant impact on the future of American illustration.

As the publishing industry was becoming more demanding, art editors searched constantly for creative talents. Pyle was well aware of the shortage of talented artists prepared to serve. He attributed this paucity to the outdated and mediocre education the younger artists were receiving at the time, and he resolved to share his talents and experience with those who were eager to learn.

Pyle was critical of the current art programs because they tended to emphasize copying rather than imagination. Students were expected to draw from a model who posed stiffly before them in a position that could be held for the long, tedious hours of class. The results produced by the students tended to be as inert as the model. Pyle's own interest in the Impressionists, moreover, had convinced him that the constant and unvarying north light prevalent in these classroom studios tended to encourage a certain mechanical monotony in the students' work. The artist, according to Pyle, should learn to think beyond the model, to develop a vast storage of pictorial memories—awakened by the changing mysteries of light and atmosphere—upon which to draw.

Fortified with an almost missionary zeal, Pyle applied for a teaching post at the Pennsylvania Academy of the Fine Arts, and was refused (a decision the Academy was to sorely regret years later). He taught instead at Philadelphia's Drexel Institute of Art, Science and Industry. The small fee required for the class combined with Pyle's wide reputation meant that the enrollment immediately reached its maximum limit of thirty-nine.

From the outset Pyle found the contact with the students enormously rewarding. His magnetic personality quickly earned him a reputation as a fine instructor and, by the second year at Drexel, students from many miles away ventured to Philadelphia to study in his class. Drexel reorganized the curriculum of the art department, making illustration the most important course. Pyle agreed to increase his teaching from one half day to two full days a week, yet he never reduced his output for the New York publishers, in spite of the extra demands on his time. He continued until 1900, when he left Drexel to establish a school of his own.

Pyle's teaching reflected his zest for experimentation. Unlike the traditional approach to teaching art—in which technical skill was stressed—Pyle's approach placed the greatest importance on developing a pictorial sense, building upon the student's latent imaginary powers. "My final aim in teaching," Pyle reported to his friend Edward Penfield, "will not be essentially the production of illustrators of books, but rather the production of painters of pictures. For I believe that the painters of true American Art are yet to be produced. Such men as Winslow Homer and [George] Fuller in figure painting, and a group of landscape painters headed by George Inness as yet are the only occupants of the field. To this end, I regard magazine and book illustration as a ground from which to produce painters."

One of Pyle's experiments was to result in the formation of his own school. Desiring a more total atmosphere for study, Pyle selected his most gifted students for a summer session in 1898 and again in 1899. With funds he managed to acquire from Drexel, Pyle awarded ten scholarships so that these students could study with him at Chadds Ford, ten miles from Wilmington along the Brandywine River. He worked with this small group, living from day to day in an outdoor environment that stimulated both teacher and students and seemed to enhance the impact of his words. Teaching under these conditions, Pyle decided, was the ideal method of inspiring the student to do his best work. Based on this conviction, Pyle resigned from Drexel in 1900 to establish his school. It became one of the earliest examples of experimental education in this country.

H. Pyle.

11. "She Saw Herself for What He had Said, and Swooned." 1909 (From *The Castle on the Dune* by J. Bacon. Published in *Harper's Monthly*, September, 1909) Oil on canvas, 27 x 18″. Private collection

12. *Nero Holding a Golden Lute, with Rome in Flames.* (From *Quo Vadis* by Henryk Sienkiewicz, vol. 2. Little Brown & Co., 1897) Oil on canvas, 26 x 16⅝″. The Delaware Art Museum, Wilmington

Pyle had grown impatient with the dilettantes he was obliged to instruct at Drexel, and was convinced that only the students' total commitment to work could produce superior artists. The forty-seven-year-old Pyle handpicked candidates for his experiment, and turned full attention to his new school. He financed the building of studios in Wilmington where the students lived and worked. In effect, this was actually more than a school: it was Howard Pyle's vision, a colony of dedicated students eager and willing to develop under the demanding yet loving tutelage of the master of American illustration.

Restricting the number of students to under twenty, Pyle was a stern admissions officer. The prospective student was expected to submit examples of his work and to have a personal interview with Pyle. If Pyle considered the applicant promising, he accepted the student on a trial basis. The student paid for his own room, board, and supplies, but there was no charge for tuition.

The student was expected to live a Spartan existence in order to develop all the disciplines necessary for good work. Winters were spent in Wilmington and summers in Chadds Ford. The students worked in their studios six days a week, from eight in the morning until five or six in the evening, and during the summers Pyle had them work outdoors, a revolutionary concept during a time when traditional art training permitted only indoor work.

He spelled out the course of instruction in a letter to his friend Edward Penfield as follows: "The students who come to me will be supposed to have studied drawing and painting as taught in the schools. My first object shall be to teach them to paint the draped and costumed model so that it shall possess the essentials of a practical picture. To teach this requires considerable knowledge not usually possessed by the artist-teachers in the schools, and this knowledge I feel myself competent to impart. I believe I am not devoid of a sense of

49

H·Pyle.

13. *The Coming of Lancaster* (also called *Lord of the Earth*). (From *The Scabbard* by James Branch Cabell. Published in *Harper's Monthly,* May, 1908) Oil, 35½ x 23¼ ". The Delaware Art Museum, Wilmington

14. *In Knighthood's Day.* Oil on canvas, 24 x 16″. Courtesy Walt Reed, Connecticut

15. "We Started to Run Back to the Raft for Our Lives" (also called *The Burburlangs*). (From *Sinbad on Burrator* by A. T. Quiller Couch. Published in *Scribner's Magazine*, August, 1902) Oil, 23¾ x 14¾". The Delaware Art Museum, Wilmington

16. *The Buccaneer Was a Picturesque Fellow.* (From *The Fate of a Treasure Town* by Howard Pyle. Published in *Harper's Monthly*, December, 1905) Oil, 30½ x 19½". The Delaware Art Museum, Wilmington

color and I trust that I will be able so to instruct the pupil as to preserve whatever color talent he may possess. My experience is that within a year of such teaching the pupil will be sufficiently grounded in a practical knowledge of painting to be able to embark upon illustrative work."

Beyond these fundamentals, Pyle imparted his notions of good picture-making. The commanding teacher possessed a great talent for communicating the fundamental qualities inherent in all superior work, yet in tune with the individual qualities in the student's character. As N. C. Wyeth described his teacher, "Howard Pyle's extraordinary ability as a teacher lay primarily in his penetration. He could read beneath the crude lines on paper, detect therein our real inclinations and impulses; in short, unlock our personalities. This power was in no wise a superficial method handed out to those who might receive. We received in proportion to that which was fundamentally within us."

In his weekly composition classes—during which time Pyle reviewed the work of the students—he conveyed to his students the importance of total immersion, a kind of physical and mental projection *into* the picture until the artist senses that he has actually *become* the object. Only in this manner, Pyle emphasized, can the subject come to life in the painting. "Pictures are the creations of the imagination," he once said, "and not of technical facility....I subordinate that technical training entirely to the training of the imagination."

But imagination was not stirred simply by standing before an easel. Pyle urged his students to meet all facets of experience with an equal degree of delight and intensity, in work as well as in play. After all, both mind and muscle needed release. And so Pyle organized picnics, swimming parties, musical performances, costume parties, bicycle, sleigh, and buggy rides throughout the year.

These years of the Howard Pyle school probably represented the most joyous and

17. Headpiece 3 for *By Land and Sea*. (Published in *Harper's Monthly*, December, 1895)

18. *Then the Real Fight Began.* 1908. (From *Pennsylvania's Defiance of the U.S.* by H. L. Carson. Published in *Harper's Monthly,* October, 1908.) Oil on canvas, 30⅛ x 21½". Collection Mr. and Mrs. W. Sipple

19. *Blackbeard's Last Fight* (From *Jack Ballister's Fortunes* by Howard Pyle. Published in *St. Nicholas,* July, 1895 [also in bound form by Century Co., 1895]) Oil, 15⅛ x 10". The Delaware Art Museum, Wilmington

productive period of the artist's life. Some of his former pupils had already become established professionals in the city, Violet Oakley and Jessie Willcox Smith, for example. Maxfield Parrish, who studied only briefly with Pyle at Drexel, had also moved on to great success. To the Wilmington school came N. C. Wyeth, Frank Schoonover, Harvey Dunn, illustrators who would rise to fame within the next decade. Pyle also extended his teaching further by lecturing in New York and in Chicago.

In their work these students tended to reflect the various components of their teacher. His women students reflected his leanings toward the decorative, but the majority of the male students produced paintings endowed with what Pyle termed "experienced knowledge," a realism abundant in rich, romantic imagery as well. Pyle explained his purpose by saying, "My objective in teaching my pupils is that they should be fitted for any kind of art, whether of easel painting or even the minor uses of portrait painting.... Among my older pupils, for instance, are Miss Violet Oakley, whose trend is entirely in the direction of mural work and glass; Mr. F. E. Schoonover who, while his work is only just beginning to make an impression, has already received a commission to paint a picture of his own choice of subject."

The small city of Wilmington had become an important center for American illustration, and before long no American publication was without some indication of Pyle's influence as a teacher. For years to come publishers would be eager to commission work from Pyle students. The "Pyle look" became evident in paintings that depicted cowboys and Indians, seafaring life, American history; it was apparent in illustrations of the classics and interpretations of the contemporary scene. Moreover, several of his students went on to become teachers themselves, passing along Pyle's principles to younger generations of artists. The so-called Brandywine School has continued to this day, still flourishing under the brush of the Wyeth family—Andrew, Carolyn, Henriette, and Jamie—and evident in the work of other

H. Pyle.

21

20. *An Attack on a Galleon* (From *The Fate of a Treasure Town*. Published in *Harper's Monthly*, December, 1905) Oil, 29½ x 19½". The Delaware Art Museum, Wilmington

21. *Extorting Tribute from the Citizens* (From *The Fate of a Treasure Town*. Published in *Harper's Monthly*, December, 1905) Oil, 29½ x 19½". The Delaware Art Museum, Wilmington

22. *So the Treasure was Divided* (From *The Fate of a Treasure Town*. Published in *Harper's Monthly*, December, 1905) Oil, 19½ x 29½". The Delaware Art Museum, Wilmington

22

contemporary artists drawn to the beauty of the Brandywine region.

Even while his school was in full swing, there was no lessening in Pyle's own creative output. By now the publications were capable of reproducing oils and watercolors (primitive though it was, the photo-mechanical process of halftone reproduction had been introduced), and Pyle painted as long as the daylight sun poured into his studio. Although Pyle tended to relegate questions of technique to a secondary position, his own technical facility in oil painting was acute. He painted rapidly, with great ease, but avoided any self-conscious display of his skill—a restrained Puritan even here—seldom piling on the pigment in an impasto technique or revealing his dexterity with the brush in a showy manner. These hours standing at the easel (he called it "his only real exercise") were terminated as dusk drew near, when he would leave his studio and devote the balance of the day to his students and family, or resume his work on a manuscript. An average working day was ten or eleven hours.

On entering the first years of the twentieth century, however, Pyle encountered the sudden jolt of changing times. The publishing world, once so innocent and incorruptible, was undergoing profound changes which troubled Pyle. A new generation of artists nad begun to capture the imagination of a vast American public—artists whose talents were eagerly sought by the magazines at any cost. The bitter competition for talent elevated fees to levels that would have been unimaginable just ten years before. Charles Dana Gibson had emerged as the new star, and with him came a new wave of sophisticated fashions and fancy imitators. Pyle sensed he was growing out of date, was repeating himself, had gone stale. Looking back, he had written and illustrated twenty-four of his own books, illustrated well over 100 other books, and every major magazine in America— *Century, Collier's, Harper's Monthly, Harper's Weekly, Harper's Young People, Ladies' Home Journal, St. Nicholas, Scribner's*—had printed hundreds of his stories and illustrations. What was left for him to do?

No one quite believed it in 1906 when they heard that Howard Pyle had accepted a position as art director of *McClure's* for a salary of $36,000 a year. Just why he accepted this post—whether it was his anxiety over mounting expenses at home, or his fear of losing the esteem of the American public—is not really known. It was an impossible arrangement from the start, and his term lasted only a few months. This was Pyle's only conspicuous failure in a long line of successes.

If Pyle had been uncertain about his creative powers before taking the position with *McClure's,* his failure as art director seriously shook his self-assurance even further. He was fifty-three years old, restless, consumed with self-doubt. His gifted students had moved on to their own professional triumphs and the newer generation of students coming to Wilmington failed to interest him.

Although he continued to receive a steady stream of assignments, he considered them mediocre and felt that this reflected the fatigue that was setting into his work. In a letter to the *Harper's* editor, Pyle wrote in 1907, "I am in great danger of grinding out conventional magazine illustrations for conventional magazine stories."

Pyle searched within himself for newer challenges, for greater pictorial possibilities, anxious to prove that his creative abilities had not dwindled with middle age. Mural decoration offered him just such a challenge. He happily accepted several commissions offered to him. Pyle discovered that the projects challenged all his faculties as he made adjustments to the scale and lighting that were so different from the conditions imposed on his studio work.

But Pyle's first efforts disappointed him. In a serious effort to master the art of mural decoration, Pyle decided to venture to Europe, where he could study the Italian masterpieces and learn what only the great muralists of the Renaissance could teach—an experience he was certain would renew his creative powers. In 1910 Pyle and his family sailed for Italy.

We will never know whether the Italian journey would have accomplished for Howard Pyle all that he had intended. While still on board the trans-Atlantic liner, only a week after his departure from New York, his health began to fail. Although good health returned to him a few weeks after his arrival in Italy, the illness hovered over him for the following months. Successive disappointments from his editors in New York, combined with his weakened physical state, must have contributed to his rapid decline. Less than a year after his arrival in Italy, Howard Pyle passed away. He was fifty-eight years old.

H·Pyle.

23. *The Flying Dutchman* (Published in *Collier's Weekly,* December, 1900) Oil, 71⅜ x 47½″. The Delaware Art Museum, Wilmington

24. *Marooned*. 1909. Oil, 40 x 60″. The Delaware Art Museum, Wilmington

25

26

27

25. "A Wolf Had Not Been Seen at Salem for Thirty Years." (From *The Salem Wolf* by Howard Pyle. Published in *Harper's Monthly*, December, 1909.) Oil, 17½ x 29½". The Delaware Art Museum, Wilmington

26. *The Battle of Bunker Hill.* (From *The Story of the Revolution* by Henry Cabot Lodge. Published in *Scribner's Magazine*, February, 1898.) Oil, 23¼ x 35¼". The Delaware Art Museum, Wilmington

27. "Once it Chased Dr. Wilkinson into the very town itself." (From *The Salem Wolf* by Howard Pyle. Published in *Harper's Monthly*, December 1909.) Oil on canvas, 28 x 18". Collection Mr. and Mrs. Howard Pyle Brokaw

28. "Old Jacob Van Kleek Had Never Favored Our Hero's Suit." (From *The Mysterious Guest* by Howard Pyle. Published in *Harper's Monthly*, December, 1908.) Oil, 29½ x 19½". The Delaware Art Museum, Wilmington

29. *Soldier of Fortune* (Published in *Harper's Monthly*, December, 1893). Oil on canvas, 24 x 16". Collection Walt Reed, Connecticut

28

29

31

33

30. *Peractum Est!* (From *Quo Vadis* by Henryk Sienkiewicz. Little Brown & Co., 1897.) Oil, 26 x 16¾". The Delaware Art Museum, Wilmington

31. *Prince and Priest.* Oil on canvas, 24 x 16". Collection James Cushing, Jr.

32. Pen drawing for *Harper's Young People*

33. Pen drawing for *Harper's Young People*

32

1. *He Blew Three Deadly Notes.* 1917. Oil on canvas, 40 x 32″. Private collection

N. C. Wyeth

2. *Eseldorf Was a Paradise for Us Boys.* 1916. Oil on canvas, 42¼ x 33¼″. Collection Mr. and Mrs. Peter Hurd

3. *Self-Portrait.* 1914. Oil on canvas, 18¼ x 14¼". Collection Mr. and Mrs. Nicholas Wyeth

4. *Self-Portrait in Top Hat and Cape.* 1928. Oil on canvas, 41¼ x 36¼".
Private collection

𝒴oung N. C. Wyeth wrote to his mother the day after his arrival, "I think I shall like the place better than I expected." He had just embarked upon the most memorable journey of his life. On October 19, 1902—exactly three days before his twentieth birthday— Newell Convers Wyeth bid farewell to his parents in Needham, Massachusetts, boarded the Century Express out of Boston, and made his entrance into the finest school of illustration in the country: The Howard Pyle School of Art in Wilmington, Delaware. Admission to the school was no small feat for the eager young man, and he felt a warm sense of gratitude for the support he received from home.

Always sensitive to the yearnings of her son, Henriette Zirngiebel Wyeth understood the significance of young Convers' passion for drawing. She had urged her husband to allow their oldest boy to leave the school he disliked and instead study drafting at the nearby Mechanic Arts School in Boston. When he graduated in 1899, N. C. Wyeth borrowed money from his reluctant father to continue his studies at the Massachusetts Normal Arts School. Encouraged by an instructor to study illustration, Wyeth went on to the Eric Pape School of Art in Boston and studied further under George L. Noyes and later Charles W. Reed. He knew of Howard Pyle's school (which was then three years old) in Wilmington through a friend, Clifford Ashley, and, at Ashley's effective persuasion, N. C. applied to the school.

Because the enrollment to the school was restricted to twenty, Pyle handpicked his pupils carefully, examining examples of the candidates' work and evaluating their character in a personal interview. Even then, the student was accepted only on a trial basis. The twenty-year-old N. C. Wyeth knew how privileged he was to be attending this extraordinary school, studying under the man whose work he had admired since boyhood, and he understood he would have to apply himself. He was expected to live a Spartan existence in order to develop all the disciplines necessary for good work. Winters were spent in Wilmington and summers

Reprinted with permission from *American Artist*, "Three Generations of the Wyeth Family" by Susan E. Meyer. © 1975 Billboard Publications, Inc.

67

N·C·WYETH

just ten miles away on the Brandywine River in the open country of Chadds Ford, Pennsylvania.

Dedicated to the notion that art and life were inextricably linked, Howard Pyle introduced young Wyeth to a schedule that included both hard work and pleasant festivities. Picnics, swimming, and parties were organized in the spirit of camaraderie. A fine horseman, N. C. Wyeth was called upon to hitch up the horses and drive the group through the countryside.

Pyle recognized Wyeth's artistic talent and encouraged him through the years. "Pyle emphasized that hard work, constantly applied, and the living of the simple life were two things that would bring about my making," N. C. Wyeth recalled years later.

When he descended from the train in 1902, young Newell Convers Wyeth knew that years of hard work lay ahead. Yet how could he foresee that this region of America would be his home for the remainder of his life? Through the years he wrote carefully considered letters to his family several times a week. This enormous correspondence, which provides a personal insight into the artist, was meticulously compiled twenty years after the artist's death by his daughter-in-law Betsy James Wyeth. Published in 1971, *The Wyeths* documents the emotional and intellectual development of one of America's finest illustrators. Through this correspondence the reader comes to know, admire, and love this great and complex man who was driven by a vision of life that he nevertheless felt incapable of obtaining.

N. C. Wyeth's trial period at the Pyle school lasted only a few months before he was elevated to advanced standing; he progressed rapidly. He was naturally responsive to the rigors of long hours of concentration, and both his talents and exuberant personality won him the respect and affection of his colleagues and his Master. Before long he was receiving commissions from the magazine publishers in New York and Philadelphia and sending money home to Needham to repay his family for their support.

Early in his career he was attracted to the potential of illustrating the cowboys and Indians of the West. Understanding the value of first-hand knowledge, he made a three-and-one-half-month trip to the West in 1904, earning his way as he traveled by working on a ranch in Colorado and as a mail rider in New Mexico. During this trip he gathered costumes and props from the cowboys and from the Navajo Indians, the beginnings of a collection that was to grow through the years, material vital to the authenticity of his illustration. This trip to the West—and the second that followed two years later—made an indelible contribution to his reservoir of images and impressions, a rich supply from which he would draw again and again.

But N. C. Wyeth was too searching in nature to restrict himself exclusively to the Western scene. Unlike many of his contemporaries, Wyeth sought to expand his subject matter—and with that his own education—into many areas. And so he read voluminously, collected costumes and props of all periods, and went on to illustrate subjects as vastly different from each other as Colonial America, Biblical Judea, and Medieval England.

Although Wyeth was attentive to historical details in his illustration and researched thoroughly the periods he was depicting, history was not simply an accumulation of facts: history was *experience*. He found in history those very moments that corresponded to something true within him, an emotional truth. For him the past contained vital stories of romance, of triumphs and failures, of expectations and disappointments, but these experiences were not buried with the past; only the setting changed. All experience could be reawakened.

Intensity of feeling was a quality he valued in himself and nurtured in his family: it was the lifeblood of the artist, the prize for being alive. All experience—if intensely felt—was precious, and the artist could summon and express those feelings in limitless ways. Building experience upon experience, the artist creates an abundant repository of impressions upon which he can play over and over: the richer this reservoir, the more precious.

"How desperately I cling to memories!" he wrote in 1917. "They are shrines to which I constantly attend! They bring to me more vividly than by any other means of contemplation the significance of the eternal past, the eternal future—and our place between the two eternities. As I look back over my experiences, for the recent sharp and defined ones and

5. *Robin Hood*. 1917. Oil on canvas, 40 x 32". (Cover painting for *Robin Hood* by Paul Creswick, David McKay, 1917.) Collection The Central Children's Room, Donnell Library Center, The New York Public Library

6. Indian Drawing. 1904. Pencil. Private collection   7. Indian Drawing. 1904. Pencil. Private collection

follow them as they recede in the rapid perspective of only thirty-four years, it has the effect of precipitating my imagination down the countless ages of *all* experience!"

And from this repository of images and associations N. C. Wyeth could transform a grove of trees in Chadds Ford into a Sherwood Forest, a sloping bank along the Brandywine River into a Civil War battle scene, a young woman into a bearded woodsman. From his imagination emerged the vivid characterization of Robin Hood, Bill Bones, Long John Silver, individuals as human as the artist's uncle or the postman who delivered the mail each day.

In addition to the hundreds of articles, the countless calendars, posters, brochures, and advertisements he illustrated, N. C. Wyeth illustrated over one hundred books. To name only a few of these: *Drums* by James Boyd; *The Parables of Jesus*; *The Mysterious Stranger* and *Tom Sawyer* by Mark Twain; *The Last of the Mohicans* and *The Deerslayer* by James Fenimore Cooper; *Robin Hood* by Paul Creswick; *Robinson Crusoe* by Daniel Defoe; *Horatio Hornblower* by C. S. Forester; *The Boys' King Arthur* by Sidney Lanier; *Treasure Island, Kidnapped*, and *The Black Arrow* by Robert Louis Stevenson.

N. C. Wyeth's painting was as much an expression of his physical nature as it was of his mental powers. His own outward appearance was distinctive: at 6 feet 2 inches he was normally the tallest person in the room, and he weighed 210 pounds, more or less. (Periodically he would control his healthy appetite and reduce.) His broad chest was the most expansive section of his frame, which narrowed at the hips and was supported by surprisingly slight legs. His arms were also slender, and his hands were rather small for his size and extremely delicate. His body, therefore, was a kind of contradiction of extremes: large and small, delicate and massive, refined and rugged. He was graceful when he moved, an excellent dancer, yet was a rugged athlete (a horseman and hiker) in his younger days. He was assertive and commanding, yet his voice was surprisingly high for a man of his size. Several people observed that his entrance into a room would bring voices to a hush. Yet he was not overbearing. N. C. Wyeth was a man whose mere physical presence charged the room with energy, a kind of vitality one seldom encounters.

When he painted, Wyeth was continually in motion. Although in reproduction his illustrations would be reduced to page size—8 x 10", perhaps—he preferred painting the original oil on a large surface—frequently 32 x 40"—with broad brushes and occasionally a palette knife. He applied his juicy pigment in assertive strokes to the canvas, a movement that

70

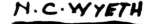

involved his entire body, like a fencer striking out in a duel. He would then back away from the canvas to study the composition through squinting eyes, returning swiftly on the attack to make the necessary alterations and additions. He worked rapidly, frequently completing an illustration in one day, and rarely in more than three. The subjects were generally men—seldom women—massive and bulky like the artist himself. Heroic and violent action—dueling, buffalo hunting, bronco busting—was part of his vast repertoire of work, but it was not the essence of his power as an artist, for he created a total world within the confines of his canvas, an atmosphere, a mood that endured after the battle was over. Action itself was secondary: tension, expectation, melancholy, fear, or triumph—these were the moods children recalled long after the pages of the book were closed.

N. C. Wyeth was a big man, and his paintings were big in both scale and in vision. It was natural, in view of this preference for large scale, that N. C. would be attracted to a still larger format, so he gladly accepted commissions to paint murals, and he completed some forty murals and large decorations for institutions, banks, and public buildings. To accommodate the size of his mural work, he built an addition to his studio and outfitted the large wing with ladders and scaffolding, which he would climb up and down vigorously—again, he was always in motion.

N. C. Wyeth learned from Howard Pyle the value of what could be termed "corporal identification" with his subject, an empathy in which the artist and subject would palpitate with the same life force, would actually become the same. If N. C. Wyeth's paintings bear a certain physical relationship to N. C.'s own physical presence, therefore, it is no accident. He consciously worked to transform himself into his subject. As he explained the process:

"My brothers and I were brought up on a farm, and from the time I could walk I was conscripted into doing every conceivable chore that there was to do about the place. This early training gave me a vivid appreciation of the part the body plays in action.

"Now when I paint a figure on horseback, a man plowing, or a woman buffeted by the wind, I have an acute sense of the muscle strain, the feel of the hickory handle, or the protective bend of head and squint of eye that each pose involves. After painting action scenes I have ached for hours because of having put myself in the other fellow's shoes as I realized him on canvas."

During his forty-three-year career, his illustrations numbered well over 2,000. But, between assignments and commissions, he devoted his time to a pursuit even more precious to him: his easel painting. He would leave behind his world of heroes and villains, of bucking horses and raging storms, and tramp off into the countryside to paint his beloved Brandywine Valley (and later the coast of Maine), gentle scenes of a newborn calf, a silent ripple of the river's current, a farmer's travail.

If the bulk of his time was devoted to illustration, his heart was with his non-commercial painting. The conflict between his illustration and his easel painting continued to plague him through the years, at times subsiding somewhat perhaps, but at other times driving him into black moods of depression. The man who had elevated illustration to a new dimension of excellence was the very same man who tortured himself with uncertainties and regrets. In 1909 he wrote his family, "It undoubtedly seems strange to you to hear me say that the very source of my livelihood (and a good one it is too) is the very thing that is standing in my way. All that I have done in the past, all that I could do in the future (in illustration) would be utterly forgotten in a preciously few years except by a few friends and relatives perhaps. It is my purpose to create pictures that will last, like the works of men like Michelangelo, Raphael, Millet, and scores of others." A few months later he continued this thinking in another letter: "The same love, the same enthusiasm that goes to make illustration goes to make painting—the one is born into the world under limitations that choke and distort and soon die—the other is born full and free as the air; if it ripens it will stand as a perfect expression of those loves and will last forever."

On April 16, 1906, N. C. Wyeth married Carolyn Bockius of Wilmington, Delaware. When he first began courting the young woman in 1904, he found her rather frail. He described her, somewhat unflatteringly to his parents, "She is timid—but her mind is alert,

N·C·WYETH

and although she may seem rather backward to comprehend [something] and more so to put [it] into immediate practice, she will store it in her head and shall make good use of it later." Whether Carolyn Bockius actually improved with age, or whether N. C. himself grew to see her differently, we will never know. Yet we do know that N. C. Wyeth married an extraordinary woman. Through the entire span of their marriage, and through the nearly thirty years she survived him after his death, Mrs. N. C. Wyeth remained an intuitive and sensitive woman, the constant strength of the family. She saw her husband through his moods, gave him the constant support and approval he so badly needed, and bore him six children.

Their first baby died shortly after birth. On October 22, 1907, the Wyeths announced the birth of Henriette (named after N. C. Wyeth's mother). Two years later, in 1909, Carolyn was born. Their first son, Nathaniel, arrived two years later, in 1911, and sister Ann in 1915. Finally, in 1917, their last child, Andrew, was born.

It was not long after their marriage that the Wyeths decided to leave the city of Wilmington and settle in Chadds Ford, Pennsylvania. Here N.C. felt he could make his "simple life" by remaining close to the countryside he loved. ("The city is no place for any artist, young or old," he was known to have said many times.) Much as he may have yearned for his native New England, N. C. had planted his roots in Chadds Ford permanently. (In 1921 the family did move to Needham, only to return two years later to Chadds Ford, persuaded at long last that the ties to Delaware County, Pennsylvania, were too strong to sever.) In 1911 N. C. bought eighteen acres of wooded land and designed a simple red-brick house. Behind the house, perched on a gently sloping hill, N. C. built the studio of his dreams, the Palladian windows facing north and overlooking the house and family he adored.

In the twenties the Wyeths began to spend their summers in Port Clyde, Maine. And so it was that by the late 1920s the route between Chadds Ford, Pennsylvania, and the Maine coast became well-worn by the Wyeths and their offspring.

From the depths of his soul, N. C. Wyeth understood Howard Pyle when the elder illustrator extolled the virtues of a simple life. A simple life meant that the artist would not be subjected to continual distractions from his work. But it meant more than that to N. C. His New England predecessors—writers such as Ralph Waldo Emerson and Henry David Thoreau, whose works he devoured passionately—had written of the simple life in more profound terms. Like Thoreau, N. C. Wyeth saw in nature a cosmos, inexhaustible in its potential for beauty. He wrote, "I am beginning to think that people of today are divided into two classes: those that accept elemental Nature casually, as a mere accessory to the important business of *trivial living*; and those who sense the perfect amalgamation of elemental nature and human life, that *cosmic relationship* which if not felt leaves us superficial and at bottom *useless* to ourselves and to the world."

And to nature he returned time and time again as his source of inspiration. Yet it would be inaccurate to say that he regarded nature as his "subject matter," so hostile was he to the so-called landscape painters who tramped through the fields "like hunters with guns over their shoulders, to 'shoot landscape,' and nothing more." Just as Pyle had taught him to project himself into his subject, so had N. C. applied this to his painting of nature. As he wrote in 1921, "To paint a landscape wherever one is endeavoring to represent with passionate emotion the hot molten gold of sunlight, the heavy sultry distances and the burning breath of soft breezes, one returns home in the evening proud and happily sympathetic in sweaty clothes and burned arms and neck. To feel thus completes one's sense of identification and unity with nature."

And so the walks through the countryside became a family ritual: a team of explorers— N. C. and the children—out to discover the wonders of their land. The aroma of moist, spring blossoms, the mud that oozed between bare toes, the sunlight flickering on the water lilies...a morning's walk was an excursion into the world of the familiar and the unknown, the world of mushrooms and goblins, clouds and princes, romance and reality ever entwined within the woods of Chadds Ford, along the banks of the Brandywine River. A leaf falling from a tree was a magical event, and N. C.'s contagious enthusiasm intoxicated the children as they shared in the mystery of those rapturous moments, building upon those experiences the rich

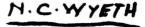

8. *Where the Mail Goes, Cream of Wheat Goes.* 1906. Oil on canvas, 44¼ x 30½". The Minneapolis Institute of Arts

9. *The Bronco Buster.* 1906 (Advertisement for Cream of Wheat.) The Minneapolis Institute of Arts

repository of associations N. C. found so vital to the development of the artist within.

"Among those misty gray hills of Chadds Ford," he wrote, "along the stretches of those succulent meadows with their peaceful cattle, in those big sad trees, and the quaint and humble stone farmhouses tucked underneath them there is that spirit which exactly appeals to the deepest appreciation of my soul. To me it is all like wonderfully soft and liquid music." Each of the children emerged from youth with that profound feeling for the mystery of nature, and each has expressed that love in a highly personal way.

If so much richness lay just beyond the threshold of his home, there was no need to travel farther for inspiration. In fact, too much travel represented a hazard to the artist: the loss of his integrity. Like Thoreau, Wyeth spurned travel, fearing the evil effects of fragmentation or, as he put it, "the profound risk of being adulterated by others." Only five years after arriving in Wilmington, N. C. wrote:

"I don't believe any man who ever painted a great big picture did so by wandering from one place to another searching for interesting material. By the gods! There's almost an inexhaustible supply of subjects right around my back door, meager as it is.

"I have come to the *full* conclusion that a man can only paint that which he knows even more than intimately; he has got to know it spiritually. And to do that he has got to live around it, in it, and be a *part* of it!

"I feel so moved sometimes toward nature that I could almost throw myself face down into a ploughed furrow—*ploughed* furrow understand! I love it so."

If at times he berated himself for, as he wrote, "living too well, too luxuriantly, for the proper disciplining of my nature," he never lost sight of the basic ingredients needed for the proper working environment and for a wholesome family setting. He was a devoted if

73

N·C·WYETH

10. *The Crystal Depths.* 1907. Oil on canvas, 38 x 26″. Private collection

11. *Deerslayer Threw All his Force into a Desperate Effort.* 1925. Oil on canvas, 40 x 32″ (From *The Deerslayer* by James Fenimore Cooper © 1925 Charles Scribner's Sons, renewed 1953.) Formerly Collection Mrs. N. C. Wyeth

12. *The Hunter.* 1907. Oil on canvas, 39 x 27″ ("The Indian in His Solitude," cover painting for *Outing Magazine,* June, 1907) Collection the Brandywine River Museum, Chadds Ford, Pennsylvania

somewhat unorthodox parent, an inspiration to each of the children. Perhaps his greatest gift as a father was his own childlike nature, his exuberant personality—"his charisma," some have called it. Wyeth's interest was swiftly ignited—by an abstract aesthetic theory, perhaps, or the child's first steps, or a budding bluebell on the Brandywine. These were miracles to him; he responded to them with a joyful outburst of enthusiasm. This spontaneous curiosity, this recurring state of wonder at even the simplest phenomenon, never diminished with the years. And nowhere was his delight in life more evident than where his children were concerned. Just moments after the birth of a new child, N. C. was alert to what was inherently unique in the infant, instantly sensitive to a certain revealing expression in the eyes or a decisive movement in the body. Preserving this individuality and even expanding the singular qualities in each child was to be his primary mission as a parent. He took a passionate interest in their training, beginning with the earliest years of walking through the countryside. "We make a great deal of these simple experiences," he wrote a year after the birth of his fifth child. "I believe them to be the real foundation of one of the most profound ethical ideas in regard to early training, to obtain the utmost of pleasure and inspiration for the simplest and homeliest events of the life about us."

Long before educational experimentation was fashionable, the Wyeths sent their young children to a nearby Montessori school, where classroom work was tailored to the individual child's particular interests and gifts. When they were too old to continue in the school, and experiences with public education proved unsatisfactory, Wyeth withdrew them from the formal classroom setting and hired tutors for individual work. "Every mother's son of us is born with that supreme gift of individual perception," he wrote, "but the sheeplike tendency of human society soon makes inroads on a child's unsophistications, and then popular

education completes the dastardly work with its systematic formulas, and *away* goes the individual, hurling through space into that hateful oblivion of mediocrity." Each of the five Wyeth children received individual instruction, liberated from the "menace of all organized schools and colleges."

Wyeth's theory did not imply, however, that the children would be liberated from study. On the contrary, their training was even more rigorous, because it was designed to awaken dormant talents, to amplify the gifts that set each child apart. Having a natural gift, after all, was only the beginning: "All the 'natural' talents of youth cannot take the place of *disciplined training.* Beethoven was a prodigy as a boy pianist, but witness the infinite and painstaking training which followed his initial flowering. Without this exhaustive discipline we would not have had the Beethoven of the nine symphonies."

Henriette, Carolyn, and Andrew, by revealing their preference for art, worked with N. C. Wyeth in the studio for several hours each day. Ann, showing an early gift for music, studied piano with a tutor, then continued on to study composition. As a boy, Nathaniel exhibited his affinity for mechanical structure by building elaborate ship models. N. C. predicted that his son would create, "but not in art," and he was correct. Because his interest lay in the sciences, Nat went on to college to study engineering. Now he is a design engineer, one of the few in this country hired by a major corporation to design whatever new system interests him.

N. C. Wyeth, like Howard Pyle, deplored dilettantism. It was better not to work at all than to dabble; work was a total commitment, regardless of the chosen field. This attitude made N. C. a formidable teacher. From the day his student first entered the studio, disciplined training began. Scornful of the leniency most art schools permitted, N. C. was a strict and exacting instructor. First, the basics: "It makes me weary to see how students insist upon avoiding the one thing that will fundamentalize their work throughout their lives—that vital necessity of knowing how to draw." Each student began with the basic geometric forms (cone, sphere, etc.) and would draw—until achieving near perfection—plaster casts, then still life, then landscape exercises. Only through knowledge can creative interpretation begin, he maintained. "A thing done right is done with the authority of knowledge (coupled with temperament). One has difficulties only when one lacks the knowledge of *truth,* which includes the knowledge of craft as well as of nature—a clear vision is absolutely necessary before the creation of a piece of art is undertaken and the power to execute said piece of art with precision and fluidity is just as necessary."

Before becoming N. C.'s student, Andrew favored pen and ink, so the elder Wyeth required that the boy switch to charcoal to avoid becoming too facile with his tools. When Carolyn arrived for her work in the studio an hour later than usual, N. C. abruptly sent her away: "Don't bother coming at all if you're going to be late," he insisted. He may have been tough, but he did not have time or interest for training dilettantes, and they knew it. His discipline proved invaluable for each of the Wyeth children, and they developed skills and working habits that laid the groundwork for their future creative work.

As the children advanced from their early training, they found in their father a brilliant teacher; he had a special gift for analytic simplification. He urged the children to empathize with their subjects as he had learned to do from Howard Pyle—to plunge into their picture, to become a physical part of their subject. A sleeve was not just a piece of cloth; there was an arm beneath: palpitating, tense from fear, perhaps, or fatigued from overwork. Each of the children learned to build a good design (a composition that would hold together even if the picture were held upside down). From his work as an illustrator, he knew how to single out the dramatic feature of the story and depict it—in the simplest, most undistracting terms—on the canvas. He had much to teach his children regarding the use of light, the capturing of the passing moment, the necessity for an uncluttered statement.

In his hands the students grew in a deeply personal way as well. Wyeth did not approve of "picture making." Creative expression, after all, is simply a visual statement of the artist's soul. And cultivation of that soul was even more important than training the eye and hand.

Listening to any one of the Wyeths today—hearing Henriette, Carolyn, Nat, Ann, or Andy recall those childhood experiences—one is transported into a kind of storybook world.

N·C·WYETH

14

13. *Summer* (From "The Moods" by George T. Marsh. *Scribner's Magazine,* December, 1909) Oil on canvas, 33½ x 30″. Private collection

14. *Winter* (From "The Moods" by George T. Marsh. *Scribner's Magazine,* December, 1909) Oil on canvas, 33½ x 30″. Private collection

There was "Pa," the driving generating force of the family, whose intense emotional responses vaulted from formidable eruptions of passion to quiet moments of tenderness. And there was "Ma," always constant and supportive, intuitively sensitive to the yearnings in each of them. Tramping through Chadds Ford countryside, the children discovered a world of marvelous fantasies at every turn. In the evenings N. C. read aloud to the family, or a record was played on the Victrola, the large living room suddenly filled with the splendid music of Sibelius or Beethoven. N. C. was a gifted musician himself, capable of improvising casually at the piano. Through the years the family entertained many guests, writers and artists who brought into the Wyeth home the stimulating world of another life.

The holidays, in particular, were events of even heightened pleasure. In the studio N. C. possessed a treasure trove of costumes and props, a collection that he had accumulated through the years for his illustration. At no time was fantasy more real than on those occasions when the costumes came to life as part of the pageantry of celebration. On Halloween in 1918, the studio was festooned with pumpkins, field corn, and Chinese lanterns. After the room was darkened, the children were permitted to enter, and N. C. marveled at the delighted response. In writing to his family about this occasion he described it: "Halloween favors were at each place, and with the smirking and ogling pumpkins peeking through the ranked cornstalks and the fire on the hearth flickering over it all, another valuable impression has been registered on these children's minds—and *ours*!!"

N. C. was convincing in his impersonations of imaginary characters. Christmas never passed without a visit from "Old Kris"—N. C. Wyeth in costume, of course—who climbed from the rooftop, ringing his bells jubilantly, tromping down to the living room, where he handed out his special gifts each year. These were the intense occasions, the magic and mystery of fantasy come true, when N. C.'s storybook characters entered the home and came to life.

N. C. nurtured these experiences, knowing that they would be part of the reservoir of images that would foster "that strange love for things remote." The music, the fine literature, the costumes and masks are all part of the rich associations that continue to nourish their imaginations today.

N. C. Wyeth wrote his family about these events: "I'll tell you these things are significant to me and offer me great relief in that they show an ability that will always give the children a foundation reason why it is worthwhile to live, and secondly as they weave the textures of their lives, the background of memories will give them untold pleasures and perhaps be the basis upon which they can build an important work."

The children advanced rapidly in their personal and creative development, ever under the watchful eye of their proud father. Henriette, Carolyn, and Andy were showing great promise in their painting, each embarking on very different avenues of expression. By 1935 two more artists had joined the family by marriage, both of them painters who had studied with N. C. Wyeth: Peter Hurd and Henriette Wyeth were married in 1929, and John McCoy married Ann Wyeth in 1935.

"This watching of the unfolding of all the younger members of the family is a glorious episode of my life," N. C. wrote in 1939. "... I am asked interminably, 'Aren't you proud of it all?' Of course I am, beyond the expression of any words. But my answer is always restrained because I am still in the battle myself, in spirit at least, and I still have a fairly clear vision of what lies ahead to be done before a real mark is achieved."

N. C. Wyeth did not live long enough to enjoy the full measure of his children's attainments. Nor did he meet the next generation of artists to emerge in the family—George Weymouth (married to Ann, the daughter of Mr. and Mrs. John McCoy) and Jamie Wyeth (the son of Mr. and Mrs. Andrew Wyeth). On October 19, 1945—exactly forty-three years from the day N. C. first arrived in Wilmington, Delaware—he and his grandson Newell Convers II were driving just two miles from home. N. C. approached a railroad crossing, which was obstructed by foliage, and an oncoming train struck the car he was driving. N.C. and his four-year-old grandson both died only moments after the collision.

N·C·WYETH

15. *Spring* (From "The Moods" by George T. Marsh. *Scribner's Magazine,* December, 1909) Oil on canvas, 33¾ x 30″. Private collection

16. *The Ore Wagon.* 1907. (From *The Misadventures of Cassidy* by E. S. Moffatt. Published in *McClure's Magazine,* May, 1908.)
Oil on canvas, 38 x 25″. Collection Southern Arizona Bank and Trust Company, Tucson

17. *Old Kris.* 1925. Oil on canvas, 41½ x 31". Collection John Denys McCoy

18. *Captain Bill Bones* (from *Treasure Island* by Robert Louis Stevenson, Scribner's, 1911) Oil on canvas, Collection Mrs. Brigham Britton

19. *The Giant*. 1923. Oil on canvas, 71½ x 56½". Collection Westtown School, Westtown, Pennsylvania

20. *The Passing of Robin Hood.* Oil on canvas, 40 x 32″. Collection The Central Children's Room, Donnell Library Center, The New York Public Library

21. *Robin Hood and His Companions Lend Aid from Ambush.* 1917. Oil on canvas. Collection The Central Children's Room, Donnell Library Center, The New York Public Library

1. *Lieutenant S. C. Robertson, Chief of the Crow Scouts.* 1890. Watercolor on paper, 18⅛ x 13⅛″. Amon Carter Museum, Fort Worth, Texas

Frederic Remington

2. *Coming Through the Rye*. c. 1902. Bronze, 27½″ high. Whitney Gallery of Western Art,
Buffalo Bill Historical Center, Cody, Wyoming

3. *Smugglers Attacked by Mexican Customs Guards.* 1901. Oil on canvas, 40 x 27⅛″. Amon Carter Museum,
Fort Worth, Texas

4. *A Cracker Cowboy of Florida.* 1895 (Published in *Harper's Monthly*, August 1895). Oil on canvas, 24⅛ x 20″. "21" Club Collection, Peter Kriendler President

*I*t was known the world over that the Americans were a rowdy bunch. They were naive and unrefined, with an undaunted pioneering spirit—they would take on any Goliath standing in their way—a rugged lot, indeed. Some of the best in American illustration contains these very qualities: a vigor and energy, if somewhat crude at times; an honesty unembellished with dainty refinements.

In his art and in his life Frederic Remington stands as the archetype of the rugged American individualist. His subject—the American West—is the symbol of that robust American personality, and his paintings and drawings represent the best examples of what made American illustration unique. Only in America could a man live in an urban environment six months of the year—hobnobbing with the most sophisticated artists, publishers, and writers of the day—and live six months in the saddle with the cavalry, cowboys, and tramps on the Western frontier. Yet Remington was equally at home in both environments and both environments accepted him equally. Only in America.

Remington came by this unorthodox mixture quite naturally from his father. The senior Remington, Seth Pierpont (known as "Pierre"), was a newspaper publisher and a hero in the Civil War, and set a fine example for the boy. Born in Canton, New York, in 1861, Frederic was only a few months old when his father sold his newspaper, recruited a company for the mounted regiment that became the famous fighting Eleventh New York Cavalry, and left home for four years to fight campaigns in Virginia and Louisiana. Returning with a distinguished military record, his father ultimately repurchased his newspaper, the *St. Lawrence Plaindealer,* and resumed his life as a patriotic crusader for the Republican Party.

At the same time, Frederic's father also continued to indulge his passion for horses by investing in the training and racing of thoroughbreds and standard-breds for the track. His

FREDERIC REMINGTON

5. *An Ox Train in the Mountains* (Published in *Harper's Weekly,* May 26, 1888). Oil on canvas, 21 x 28″. "21" Club Collection, Peter Kriendler President

son frequently joined him in making the rounds of the fairs, stock farms, and races, acquiring a basic training in how to evaluate horseflesh and how to handle even the most spirited of horses. All during his boyhood, young Fred could be seen galloping over the countryside on his own horse, under the proud, watchful eye of "the colonel," as his father was called.

The younger Remington continued to be a sportsman all his life; more sportsman, that is, than student. He was a rebellious boy—at military school and later at Yale—and was more inclined to engage in fist fights and pranks than in studies. As one classmate, Julian Wilder, recalled years later in a 1910 article in *Collier's*: "I should always have remembered Remington without his rising to fame, for a little wrestling match in which we once indulged resulting in my receiving a broken shoulder blade, a broken collar bone and a dislocation of the arm." Military school failed to harness him, and later at Yale's School of Fine Arts, Remington complained of the stuffy atmosphere he found so boring.

Just when he decided to become an artist is not certain. He had begun to take an interest in drawing while at the military academy. From the outset he seems to have preferred scenes of adventure and action: Cossacks, scouts, and frontier troopers on horseback populated the rather crude pen sketches he made at the time. The classes at Yale were too restricting for the restless young Remington. The dreary exercises in drawing from plaster casts held little kinship with his zeal for action.

Although he endured the academic rituals of his art classes painfully, he relished football with a passion. He excelled on the varsity team as a "rusher" and, between his bouts on the playing field, also became Yale's heavyweight boxing champion.

Remington's art was always connected to his love for sports and outdoor life. Although he

FREDERIC REMINGTON

is best remembered for his depictions of the West, he also wrote some splendid stories on the theme of sports—all true incidents in which he participated—and created a number of paintings and drawings on sports subjects as well, including football, horsemanship, canoeing, and hunting. His drawing called "A Tackle and Ball Down," in an 1887 issue of *Harper's Weekly*, is one of the first pictures published of football players in action.

Remington did not remain at Yale for long. Much to his mother's disappointment, he left the school after his father died, in the middle of his second year. (Several years later, in 1900, Yale awarded him an honorary degree, a gesture Remington found very touching.)

Although his father had left him a modest inheritance, Frederic was obliged to wait for nearly three years until he was of age before he could control the patrimony. For a brief time he took a clerical position at the Governor's office in Albany, but tended to pass the better part of his day making pictures rather than attending to his clerical duties. He clearly did not have the temperament for an office job, having instead a marked preference for his spare-time activities of horseback riding and boxing.

In the meantime he had fallen in love with Eva Adele Caten and, with characteristic impetuousness, asked for her hand in marriage just a few days after meeting her. With little prospect of a secure future seen for his daughter, Lawton Caten withheld his consent to the marriage. Young Remington was resolved to win his bride by going to the West to seek his fortune and prove his worthiness.

Actually, this was just the excuse Remington needed to make the trip he had dreamed of all his life. It was 1881. The allure of the West was most tantalizing to a hearty and robust boy with a rich imagination: the cattle industry was flourishing; new gold fields were reported; his mind was filled with the romantic tales of adventure he had read, and he was eager to retrace the steps of his heroes, Lewis and Clark and George Catlin. He embarked on his great adventure with visions of glory before him.

The notion of combining his lust for the West with his artistic gifts did not occur to him until after his arrival in Montana. Years later Remington recalled his moment of awakening: "Evening overtook me one night in Montana and by good luck I made the campfire of an old wagon freighter who shared his coffee and bacon with me. I was nineteen years of age and he was a very old man....During his long life he had followed the receding frontiers, always further and further West. 'And now,' said he, 'there is no more West. In a few years the railroad will come along the Yellowstone and a poor man cannot make a living at all'....He had his point of view and he made a new one for me....I saw men all ready swarming into the land. I knew the derby hat, the smoking chimneys, the cord-binders, and the thirty-day notes were upon us in a restless surge. I knew the wild riders and the vacant land were about to vanish forever...and the more I considered the subject, the bigger the Forever loomed. Without knowing exactly how to do it, I began to try to record some facts around me, and the more I looked the more the panorama unfolded."

For the remaining years of his life, Remington devoted himself to the mission of recording those facts.

Frederic Remington returned from his first trip to the West a few months later, but certainly not with a fortune in hand. Instead he had a sack full of drawings, most of them crude, of the sights he had seen as he "hobnobbed with scouts, miners and freebooters of the plains." *Harper's Weekly* purchased one drawing—which was redrawn by William A. Rogers—and devoted a full page to its reproduction.

Convinced that there was a future for him in this business, Remington returned to the West in 1882, now having control of his father's modest inheritance. He invested in a sheep ranch in Kansas and spent a year operating the spread, an experience which provided the kind of intimate knowledge of the West he would utilize throughout the remainder of his life. During this time he made hundreds of sketches and set down to serious painting in his improvised studio on the ranch. Eva Caten's father must have been softened by Remington's seriousness of purpose and by the sincerity of the couple's mutual ardor, and he finally consented to their marriage in 1884.

The newlyweds settled in Kansas City, a booming city on the threshold of the West. Here

FREDERIC REMINGTON

6. *Don Gomez and His Lancers at Ochoa Springs.* Oil on canvas, 27⅛ x 40⅛". "21" Club Collection, Peter Kriendler President

Remington invested his savings in a thriving saloon, only to find soon after that his partners had swindled him out of his money. His efforts to sell his material to the New York publishers had failed and the couple was penniless. In a final resolve, Remington disposed of all their possessions, returned his wife to the East, and took off on horseback, committed to the task of succeeding—once and for all—as an artist of the West.

And so he did. In 1886 he finally sold his drawings in succession to *Harper's Weekly, St. Nicholas,* and *Outing.* Success came very rapidly to him after these appeared. He never had to worry about finances again. In five years he had already seen more of the West than most men see in a lifetime, and with his uncanny ability to remember details, he possessed a reservoir of images and associations that he could draw upon repeatedly over the years ahead.

But Remington was not content simply to paint and draw what he had seen in his youth. He was driven by a compelling urge to return to the West over and over again. The sport of it, the rugged men he met (men "with the bark on," as he was fond of saying), the saloons and campfires, the dust, open ranges, and big sky overhead were too important for him to abandon in exchange for a routine life in a New York studio. The frontier life was so close to his own character that he was incapable of adopting any substitute. Returning to the West each year—and in some periods making as many as four trips in a year—Remington collected new material for his illustrations and reported on current events, but these trips were more than assignments to him: they also satisfied his restless spirit. "If I sat around the house all the time," he observed, "I couldn't do it....I travel a third or half my time. I can't work steadily more than two or three months. I must go somewhere and see something new. Then when I see what I want I think it over and kind of get my idea of what I am going to do. Then the rest is nothing."

This was the schedule he maintained for the duration of his career. Returning from the

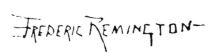

7. *How Order Number Six Went Through* (Published in *Harper's Monthly,* May 1898). Oil on canvas, 27⅛ x 40″. "21" Club Collection, Peter Kriendler President

West to his home outside New York City in New Rochelle, Remington would work every day for several weeks. He would arise at 6:00 A.M., paint from 8:00 to mid-afternoon, and culminate the day with exercise, either walking or horseback riding. He adhered to this daily schedule until he was off again to the West or to his summer home on an island he purchased on the St. Lawrence, not far from his childhood home.

Until the early twentieth century—when his work became more lyrical as he turned toward becoming a fine artist—his paintings and drawings were intended to serve one purpose alone: to record and document the changing West. He was a journalist, like his father, but without a visible crusade (although he was inclined to side with the military in their efforts to bridle the Indians). He objectively recorded current events and reconstructed historical episodes: the explorers of the West, the trailfinders, the pioneers, the Plains Indians, the cavalry, and cowboys. To the most minute detail, Remington's paintings illustrated the life on the reservations, the wagon trains, the Indian wars, the European immigrants establishing their settlements, the frontier trappers, buffalo hunters, and cattle ranchers. The subjects were unending and entirely in tune with Remington's own free spirit. As he commented in an interview in 1900, "Western subjects for art? Why, I don't consider that there is any place in the world that offers the subjects that the West offers. Everything in the West is life, and you want life in art. There is a freedom about the West that is inspiring: it is still comparatively new, invigorating. The field to me is almost inexhaustible, although I've been painting and drawing Western life for a great many years."

This animated quality in Remington made him immediately likeable. A robust and energetic man—he weighed over two hundred pounds—Remington swaggered as he walked and spoke his mind freely. While accompanying the cavalry as a reporter on an Indian mission, Remington was always a welcome member of the troop. A young lieutenant observed

that the artist was "a big, good-natured, overgrown boy—a fellow you could not fail to like the first time you saw him—that was the way he appeared to us."

He was the personification of the American spirit, a man's man, an athlete, story-teller, adventurer: in short, an American hero. An invitation to travel in Europe, for example, was made palatable to him only because of the opportunity it offered to canoe down the Volga. Although this did not work out as expected, he found another attraction in Europe to make up for the loss: in London he was able to attend Buffalo Bill's famous Western show.

If his personality seems to resemble that of another figure who was prominent at the time—Teddy Roosevelt—it is not surprising to learn that they were friends. Their mutual love for the West could not fail to draw them together. Roosevelt had been the owner of his own cattle ranch in North Dakota in the early 1880s and wrote a series of articles about his experiences for *Century* a few years later, requesting that Remington be the man to illustrate these stories. Thus ensued a lifelong friendship. Roosevelt was one of the few to recognize Remington's exceptional talents as a writer: "You come closer to the real thing with the pen than any other man in the western business. . . . Without stopping your work [in art], I do hope you will devote more and more time to the pen." And in a eulogy for Remington, Roosevelt prophesied, "The soldier, the cowboy and rancher, the Indian, the horse and cattle of the plains will live in his pictures, I verily believe, for all time."

While his contemporaries were concerned primarily with illustrating fiction, Remington was recording the facts, a reporter on horseback documenting a changing civilization. His paintings and drawings were designed to tell a true story, to narrate the events as they unfolded before him, chronicles of their time. Any historian of the West cannot fail to benefit from a close study of these documents.

Determined to achieve authenticity in everything he created, Remington developed a mind capable of retaining the most minor details from observation. He was also able to record essential facts in rapidly executed pen sketches. Moreover, he amassed a large collection of Western paraphernalia to use for reference once he returned to his New York studio—costumes, saddles, weapons—props he repeatedly worked into his paintings and drawings over the years. In his travels West, Remington never failed to bring with him a camera for recording additional details to supplement his sketches. This, he claimed, was its only merit, capturing the fleeting moments of a scene more effectively with a pen than with the camera: "The best reason why I use them [photographs] so little is that I can beat a Kodak—that is get more action and better action because Kodaks have no brains—no discrimination."

Regarding his work as a document, Remington avoided any temptation to romanticize the West while on these assignments. (Later, when he turned to fine art, he was more inclined to do so, but surely not in his illustrations of the time.) He demonstrated in his art the very qualities he respected most in the men of the West: he was a painter "with the bark on." Remington was disinterested in the romantic landscapes that had attracted Thomas Moran or Albert Bierstadt, and he refused to sentimentalize the cowboy and Indian as his Eastern colleagues tended to do. He captured instead the hard-bitten reality of the rugged life in the West. The men in his illustrations are dusty and sweaty, the horses frequently scrawny, the Indian more human than villain. If some of these early illustrations seem to suffer from a certain crudity in execution—lacking the technical polish evidenced by his colleagues—they excel in authenticity, a raw truth brutally expressed and so characteristic of the rugged American pioneer they described.

Although he was a consummate painter of nature, Remington subordinated landscape to the human figure, regarding it simply as a setting for the dramatic events occurring between man and beast or between man and man. (Not surprisingly, Remington's paintings rarely included women.) Over the years he developed a great facility for rendering—entirely from imagination—the human figure in any pose. He was equally skilled at depicting animals, particularly the horse, portraying convincingly the powerful agility of his lifelong friend. His father would, no doubt, have been proud to have seen how well his son had come to know the horse, from the saddle and at the easel.

FREDERIC REMINGTON

8. *"Howdy Pard," The New Year's Stag Dance at Headquarters* (Published in *Collier's Weekly,* December 1901). Oil on canvas, 27 x 40″. "21" Club Collection, Peter Kriendler President

9. *The Last Three.* Oil on canvas, 21¾ x 34″. "21" Club Collection, Peter Kriendler President

10

11

12

10. *Drum Corps, Mexican Army.* 1889. Oil on wood, 18⅛ x 28⅛". Amon Carter Museum, Fort Worth, Texas

11. *Through the Smoke Sprang the Daring Young Soldier.* 1897. Oil on canvas, 27¼ x 40⅛". Amon Carter Museum, Fort Worth, Texas

12. *Bronco Buster.* 1895. Bronze, height 23¼". Whitney Gallery of Western Art, Cody, Wyoming

13. *His First Lesson.* 1903. Oil on canvas, 27¼ x 40". Amon Carter Museum, Fort Worth, Texas

13

14. *A Merry Christmas in a Sibley Tent* (Published in *Harper's Weekly,* December 1891). Oil on canvas, 23⅛ x 33″. "21" Club
Collection. Peter Kriendler President.

15. *The Old Stage Coach of the Plains.* 1901 (Original illustration for *The Century Magazine,* January 1902). Oil on canvas, 40¼ x 27¼". Amon Carter Museum, Fort Worth, Texas

16. *Hunters Camp in the Big Horn.* 1909. Oil on canvas, 27 x 30″. National Cowboy Hall of Fame, Oklahoma City

17. *In From the Night Herd.* Oil on canvas, 27 x 40″. Albert K. Mitchell Collection, National Cowboy Hall of Fame, Oklahoma City

Remington's discovery of sculpture in 1898 had an immeasurable effect on his development as an artist. Always an admirer of sculpture, he was urged to try it by a sculptor friend, Frederic Ruckstull, who sensed Remington's ability to see the figure three-dimensionally. Remington's first attempt at sculpture resulted in *The Bronco Buster*, a piece displaying his natural talent for the medium. "I always had a feeling for mud," he explained, "and I wanted to do something a burglar wouldn't have, moths eat, or time blacken."

His success with the first piece encouraged him to try others, recognizing the potential for success in what he termed "the mud business." During the following years, he created nearly twenty pieces. His technical ability for sculpture was a marvel. He was virtually the first artist in America to use the lost wax process—brought to this country from Europe by Riccardo Bertelli—which enabled him to create pieces of great delicacy and movement, unobtainable by the traditional sand-casting process commonly used until then. (Bertelli could be exasperated with this ambitious artist at times. Remington would push the medium to great extremes in order to accomplish the effects he desired. According to Bertelli, Remington "always wanted to have his horses with all four feet *off* the ground!")

In the relatively short period that he was a full-time illustrator, Remington managed to compress a volume of work most artists would have been pleased to produce in a lifetime. (By the time he died he had painted something like 3,000 oils.) He worked fast and deliberately, eager to "get on with it," dividing his time between his work in the studio and his travels. His illustrations appeared regularly in all the major magazines until 1903, when he signed an exclusive contract with *Collier's*, an arrangement that lasted only for a little more than a year. After this, Remington turned his efforts exclusively to working for exhibition rather than reproduction. He had been an illustrator for eighteen years.

The transition from illustrator to fine artist had been gradual, and a number of incidences accounted for the change. Always eager for recognition by his peers, Remington had entered his works regularly in exhibitions in the New York area, with some degree of success. Just six years after the publication of his first illustration, Remington was elected to associate membership in the National Academy, a distinguished honor for any artist, particularly an illustrator. His early efforts at exhibition did not prove so financially successful that he was able to exchange his lucrative career as an illustrator with an uncertain future as a fine artist. But new developments altered his course.

Once champion in his field, Remington began to encounter competition from a newer generation of illustrators who were eclipsing him in popularity, a development Remington found threatening to his pride and self-esteem. A young painter, Charles Schreyvogel, had become particularly popular and Remington's jealousy of this artist, his outspoken hostility to what he called Schreyvogel's "half baked stuff," created a foolish image in the public eye. Humiliated at having exposed his hurt pride so publicly, Remington withdrew from battle to devote himself entirely to his painting and sculpture.

During the five years Remington painted exclusively for exhibition, his approach changed quite markedly. He was less concerned with literal reporting, and more inclined to romanticize. Disappointed with the changes he was witnessing in the West, Remington observed that his beloved territory was being taken over by "derby hats and blue overhauls." Consequently, his work became more reflective, more painterly, more emotional, far less reliant upon observed facts. Moreover, Remington had become clearly influenced by the American Impressionists (several of whom were his friends), who were exhibiting their work widely. He began to incorporate some of their techniques into his own work. He experimented with a brighter palette, a freer brushstroke, and became particularly fascinated by the mysterious qualities of nocturnal light and color, which he tried to capture over and over in his paintings.

Remington's new efforts as a fine artist were just beginning to enjoy the acceptance of the critics when he died suddenly at forty-eight, stricken with an acute attack of appendicitis and never recovering from the emergency surgery performed on him. It seems incongruous that such an early death should come to this hardy and robust man whose brief career left so enduring a contribution to our American heritage.

18. *Infantry Soldier.* 1901. Pastel on paper, 29 x 15⅞". Amon Carter Museum, Fort Worth, Texas

19

19. *The Last Stand.* 1890. Oil on canvas, 64 x 47″. Collection of Western Art and Artifacts at Woolaroc Museum, Bartlesville, Oklahoma

20. *An Indian Trapper.* 1889 (Original illustration for *Harper's Monthly,* May 1891). Oil on canvas, 49⅛ x 34¼″. Amon Carter Museum, Fort Worth, Texas

21. *Register Rock, Idaho.* c. 1891 (Original illustration for *The Century Magazine,* July 1891). Oil on canvas, 17⅛ x 27¾″.
Amon Carter Museum, Fort Worth, Texas (following spread)

FREDERIC REMINGTON

22

23

22. *Sign of the Buffalo Scout.* 1907. Oil on canvas, 27 x 40″. Albert K. Mitchell Collection, National Cowboy Hall of Fame, Oklahoma City

23. *The Smoke Signal.* 1905. Oil on canvas, 30½ x 48¼″. Amon Carter Museum, Fort Worth, Texas

24. *Cheyenne Buck.* 1901. Pastel, 28½ x 24″. Joe Gordon Collection, National Cowboy Hall of Fame, Oklahoma City

1. *The Reluctant Dragon.* 1898. Oil on stretched paper. Collection Mr. and Mrs. Daniel W. Dietrich II

Maxfield Parrish

2. *Baa Baa Black Sheep.* 1897 (From *Mother Goose in Prose* by L. Frank Baum).
Drawing in lithographic crayon and india ink on white paper, 12¾ x 10¾".
Fogg Art Museum, Harvard University, Cambridge, Massachusetts. Gift of
Charles Bain Hoyt

3. *Autumn Brook.* 1948. Oil on panel. Private collection

4. *Evening Shadows.* 1960. Oil on panel, 11 x 13″. Collection Quintin Magbanua. © Brown & Bigelow, a division of Standard Packaging Corporation

4

*M*axfield Parrish wrote in 1943, "There is nothing I dislike more than any kind of personal publicity, the so-called write up or 'story'.... There isn't any story here. So many in the past have tried to find one; jumped at the conclusion that because I painted pictures of a certain kind there must be something decidedly interesting about the artist; he must live in a tree, eat nuts and berries, or something."* So Parrish expressed himself in a letter to Brown & Bigelow (for whom he had been painting landscapes since 1936), in response to their suggestion that a free-lance writer be sent to Cornish to interview him.

In fact, Parrish was an intensely private man, preferring to keep others at a distance at all times. Consequently, the image of the artist as presented in print tends to be like his art—orderly and well balanced, yet without revealing any glimpse at the inner life of the creator. He always presented himself as a charming gentleman, and his astonishingly handsome appearance was consistent with his energy and gift for conversation. In his art and in his personality, he could charm his public with a sharp sense of humor which could range from being devilishly wicked to gently whimsical. But emotions were not a matter for display.

In general, Parrish was not given to passion or impulse—to the unpredictable twists and turns in life—as so many of his colleagues tended to be. He suffered no financial hardships, even before he became a professional artist, and his brilliant artistic gifts were recognized early in his career, with no later reversals. In what was no doubt a profound aspect of his character, Parrish conserved his energies, devoting his most intense concerns to his work, unwilling to let distractions deter him from his deliberate course. With this single-mindedness of purpose, Parrish's creative powers expanded, rather than diminished, during a career that spanned sixty-five years of uninterrupted work.

Parrish was fortunate even by birth. Not many artists are lucky enough to be born into a family where artistic pursuits are so cherished as they were in the Parrish household. His father, Stephen Parrish, earned a distinguished reputation as an artist—particularly for his etchings—having courageously given up his stationery store in Philadelphia to commit himself totally to his art. Young Maxfield (who was actually born Frederick Parrish, but later assumed his paternal grandmother's maiden name as a middle name, by which he came to be known professionally) never felt a conflict between his parents' expectations for him and his own particular yearnings. Music, literature, and art were an important part of his boyhood.

*Except where otherwise noted, quotations appearing in this chapter have been excerpted from the only major study ever completed of Maxfield Parrish, an excellent book by Coy Ludwig, *Maxfield Parrish,* Watson-Guptill Publications, 1973.

M . P

5. *Villa Medici, Rome* (From *Italian Villas and Their Gardens* by Edith Wharton, 1904). Oil on panel. Collection Union Oil of California

6. *Vicobello, Siena* (From *Italian Villas and Their Gardens* by Edith Wharton, 1904). Oil on paper. Collection John D. Merriam

The boy's exposure to this heritage was reinforced in 1884—when he was fourteen—by a two-year trip to Europe with his parents, during which time his father painted, Maxfield studied in Paris, and all three attended concerts and museums regularly.

Maxfield had already shown indications of talent in drawing by the time he was three, a gift the father encouraged by giving him instruction and helping him develop a critical eye toward art and nature. Years later Stephen Parrish continued to instruct Maxfield when they shared a studio for two consecutive summers in Massachusetts. Parrish always maintained that his father was his most influential teacher.

One senses that art for Maxfield Parrish was a perfectly natural outcome of his youth. Except for a brief flirtation with architecture, while studying at Haverford College, Parrish's choice of art as a career was logical. (He never altogether abandoned architecture, however, incorporating the interest in various aspects of his work throughout his life.) After his graduation from Haverford he studied for two years at the Pennsylvania Academy of the Fine Arts and attended some classes of Howard Pyle's at the Drexel Institute. (It is reported that Pyle, after an examination of Parrish's portfolio, announced there was nothing more he could teach the young artist, recommending only that Parrish develop a more individual style in his work.)

So these early years were not consumed with self-doubt and uncertainties, economic deprivation or family pressures so commonly associated with the beginnings of an artist's career. He married in the same year he received his first commission—a cover design for

M . P

Harper's Bazar in 1895—and never suffered for lack of work opportunities from that point on. His single mission and sense of purpose must have been the reason he left for Europe, alone, to visit its museums and salons only days after his marriage to Lydia Austin. Upon his return two months later, he settled into a Philadelphia studio to work. The couple lived in Philadelphia only three years before moving to a new home near Cornish, New Hampshire.

Cornish was an ideal choice. During the 1890s, it was well known as a summer colony of artists and writers, a lively community of intellectuals. The first of this group to settle there was Augustus Saint-Gaudens—the eminent sculptor of the day—who was later followed by artists Thomas Dewing, Herbert Adams, Paul Manship, Kenyon Cox, and writers Percy MacKaye, Hamlin Garland, and Norman Hapgood. Parrish's parents had already settled there and Maxfield decided to build a home nearby.

This was no ordinary home, however. Having studied classical architecture closely, with the intention of becoming an architect himself, Parrish was determined to apply to this new structure the kind of resolution that was so characteristic of the man. He designed *and* built the house himself, with only the assistance of a local carpenter. When completed, the home was cited in a number of magazines as a remarkable architectural achievement. Like everything else Parrish designed, "The Oaks" (as the residence was called) is elegant, demonstrating the artist's brilliance for spatial balance, detail, and fine craftsmanship. As the family enlarged, so did the dwelling in which they resided, and the home became still more original in concept and construction. In addition to the house itself, he constructed a sizeable building for his studio, one that contained rooms for a fully equipped machine shop, darkroom, painting studio, as well as a living room, kitchen, two bedrooms, and garage.

"The Oaks" remained Parrish's home for the duration of his life. He was content to remain in New Hampshire all year round, even though Mrs. Parrish preferred to travel south in the winter. For over twenty of these winters she would journey to Saint Simons Island, a small island off the coast of Georgia, to research the songs and dances the natives had inherited from their slave ancestors. (She compiled her findings in a 1942 book called *Slave Songs of the Georgia Sea Islands*.) Unlike his wife, Parrish preferred the long New England winters when he could work uninterrupted by the festivities that distracted him during the summer months. For sixty-five years, except for the brief trips he made on assignment or with his family, Parrish withdrew into his studio each day at dawn.

He was not a man to combine his activities as an artist with those of a father. They were clearly separated. Unlike Howard Pyle or N. C. Wyeth, whose children ambled freely through the studio while their father worked, Maxfield Parrish did not welcome interruptions of any sort. If any of his four children entered their father's studio during the course of a working day, it was as model to the artist.

(He did, however, enjoy teaching his three sons how to use the machines in the shop below the studio. "Even when he was working, the humming of the lathe or the screech of the table saw was music to his ears," recalls one member of the family. "But, let the family's Holstein cow, in season, lift her voice in song from the pasture below his studio and he would telephone his wife at the house to 'take that God damned animal over to the west pasture!'")

If his sentiments toward family seem stern, they are consistent with the discipline he exercised in his daily routine. Always finding the morning hours most productive, Parrish would awaken early and begin immediately. During these morning hours he attended to the procedures that demanded his most intense concentration—drawing in the figures or designing compositions, perhaps—and in the afternoon he would undertake the more routine tasks, such as glazing, varnishing, or constructing panels. He never deviated from this schedule.

Parrish was highly structured. By looking closely at the art he produced over the years, it seems inconceivable that he could have been otherwise. His approach to design, and the techniques he employed to execute these concepts, demanded painstaking attention to detail and a thought pattern that was analytic and orderly. He was intrigued by mechanics and architecture, not given to spontaneous whims. "I'm no good at the little telling sketch," he remarked once, a statement that says as much about his character as it does about his art. It is

M . P

7. *Tramp's Thanksgiving* (also called *The Tramp's Dinner*). (Design for *Collier's Magazine* cover, November 18, 1905). Oil, 20½ x 15½". The Delaware Art Museum, Wilmington

8. *Concerning Witchcraft* (From *Knickerbocker's History of New York* by Washington Irving, 1900). Pen and ink with crayon. From the original in the Free Library of Philadelphia

not surprising to learn, for example, that he subscribed to a theory of design, current at the time, called Dynamic Symmetry. This theory owes its formulation to Jay Hambidge, whose analysis of Greek art determined that its evident harmony could be explained by reducing the designs to a series of rectangles. This elaborate system of designing with rectangles formed a rather rigid design principle to which Parrish adhered during the second half of his career. Only a disciplined artist like Parrish, whose thinking was so analytic and whose art so structured, could apply such a complex theory to an entire body of work as successfully as he did.

His technical approach to painting was equally exacting. Parrish possessed a deep regard for fine craftsmanship in all art, including the musical and culinary arts as well as the visual arts. His devotion to beautiful objects—regardless of how utilitarian—inspired him to create his own artifacts. For example, in his machine shop he constructed hinges, latches, and other everyday objects for his home. Shortly after Masonite was introduced on the market, Parrish discovered that the material could provide an excellent support for his paintings. His affection for Masonite was so great, in fact, that he experimented with it in other ways as well. In his workshop he built tables and chairs from the material and found it preferable to wood for his picture frames. Parrish even constructed his own boxes for shipping the panels. He painted these boxes on the inside because he was convinced that a painting that arrived in a handsome package would bring more immediate favorable reaction from a client. As a child he made wooden models and later used these skills to construct elaborate architectural models—which he illuminated—to be used as models for his paintings. Even at seventy-three years old, entirely unassisted, he installed a new roof to his studio building!

It is possible that Parrish first understood the value of relating craft to art from his father. He could have seen that Stephen Parrish's delicate etchings relied as much on technical knowledge and a craftsman's hand as they did upon a sensitive, artistic eye. In the etching process, art cannot be separated from machinery. Young Maxfield may have recognized, very

M · P

early in his life, that an artist can only benefit by using technology to his advantage.

It was logical, therefore, that Parrish would use photography as an adjunct to his art as well, constructing an array of instruments that other artists might well have found bewildering at the time. Parrish used, for example, a large 4 x 5-inch glass plate camera, developing the image in positive form on another glass plate in a darkroom located in his studio. In 1925 Parrish constructed an elaborate projector (which resembled one later introduced on the market called a Balopticon). Parrish would slip the glass print into his home-built contraption and project the image onto a sheet of tracing paper. He could adjust the size of the projected image by raising or lowering the instrument. Parrish would trace what he wanted from the photograph and transfer the image onto his painting surface. He generally combined several photographs for one painting. Parrish never painted from live models, preferring instead to photograph the model—who was generally a member of the family or a friend or himself—in a variety of poses, selecting the desired poses for projection onto the tracing paper.

This devotion to craftsmanship was nowhere more apparent than in his inventive methods of drawing and painting. Even early in his career—before he had begun to utilize the glazing technique with which he became so associated in later years—he used whatever resources were necessary to execute his concept. With a strong feeling for contour always pronounced in his work, he might cut the silhouette of a figure from a piece of heavy paper, draw in the features, and paste it down onto a highly detailed drawing he had already made on another sheet. Consequently, even his simplest black-and-white work of this early period might combine collage with pen and ink and lithographic crayon drawings, a wash or two of watercolor, and perhaps areas of Rossboard (a paper already decorated with dots or lines).

Parrish was most ingenious, however, in his oil painting technique. No other artist has ever managed to accomplish the mysterious effects of light so identified with the Parrish touch. His uncanny gift for unusual design and pattern, combined with a most unorthodox sense of color, was heightened to its best advantage by his meticulous glazing technique.

Parrish was always fascinated by the iridescent qualities of color intensified by light. Even in his early work he would outline his forms, pronouncing the design pattern through silhouetted shapes, and apply flat areas of transparent color within these contours. He called these his "colored drawings." As he developed a more sophisticated painting technique, he eliminated the contour and modeled his forms with color instead. He began to use glazes almost exclusively.

In a sense, Parrish was a Tiffany with paint. He sought the effect of stained glass in his painting or—in his terms—the brilliant effect of a Kodachrome transparency illuminated from behind with light. With his inclination to this kind of technological reference, Parrish also maintained that this method more closely approximated the printing process by placing one color over another in a succession of layers. In fact, the glazing technique is one of the most *difficult* to reproduce because it relies so heavily on the particular qualities inherent in oil paints, features bearing little resemblance to the qualities of printing inks or to the methods of halftone printing which so inadequately translate the subtleties of glazes into a pattern of dots. (One has only to compare an original Parrish with a reproduction of the same to see how much is lost.)

In spite of the technological references Parrish made in describing the glazing technique, he was also well aware that the method itself originated centuries before, with the old masters. It was, as he said, "not original with me." Simply stated, the procedure is as follows: Over a white ground several thin layers (glazes) of transparent paint are applied. By being transparent, each layer should be discernible from the top surface and the underlying color should be heightened by the reflective qualities of the white ground below. The layers of paint are like color filters, therefore, enhancing the color beneath and, in combination, forming a luminous build-up of color that is unobtainable through any other means. In theory, glazing seems quite simple. In practice, it is painstaking and laborious.

First Parrish would prepare his panel by coating it with a good white primer (he used F. Weber's Permalba). Then he would outline the drawing in pencil, indicating where the first underpainting would be placed. The underpainting was a strong treatment in monochrome—usually in monastral or ultramarine blue—designed to dominate

119

M . P

the layers placed over it and to provide a good foundation for shadows. Over this he would bring up the transparent layers, using opaque pigments only for trees. To prepare his paints, Parrish would squeeze some oil pigment from the tube onto a glass palette, without mixing it with any other paint. (In its pure state, pigment is at its maximum transparency.) Then he would add some linseed oil to the pigment, just enough to obtain the desired degree of transparency, best determined by mixing the paint on a sheet of glass placed over a piece of white cardboard. After reaching the desired consistency, Parrish would place a very thin application of the paint in small areas, then press the pigment against the surface of the panel with a rag to flatten it out completely, and to remove even the slightest trace of brushstroke left by the small brush.

Between each layer of paint was applied an equally thin layer of varnish. The varnish prevented any contamination of paint from one layer to the next, and also restored the brilliance of the original oil color which had subdued after drying. The varnishing process was almost as painstaking as the glazing. Varnish can only be applied after the layer of oil paint is absolutely dry, a process requiring as much as ten days to two weeks. Varnishing is accomplished only in a very warm room in which both painting and varnish have already been exposed to the heat for some time to eliminate any moisture. Before applying the subsequent layer of glaze, Parrish was obliged to wait for the varnish to dry thoroughly. Finally, he would roughen the varnished surface by rubbing it lightly with a pumice to create a more receptive "tooth" on which the next layer of glaze would adhere. Since so much time was required for the drying of these panels, Parrish worked on several paintings simultaneously—as many as ten or twelve at a time—drying them out in the sun's heat during the summer and exposing them to heat lamps in the winter.

Since the glazes had to be applied meticulously, Parrish adopted a number of methods for doing this. For most of his work he used a so-called stipple brush, a tool most commonly associated with painting china. Available in several sizes, the stipple brush is actually loaded only on the ends of its bristles so that the paint is deposited on the surface in a series of dots, or "stipples," rather than in a single mass of paint. The underlying surface is visible through these dots. As more pigment is added, these dots are converted into an overall layer of paint, but the artist can control the point at which he wants this to occur. Using this technique, Parrish could grade his pigments carefully from a dense concentration of color to a bare whisper of it. The final results look almost as if he had used an airbrush (which he did not), so indiscernible are the gradations from one color to the next.

Controlling these pigments and enhancing the transparent effects of the glazes were his most persistent technical challenges. He would texture the glazes with coarse paper, wipe them out with cheesecloth, clean their edges with a pencil knife, and resort to whatever methods he could devise to heighten the degree of reality in his make-believe scenes.

If an ordinary work day for Parrish included long hours of concentrated application to details, it must also have provided the single strongest outlet for his whimsical side as well. How else can we explain the images that emerged each day from those meticulously painted panels? Goblins, serpents, giants, and dragons living in a magic, gossamer world of castles and clouds. Only a mind rich in fantasy could have produced the unforgettable creatures populating his many children's books: The Reluctant Dragon in *Dream Days*, Humpty Dumpty in *Mother Goose in Prose*, Prince Agib and Sinbad in *The Arabian Nights*, Pompdebile in *The Knave of Hearts*. A never-ending parade of kings and queens, gnomes and nymphs, paupers and noblemen sallied forth from the Cornish studio, leaping and dancing, swinging and strutting throughout each season, year after year.

His characterizations, combined with his strong sense of design, made him the most popular advertising and cover design artist of his time. He was not a narrative illustrator, as Pyle, Wyeth, or Flagg were, because he was less interested in telling a story than in making a picture. His work was more decorative than literary. In recognizing that all covers for books and magazines must be regarded as posters, he made a major contribution to the development of graphics in America.

Parrish never took any shortcuts with these assignments. He established new challenges

M . P

9. *Primitive Man*. 1921 (Calendar design for General Electric Mazda Lamps). Oil on panel, 28 x 18″. Private collection

10. *Prometheus* (Calendar design for General Electric Mazda Lamps, 1920). Oil on panel. Courtesy Graham Gallery, N.Y.

whenever he suspected he was repeating himself. Wearied of the narrow vertical format imposed by the standard magazine, for example, Parrish introduced the strong horizontal line—which later became a common practice for magazines—to readjust the spatial elements for a more unpredictable arrangement. When *Collier's Weekly* offered him an exclusive contract, he accepted, not only for the excellent fee he was promised, but because with the magazine's large format (9 x 12″ rather than the usual 7 x 10″) Parrish felt he would have greater freedom to explore new avenues in his work. During the seven years (1903–10) Parrish worked under this contract, he took the opportunity to experiment rather than to repeat, and these covers represent some of his finest achievements in magazine illustration. Ten years later he agreed to paint a number of covers for the humor magazine *Life*, and here his work was altogether different again. In these covers—which he called his "odds and ends"—he painted comical characters performing their antics against a plain background.

In addition to the books and magazines he illustrated and the several murals he executed (which again called upon his knowledge of architecture), Parrish also did extensive work in the field of advertising. His Dutch boy became a virtual trademark for Colgate products, and he worked regularly for Fisk Tires, Jell-O, Cranes' Chocolates, among several other accounts. One of these assignments came every year from 1918 to 1934: a calendar painting for Edison Mazda, printed in a large and small format. No single account ever gave Parrish greater visibility to the vast American public. The success of these calendars is evident by the editions of the smaller format calendars: in 1918 with the first, Edison Mazda printed 400,000; in 1925 1,500,000 were printed! Available in two sizes, the calendar paintings also appeared on

121

M · P

11

12

13

11. *Villa Torlonia, Frascati (The Cascade)*. (From *Italian Villas and Their Gardens* by Edith Wharton, 1904). Oil on panel, 28 x 18″. Collection Mr. and Mrs. Arthur Manella, Studio City, California

12. *Little Sugar River, Noon*. Oil on panel, 15½ x 19¾″. Virginia Museum of Fine Arts, Richmond. Gift of Mr. Langbourne M. Williams

13. *Birches*. 1946. Oil, 13 x 15″. Collection Mr. and Mrs. Samuel G. Waugh. © Brown & Bigelow, a division of Standard Packaging Corporation

playing cards. Every family in America seemed to have a Maxfield Parrish in their home.

Parrish was not happy with his advertising work. With each assignment he endured constant interruptions, was frustrated by the restrictions imposed upon him, and did not feel adequately compensated for the time spent on the work. "I only want a little of this kind of work," he wrote, "for I find that the way I do it does not pay me anywhere near as well as what we may call my regular work." Moreover, he had come to see that there was a burgeoning market for art prints.

It was not unreasonable that Parrish should be called "The Businessman with a Brush." Always handsomely paid for his illustrative work, he recognized early in his career that there was also a market for his originals as well. After 1902, in fact, Parrish sold only the reproduction rights, retaining the original paintings for sale to collectors. Whenever the magazines made prints of these paintings—which was commonly done by magazines of the day—Parrish additionally received a small royalty upon their sale.

By the 1920s it had become evident to Parrish that it would be lucrative to paint specifically for the purpose of publishing art prints. He wrote: "What I am doing nowadays is to build up the print business. A successful print is a pretty good thing all round. In the first place I can paint exactly what I please, and then, if it's successful it means an income, a pretty big one, for a number of years." With this intention, he decided to reduce his work load for advertising to devote greater time to art prints.

It was not until 1923 that Parrish painted his first picture exclusively for this purpose. And his first effort in this direction was to become his most famous of paintings: *Daybreak*. Published by the House of Art, "the great picture," as Parrish called it, became the rage of its day. It was pure Parrish, executed in the characteristic Parrish blue—for which the artist had become so well known—and using as models his daughter Jean and one of his favorites, Kitty Owen, a friend of his sons. The subject was strange and arresting: two nymphettes lingering peacefully in a mysterious, dream-like setting, a suggestive painting that enchanted millions of Americans. Reproductions could be seen everywhere—in hotel lobbies, college dormitories, over mantels, in bedrooms. By 1925—only two years after it had been published—Parrish had already earned more than $75,000 in royalties!

Parrish went on to create three more paintings for art prints which were not quite so successful. By the time he had completed the third, however, his interests had already shifted, and he wanted only to paint pure landscapes. "I'm done with girls on rocks," Parrish stated flatly in a 1932 interview. "I've painted them for thirteen years and I could paint them and sell them for thirteen more. That's the peril of the commercial art game. It tempts a man to repeat himself."

Actually, Parrish had always held a special affection for landscape. His father—from whom Maxfield had learned so much—had been an excellent landscape painter and printmaker; in Maxfield's early assignments—such as his work for Edith Wharton's *Italian Villas and Their Gardens*, in 1903, for example—he demonstrated his evident skill. Throughout his life, moreover, he lived in a setting that reminded him daily of the rich potential in nature. His description of the view from his Cornish home strangely resembles the qualities of a Parrish landscape painting: "...as you descend some steps from the upper level to the house terrace, through old oak trunks and branches, through them and beyond them, you have a confused sensation that there is something grand going to happen. There is blue distance, infinite distance, seen through this hole and that, a sense of great space and glorious things in store for you, if only you go a little further to grasp it all. It takes your breath away a little, as there seems to be just blue forms ahead and no floor."

It was not until the thirties that Parrish turned to landscape exclusively. Brown & Bigelow, the calendar and greeting card company in Saint Paul, Minnesota, gave him just the opportunity he was seeking: to paint pure landscapes—with no restrictions whatsoever—for their annual calendar. Each year, from 1936 to 1962 (when he had finally become too infirm to paint any longer), Parrish delivered a new landscape to Brown & Bigelow, an astonishing array of mysterious, jewel-like scenes that seemed to have been painted from another planet, or the moon perhaps, but surely not on earth.

M . P

14

15

16

14. *Old King Cole.* Oil on canvas. The Mask and Wig Club of the University of Pennsylvania

15. *Cook with Steaming Pot of Soup.* 1923. (From *The Knave of Hearts* by Louise Saunders, 1925). Oil on panel, 8 x 18″. Collection Mr. Hans Lewald

16. *Humpty Dumpty* (*Life* cover, March 17, 1921). Oil on panel. Rare Book Division, George Arents Research Library, Syracuse University

17

17. *Lobsters and Chef* (From *The Knave of Hearts* by Louise Saunders, 1925). Oil on white card, 9 x 19½″. Collection Jeffrey T. Darbee

18. *Welcome Home, Teddy Roosevelt.* 1910. Oil on paper, 18 x 23¾″. Private collection

19. *A Swiss Admiral* (*Life* cover, June 30, 1921). Oil on white card, 15 x 12″. Private collection

18

19

20. *Man with an Apple* (*Collier's* cover, April 1, 1911). Graphite under oil on paper, 22½ x 16″. Collection Achenbach Foundation for Graphic Arts, California Palace of the Legion of Honor, San Francisco

21. *Sign Painter with Mudball (A Man of Letters)*. (*Life* cover, January 5, 1922). Oil on panel, 15 x 12″. Private collection

Parrish derived enormous satisfaction from directing his creative energies entirely toward the painting of landscapes, as he was able to do in the new phase of his career undertaken under the aegis of Brown & Bigelow. And it was a source of pleasure to him that his very first painting for Brown & Bigelow was the first landscape in the history of the company to become a leader in sales volume.

Of course, these marvelous paintings were not painted on-the-spot, but they were, like everything Parrish painted, created in his studio from props, models, photographs, and from his rich imagination. He assembled these inventively: "The tree was taken outside my studio window here," he wrote, "the brook was from the back of Windsor, the rocks were from Bellows Falls, and a mountain or two from Arizona. And yet I've heard some say that they had been just to that spot."

Ever the inventor, Maxfield Parrish might construct his landscape scenes entirely in his studio. We have an account of this procedure from Maxfield Parrish, Jr., who observed: "He had a collection of about twenty or thirty pieces of granite, schist, quartz, and other sedimentary igneous rocks weighing from a pound or two to ten pounds. These all were painted a light neutral brown. Rottenstone powder was mixed with varnish and turpentine and had the color of light-tinted mud. He would arrange these on his worktable in his studio, usually on a piece of plate glass, and pour around the bases of the rock powdered rottenstone, dry and finely powdered, and the angle of repose, after a few sharp raps on the edge of the table with a piece of stove wood, made it assume more or less the same shapes as the talus slopes one sees around the base of weathered cliffs and mountain faces. He would then close the curtains of the studio, and with a single student lamp try illuminating the synthetic landscape with this single source of light at various angles till he got the effect he wanted. The upside-down reflection of the whole from the upper surface of the glass at a low angle gave a quite realistic looking landscape surrounded by a placid body of water." Parrish would photograph this set-up, project it onto his tracing paper, and proceed as he would with any other painting.

These landscapes for Brown & Bigelow occupied Parrish until the end of his painting life. They were mysterious, iridescent scenes which he hoped would convey, "those qualities which delight us in nature—the sense of freedom, pure air and light, the magic of distance, and the saturated beauty of color."

Maxfield Parrish finally put his brushes away for the last time in 1962, and passed away four years later. Poster artist, children's book illustrator, humorist, landscape painter, designer, architect, craftsman, and muralist: a more-than-sixty-year career in which none of his creative powers ever diminished. An extraordinary feat for any man.

M · P

22. *Spring.* 1936. Oil on panel, 21 x 17". Collection Howard E. Hoffman, Harrisburg, Pennsylvania

23

24

25

26

23. *Cadmus Sowing his Seed*. 1907. Oil on panel, 40 x 33″. Private collection

24. *Garden of Allah*. 1920. Oil on panel, 15½ x 30¼″

25. *Daybreak*. 1922. Oil on panel, 26½ x 45½″. Private collection

26. *Venetian Lamplighters*. 1923 (Calendar design for General Electric Mazda Lamps). Oil on panel, 28 x 18″. Private collection

28

27. *Stars*. 1926. Oil on panel, 35⅛ x 21¾". Collection Howard E. Hoffman, Harrisburg, Pennsylvania

28. *Wild Geese*. 1924. Oil on panel, 14¾ x 19¾". Private collection

30

31

29. *Snow White (The Story of Snow Drop)*. (*Hearst's Magazine* cover, August 1912). Oil on panel, 30½ x 24½″. Fine Arts Museums of San Francisco, lent by the William G. Irwin Charity Foundation, on permanent loan

30. *Romance*. 1922. (End papers for *The Knave of Hearts* by Louise Saunders, 1925). Oil on panel, 31 x 34¾″. Private collection

31. *The Pirate Ship*. 1906. Oil glazes on paper, 18 x 16″. Detroit Institute of Arts. Bequest of Mr. and Mrs. Lawrence P. Fisher

J. C. Leyendecker

1–2. Arrow Collar advertisements. Courtesy The Arrow Company

Collier's

THE NATIONAL WEEKLY

VOL XXXIX NO 21
AUGUST 17 1907

VACATION

PRICE 10 CENTS
$5.20 A YEAR

3. Painting for *Collier's* cover, August 17, 1907

4. *The Inland Printer* cover, 1897. Courtesy Columbia
University Library

During the first decades of this century, the large magazines grew larger, the
successful illustrators became even more successful, and publishing evolved into America's
most glamorous business. The artists whose illustrations delighted the fancies of millions of
Americans each week became celebrities themselves, pre-dating the Hollywood movie stars,
but not altogether unlike them. The illustrators had become public property, good headline
copy, excellent material for gossip.

J. C. Leyendecker was a notable exception. During his life he was a withdrawn, solitary
man, whose inner conflicts—which must have been great—were kept private. He did not
leave any personal written records and only two written sources exist to provide any insight
into the artist's character: *J. C. Leyendecker* (1974) by Michael Schau and *My Adventures as an
Illustrator* (1960) by Norman Rockwell. Nor did Leyendecker's own art reveal very much of the
artist's deepest sentiments. The personalities populating his illustrations are masked by
self-possession and restraint, giving no clues to the secrets locked within the heart of their
creator.

Just as Charles Dana Gibson presented his public with the distinctive mark of the patrician
American woman, so did J. C. Leyendecker establish the prototype of the fashionable
American male. His "Arrow Collar Man" (for which he is most remembered) is the
square-jawed, aloof, unconquerable gentleman who, for decades, became the symbol of what
manhood should be. Yet the creator of this American hero was himself not a native-born
American. Nor was his own life an example of what Americans would find enviable.

Joseph Christian Leyendecker was born in Montabour, a town in southern Germany, on
March 23, 1874, the eldest son. His younger brother by three years, Frank Xavier, was born in
Germany, also; his sister Augusta was born in America after the family had emigrated to
Chicago in 1882.

By apprenticing himself to J. Manz & Company, an engraving firm in Chicago, at the age
of sixteen, Joe raised sufficient funds to study at the Art Institute. The combination of his
work and studies provided him with the foundation he needed for developing his drawing

5. The House of Kuppenheimer advertisement, 1918. Collection Alex Chasky

and painting skills on one hand, and for an education in the technology of engraving on the other—a foundation that would be invaluable to him for the duration of his career.

For five years Leyendecker continued this arrangement, saving his money, and applying himself to his work. In 1896 he won a coveted award: first prize in *The Century* magazine poster contest, his entry being reproduced on the cover of the prestigious magazine. (Maxfield Parrish won second prize in the same competition.) Thenceforth, his career was established as an illustrator. By the following year he had already illustrated a dozen covers for the eminent Chicago publication *Inland Printer*.

The award money from *The Century* poster contest, combined with his savings from the engraving company and his parent's assistance, was sufficient for him to embark for Paris to study art, and to take his brother along with him.

If Frank Xavier sounds like a footnote in Joseph's life, it is not surprising. From the very beginning the Leyendecker parents recognized Joe's talents and made whatever financial sacrifices were necessary to assist their eldest in acquiring the proper education. The younger son never received comparable encouragement, although his artistic talents must have been equally apparent at an early age. Norman Rockwell attributes this inequity to the parents' immigrant outlook: "When the boys were very young," says Rockwell in his book, "the family had decided that Joe was a genius and, like many immigrant families, had henceforth concentrated all their efforts on helping him to fulfill himself. I guess the family felt that only one of their children had a chance to distinguish himself and so they fixed on the one who had a talent and sort of sacrificed their lives to him. Many immigrant families seem to have regarded a talent as a gift from God and therefore something which was to be respected and aided, which it would be somehow sacrilegious to waste."

In spite of the marked preference given to the eldest son, Joe's own allegiance compensated for the inequalities, and he remained loyal to his younger brother. They were inseparable companions. Their relationship, in fact, was somewhat symbiotic, a mutual dependence which, no doubt, determined the outcome of later events in their lives: Frank never formed a comparable involvement with any other individual, and Joe's later attachment

6. The House of Kuppenheimer advertisement, 1918. Collection Alex Chasky

to another man would ultimately divide the two brothers irreconcilably.

Unlike several of his colleagues who were contemptuous of the academic approach to which they were subjected in art schools, Joe Leyendecker seems to have preferred the more traditional training. In Paris he studied at the Académie Julian, the most conservative of the Parisian art schools, under the directorship of Adolphe William Bouguereau. A fashionable, academic painter, Bouguereau was openly hostile to the current trends in "popular art"—the posters by Henri de Toulouse-Lautrec, Alphonse Mucha, and Jules Chéret, so widely seen throughout Paris at the time. The Leyendecker brothers seemed to display no great admiration for these contemporary artists, and they worked assiduously at the Académie Julian (and at Colarossi, where they took a few classes as well), perfecting their academic skills. Joe Leyendecker established himself as one of the most gifted artists ever to attend either school, and his student work was so highly esteemed that much of it was preserved in the permanent exhibition at the Académie Julian until a bombing raid destroyed the work during World War II. Rockwell, too, recalls that even twenty years later, when he went to Paris, the schools were still talking about J. C. Leyendecker.

Joe and Frank Leyendecker returned to America two years later and immediately set up a studio together in Chicago, soon handling a number of accounts on a regular basis. So successful did the studio become, in fact, that in less than two years they decided they were ready to take on the great colossus: New York. They moved their studio in 1900, the year after Joe Leyendecker had his first cover reproduced on the *Saturday Evening Post*. (This was the first of 321 covers for the *Post*, a number exceeded by only one other artist in history —Norman Rockwell!)

Once in New York, J. C. Leyendecker was among the city's most prominent illustrators, his work appearing regularly in national magazines. But it was his commercial work that established him most rapidly as one of the most sought-after illustrators of the day. Cluett, Peabody & Co., Inc. hired him to create the art for a campaign to advertise their Arrow brand detachable shirt collars. The so-called "Arrow Collar Man" became a star overnight, his elegant *hauteur* used to sell several hundred styles of shirt collars. The Arrow Collar man

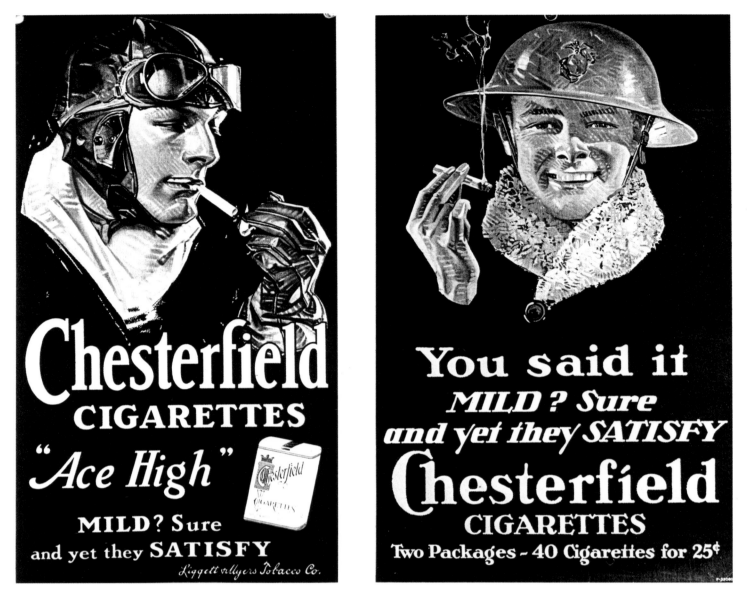

7. Chesterfield Cigarette advertisements, 1918. © Liggett Group Inc. (formerly Liggett & Myers Incorporated)

represented a phenomenon that Michael Schau, in his book *J. C. Leyendecker,* describes as follows: "Today, it is difficult to imagine the sensation created by Leyendecker's pictures. But fan mail for one model or another arrived at Cluett, Peabody by the ton, and in one month in the early 1920s the Arrow Man received 17,000 fan letters, gifts, marriage proposals, and notes threatening suicide—a deluge surpassing even Rudolph Valentino's mail at the star's apex. The term 'Arrow Collar Man' became a common epithet for any handsome, nattily dressed gent, and the Arrow Man was the subject of admiring poems, songs, and even a Broadway play. In 1918 Arrow Collar sales rose to over $32 million."

His dazzling success with the Arrow campaign attracted the notice of other clothing manufacturers as well, and before long his handsome creations were also promoting fashions by B. Kuppenheimer, Hart Schaffner & Marx, and Interwoven Socks. In addition to the commercial work, of course, Leyendecker continued to illustrate regularly for the national periodicals. From 1903 until 1943 his covers for the *Saturday Evening Post* appeared on all the holiday issues—their biggest sellers—and on many issues in between as well. The idea to use a baby to represent the New Year was Leyendecker's, and his good-natured characters strutting across the pages of the magazine obviously inspired Norman Rockwell in the creation of his first covers for the *Post.*

Leyendecker's work habits were meticulous, marred only by his tendency to rework a painting so many times that he was in continual risk of missing his deadlines. The vast amount of oil sketches he left behind is evidence of his healthy appetite for accumulating ideas, sketches made even when no specific assignment called for them. His files were filled with

sketches he had made of hand positions, heads, flowers, and babies, ideas he would use later for reference when an assignment might call for them.

His pencil or charcoal sketches were only about 2 x 3 inches, the oil sketches only slightly larger. These he would transfer to the larger canvas. Dating from his days as a student in the academy, Leyendecker relied upon the traditional method of copying by "squaring up." With a straightedge as a guide, he drew pencil lines in a grid-like pattern across the smaller sketch and bisected these squares with diagonal lines. By squaring up the larger surface with proportionately larger squares, and following the placement of the forms within each square on the sketch, he could copy the smaller version almost mechanically. For a single painting he might make dozens of oil sketches on canvas—a hand in several positions, the face in many expressions, the body posed in different ways, squaring up the sketches he preferred and transferring the detail to the larger surface with the squaring-up method. A cover, therefore, was most likely a composite of details taken from several sketches, a "picture puzzle," as he called it, which was assembled to fit into his design. Although he combined fragments, however, Leyendecker never lost sight of the whole.

Here is Norman Rockwell's account of how his friend executed a painting: "He would make endless little sketches from the model—two or three of the hands, a couple of the head, the torso, the eyes, the folds of the dress, the shoes—until he had drawn everything exactly as he wanted it. Usually he filled three or four canvases in this way. Then he would combine the sketches on another canvas and that was his finished painting. By working this way, he explained, he could forget draftsmanship when painting and concentrate on his model and the situation. In painting, the whole isn't the sum of the parts. You have to see the whole thing at once all the time you're painting."

Leyendecker was capable of fragmenting the parts because he regarded them as subordinate to the whole. Here, in fact, he was at his best: J. C. Leyendecker was a consummate pictorial designer. No other illustrator of his time—with the exception perhaps of Maxfield Parrish—was so conscious of contour, the silhouettes made within and surrounding the image. In spite of the modeling used to describe his forms, his painting is actually two-dimensional, flat shapes placed intelligently, one over the other, to form never-ending design variations. Though his style never varied, his illustrations became increasingly ornate as he took on greater challenges, a master of composition, triumphing over even the most complex design problems with a clarity of thinking that remained his hallmark for the entire duration of his career.

His brushstrokes were actually "brush thrusts," sharp stabs of oil paint, as decisive as his distinctive signature. "As a rule," he wrote simply, "I start work with a round or flat sable using a thin wash with turps as a medium. Keep shadows very transparent and as the work progresses apply the paint more thickly on lighted areas adding some poppy or linseed oil if necessary, and using a larger flat bristle brush for the heavier paint, but still keeping the shadows thin and vibrant."

Leyendecker's astonishing success as an illustrator, and the handsome income that accompanied his achievements, altered his style of life considerably. He spent his money as rapidly as he earned it, developing a pattern that Rockwell describes as "Leyendecker's credo": "Joe believed that an artist should live just a little bit beyond his means so that there would always be a challenge. 'Buy more than you can afford,' he used to say, 'and you'll never stop working or fret so over a picture that it never gets done. If every day you have to save yourself from ruin, every day you'll work. And work hard.'"

Such a credo may well have originated in his youth from growing up as the eldest son in an immigrant family, determined to survive against all odds. And later when the odds were no longer significant, he simply elevated the stakes in order to reassert a perpetual struggle for survival. Regardless of its origin, J. C. Leyendecker's thirst for luxury resulted in an elegant style of life. Frank seemed to be like him. And on the surface it appeared that the Leyendecker brothers were ideally suited for their parts, as fashionable as any Arrow Collar Man, and certainly no less handsome. Seeing them walk down the street on the way to his New Rochelle home, Rockwell recalls his first impression of the Leyendecker brothers: "They were quite

8. "Over the Top." The House of Kuppenheimer advertisement. Collection Alex Chasky

9. The House of Kuppenheimer advertisement, 1918. Collection Alex Chasky

short and walked in step, with real military precision," Rockwell wrote, "the tips of their canes and their black and white saddle shoes hitting the pavement at precisely the same instant. They wore white flannels, double-breasted blue blazers with shiny brass buttons, and stiff straw hats. One-two, one-two, one-two, they marched toward me. As they turned sharply, without breaking step, into our yard, I could see that they were both very handsome, dark complexioned with high cheekbones and straight, delicately molded noses. Like Spaniards. And trim, well built, the line of their jackets falling straight from shoulder to hip."

If the Leyendecker brothers seemed to resemble two Arrow Collar Men as they strutted down the street, they appeared even more like the illustrations when in their studio or home. After moving to an elegant house in Greenwich Village, Joe opened a large studio in midtown Manhattan. (Since Frank preferred to work at home, Joe did not share the studio with his brother.) The studio was located in the luxurious Beaux Arts Building, elegant quarters staffed by a butler in full uniform, and containing a room for painting that was described by a model as "a small Grand Central Station."

In 1914 the brothers had a mansion constructed in New Rochelle (where Remington had lived and where Rockwell would meet them as neighbors), and they moved to this New York suburb as soon as the house was ready. Designed to resemble a French chateau, the fourteen-room home was located on Mount Tom Road and the estate included several acres of land in which Joe could cultivate sumptuous formal gardens. Each day, for several years, Joe would commute to his elegant New York studio, chauffered to and from the New Rochelle station in a limousine. (It was here that Rockwell, then a teenager, would linger regularly just for the opportunity to catch a glimpse of his hero at the station.)

Living in the lap of luxury, the brothers seemed to lead an enviable life. Since childhood they had been inseparable, complementing each other in personality, the younger brother more outgoing and sociable, the older more withdrawn, in spite of his success. As a fellow artist, Norman Rockwell observed the brothers' relationship in unique terms: "They had the same friends, gone everywhere together, even painted alike, though Frank never had Joe's

10. Arrow Collar advertisement. Courtesy The Arrow Company

11. Love Songs from Wagner Operas. *The Century*, 1902

facility or technical polish. And they shared a secret medium (that's what you mix your oil paint with). Only Joe and Frank knew the formula. For years they had kept it secret, refusing even to exhibit their pictures for fear that some artist would discover it. The use of this medium gave their paintings a special quality. You could see each brush stroke in the finished painting. Very distinctive."

Yet in spite of this apparent intimacy, their differences became more pronounced with the years. Although some regarded Frank X. Leyendecker as a painter as gifted as his brother (and some even disagreed with Rockwell, feeling that Frank was *superior* to his brother), the Leyendeckers did not share the same ambitions. Frank had lived in the shadow of his older brother from the time of his youth, until his adulthood, first in the eyes of his parents, and later in the eyes of the public. Frank denied that he was even interested in commercial work, claiming preference for fine art, yet he rarely produced any work in this area either. Unlike his brother, who never missed a deadline, Frank would delay and procrastinate, refining and reworking his paintings, frequently losing the assignment altogether because of his inability to deliver.

Whatever conflicts the brothers may have had regarding their work, their differences were only compounded with the arrival of Charles Beach. The Canadian first arrived in 1901, visiting Joe in his New York studio because, according to Rockwell's account, "He had fallen in love with a girl in one of Joe's drawings and had come all the way from Canada to meet her." Leyendecker selected Beach to be the model for his first Arrow Collar ad, a decision he made because of Beach's outstanding looks. "He was tall, powerfully built, and extraordinarily handsome," wrote Rockwell. "Looked like an athlete from one of the Ivy League colleges. He spoke with a clipped British accent and was always beautifully dressed." The association between artist and model was to last over fifty years.

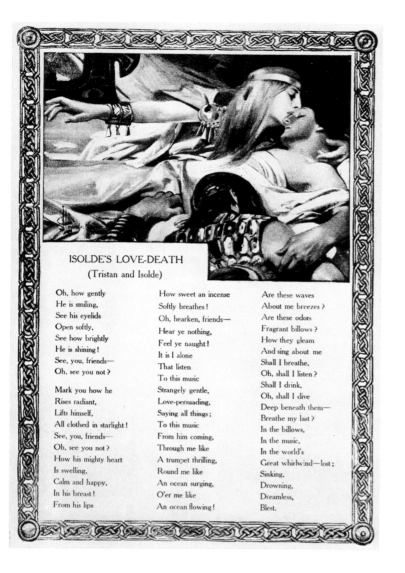

ISOLDE'S LOVE-DEATH
(Tristan and Isolde)

Oh, how gently
He is smiling,
See his eyelids
Open softly,
See how brightly
He is shining!
See, you, friends—
Oh, see you not?

Mark you how he
Rises radiant,
Lifts himself,
All clothed in starlight!
See, you, friends—
Oh, see you not?
How his mighty heart
Is swelling,
Calm and happy,
In his breast!
From his lips

How sweet an incense
Softly breathes!
Oh, hearken, friends—
Hear ye nothing,
Feel ye naught!
It is I alone
That listen
To this music
Strangely gentle,
Love-persuading,
Saying all things;
To this music
From him coming,
Through me like
A trumpet thrilling,
Round me like
An ocean surging,
O'er me like
An ocean flowing!

Are these waves
About me breezes?
Are these odors
Fragrant billows?
How they gleam
And sing about me
Shall I breathe,
Oh, shall I listen?
Shall I drink,
Oh, shall I dive
Deep beneath them—
Breathe my last?
In the billows,
In the music,
In the world's
Great whirlwind—lost;
Sinking,
Drowning,
Dreamless,
Blest.

Because of the absence of any personal records, we will never know the precise nature of their relationship. Reports given by friends and neighbors tend not to be reliable, exaggerating the extremes of each personality involved as though each was a character in a Victorian melodrama: Beach the Villain, Joe the Victim, Frank the Martyred Younger Brother. Rockwell, for example, describes Beach as "a real parasite—like some huge, white, cold insect clinging to Joe's back." But Rockwell also maintains that Joe had been a sociable, gregarious man prior to meeting Beach, his personality transformed by the evil interloper. In fact, the indications are that Leyendecker had always been a shy, introverted man, dependent on Frank for the social amenities. Nor is it evident that Leyendecker became any less social after meeting Beach than he had been before. They did entertain and travel (moderately, but not infrequently) and continued to do so for quite some time.

A more likely analysis is that Joe substituted one dependence for another. After all, Beach acted as agent, bookkeeper, messenger, apprentice, secretary, and caretaker for Joe, sparing him the distracting details of daily living that would have interfered with his work. Meanwhile Frank had become increasingly unreliable. Joe's growing dependence on Beach must have come as a great blow to Frank, but it was not a sudden transition. Twenty years had passed before the situation became unendurable to the younger brother.

All his life Joe had been bound to his family. He supported his parents until their death, and he lived with his unmarried brother and sister Augusta until 1921, continuing to support his sister until his death in 1951. Obviously, the equilibrium in the family could not remain unaffected by Beach's arrival. Over the years Frank had grown even more intensely neurotic about his work, occasionally subverting an assignment on purpose in order to lose the account. He received fewer and fewer assignments as a result. Falling behind on his contributions to the mortgage payments, he was irritated whenever Beach would make up the difference, yet he

12

E. Phillips Oppenheim—Gilbert Seldes—Mrs. Garret A. Hobart—Howard Mingos
James W. Bennett—Stewart Edward White—Kennett Harris—Oma Almona Davies

13

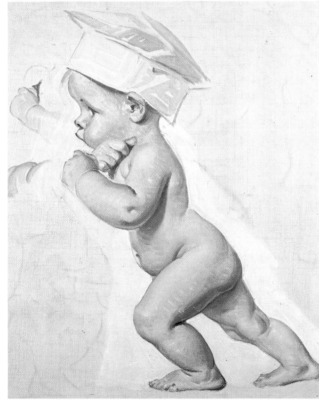

15

Isaac F. Marcosson—George Weston—Philip Gibbs—Will Irwin
George Pattullo—Princess Cantacuzène—Henry C. Rowland

16

14

12. *Saturday Evening Post* cover, January 1, 1927.
Collection Michael Schau

13. *Saturday Evening Post* cover, June 29, 1929.
Collection Michael Schau

14. *Saturday Evening Post* cover, January 20, 1940

15. Study for *Thanksgiving Baby*. Oil , 10¾ x 8¾".
Collection Walt Reed

16. Finished cover for *Saturday Evening Post*,
November 25, 1922

17. *Collier's* cover, April 27, 1907

18. *Saturday Evening Post* cover, June 8, 1929

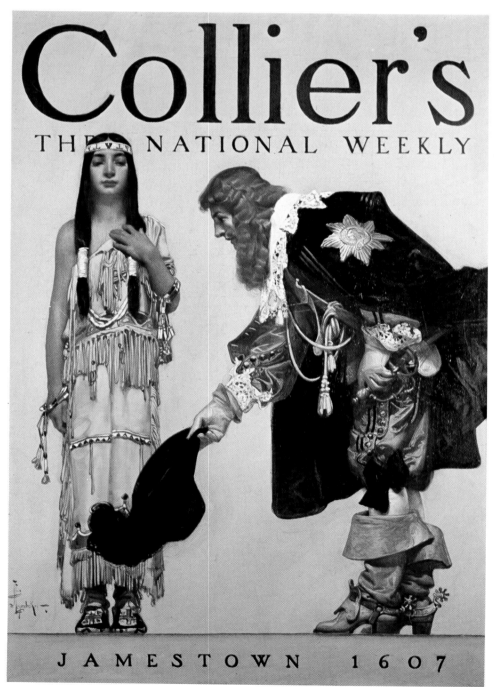

17

18

19. Study for *Saturday Evening Post* cover. Collection Walt Reed

made no effort to improve his performance. Beach was no doubt possessive of Joe, and perhaps deliberately came between the brothers, but the family remained dependent. The tensions finally erupted in 1921, and Frank moved out of the mansion, Augusta leaving with him in support. One year later—perhaps from the effects of drugs—Frank was dead. He was forty-seven years old.

Joe Leyendecker was deeply shocked by the death of his brother and became more solitary than before. He continued to live in the Mount Tom Mansion but left the premises only seldom. He no longer commuted to New York, working instead in a studio wing adjoining the house. Beach ran all the errands in New York. When Joe wasn't painting, he was seen tending his gardens, or strolling through his estate, still handsomely dressed, and with a distinguished air about him. In spite of his obvious sadness, he continued to be extremely productive throughout the twenties, and even into the mid-thirties his income was reported at an annual level of $50,000. It was not until the end of the thirties that his popularity began to wane and he was faced with economic hardships. Having lived according to his "credo," Leyendecker had not managed to save any money and was obliged to release his extensive household staff, maintaining the entire estate with only the assistance of Beach.

In 1951, at the age of seventy-seven, J. C. Leyendecker died suddenly from a heart attack while sitting with Beach on the patio overlooking his gardens. Overcome by the loss of his friend, Beach developed a severe drinking problem, and died shortly afterwards himself. The estate already had been sold and all the paintings were dispersed.

Illustrators come and go, swept along by the tide of fashions and fads. Like any celebrity, the illustrator is both victor and victim of the time in which he lives, his future ever precarious and uncertain. Norman Rockwell's reaction to J. C. Leyendecker's passing is a moving reminder of the price the great illustrator had paid for his stardom: "And that was the end of it all. It scared me. Joe had been the most famous illustrator in America. Then the *Post* had dropped him; the advertising agencies had dropped him; the public had forgotten him. He had died in obscurity. It might happen to me. When I got home I went out to the studio and looked at my picture. I was naturally depressed. Still, it wasn't a reassuring sight. But then I noticed that the eyes of the man in the picture needed just a touch of white to give them a sparkle. So I sat down and got to work. After a while I thought to myself, Well, here I am. And I can still hold a brush."

152

20

21

22

20. *Enlist Today, U.S. Marines,* 1918. Courtesy Columbia University Library

21. Poster for University of Pennsylvania, 1906. Subject used for *Saturday Evening Post* cover, November 14, 1908. Courtesy Columbia University Library

22. Study for *Saturday Evening Post* cover, November 4, 1933. Collection Walt Reed

23. *Weapons for Liberty.* War bonds poster, 1917.

23

24. Arrow Collar advertisements. Courtesy The Arrow Company

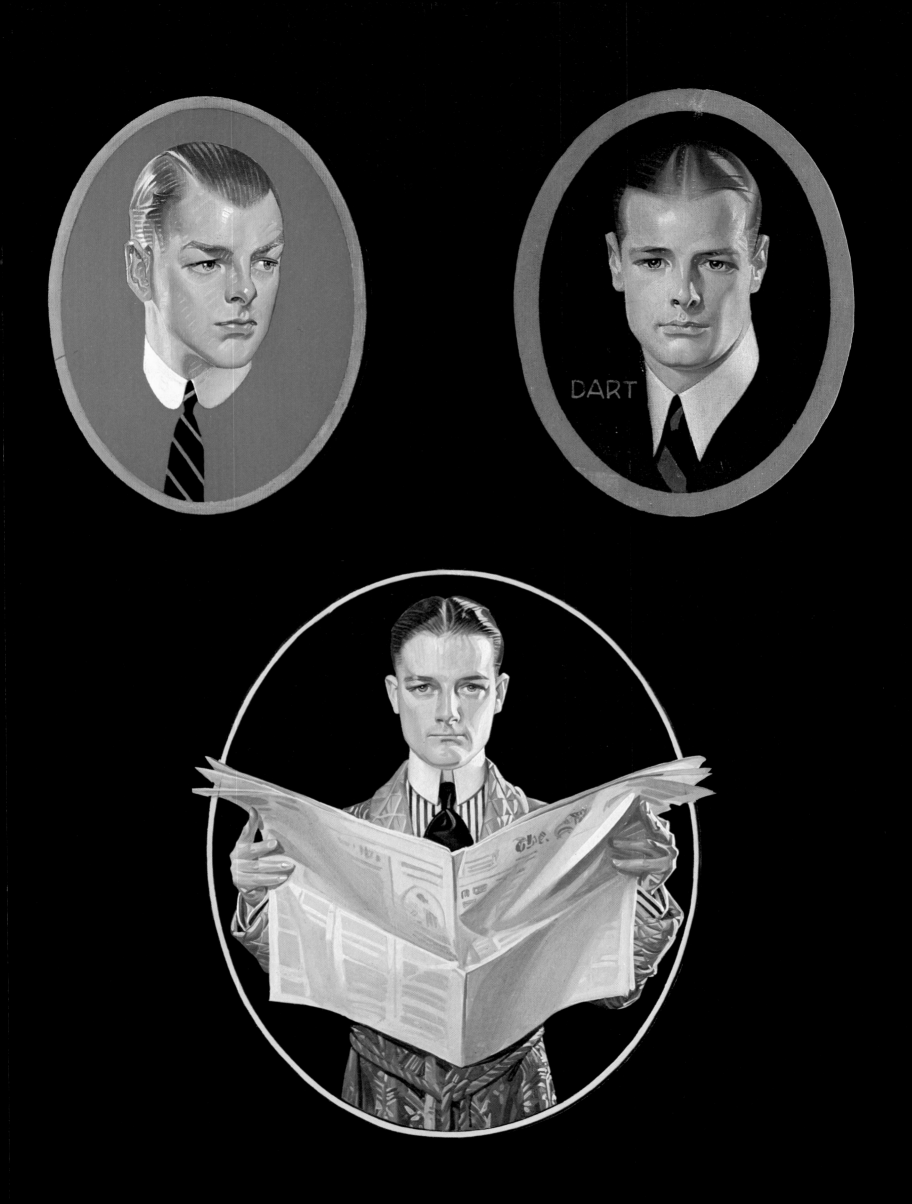

26

25–27. Arrow Collar advertisements. Courtesy
The Arrow Company

27

30

28. Arrow Collar advertisement, c. 1913.
Courtesy The Arrow Company

29. Arrow Collar advertisement, c. 1922.
Courtesy The Arrow Company

30. Arrow Collar advertisement, 1929.
Courtesy The Arrow Company

1. *The Connoisseur* (Original oil painting for *Saturday Evening Post* cover, January 13, 1962)

Norman Rockwell

2. Rockwell and his wife Molly, 1967. Charcoal.
Collection Norman Rockwell

3. *Saturday Evening Post* cover, August 23, 1930

William Wrigley, Jr.
Isaac F. Marcosson—Leonard H. Nason—Julian Street—Norman Reilly Raine
Clarence Budington Kelland—Nunnally Johnson—Frederick Hazlitt Brennan

4. *Saturday Evening Post* cover, September 13, 1930

There is no better example of a Norman Rockwell illustration than the artist himself. The qualities in his work that have endeared him to the American public for more than a half-century are the very qualities in the man that are so appealing. Considering his unparalleled success (there is no American illustrator who has ever been so adored by his audience for so long), it is remarkable that the artist remains unspoiled, displaying no trace of arrogance or cockiness. Quite the contrary, Norman Rockwell is more inclined to appear embarrassed by his fame, quietly poking fun at himself in a kindly, almost boyish manner. Over the years, he has managed to retain a genuine innocence about life, a disarming vulnerability that is the essence of what makes his illustrations enduring.

Yet Rockwell has no illusions about the content of his work: "The view of life I communicate in my pictures excludes the sordid and ugly," he wrote. "I paint life as I would like it to be....Maybe as I grew up and found that the world wasn't the perfectly pleasant place I had thought it to be I unconsciously decided that, even if it wasn't an ideal world, it should be and so painted only the ideal aspects of it."

These observations, and those quoted throughout the remainder of this chapter, appeared in his delightful autobiography, *My Adventures as an Illustrator* (1960). Totally free of braggadocio, this autobiography provides an intimate insight into the artist's true character, the ambition and self-doubts that drove him to work hard to win and sustain the approval of a wide audience. Surely, there is no better way to understand the appeal of his illustrations than to understand the nature of the man behind the easel, an approach Rockwell himself acknowledges: "The story of my life is, really, the story of my pictures and how I made them. Because, in one way or another, everything I have ever seen or done has gone into my pictures."

The idealized world Rockwell has elected to paint through the years is that of small town or rural America, not the life of the city. Although it is tempting to conclude from this that provincial life is what Rockwell knows best, in fact, the contrary is true. He was as much a part of the urban publishing world as his colleagues Charles Dana Gibson, James Montgomery

163

Norman
Rockwell

5. *Saturday Evening Post* cover, December 4, 1920

6. *Saturday Evening Post* cover, December 8, 1928

Flagg, and Howard Chandler Christy. He lived in or near New York City for over thirty years, was a neighbor and friend of the sophisticated J. C. Leyendecker in New Rochelle, and attended innumerable gatherings with his illustrator-friends whose work appeared in the same magazines of the time. Unlike his colleagues, however, Rockwell chose to depict what he knew less intimately: "I doubt that I would have idealized the country if I had grown up as a farm boy," he observed.

Rockwell was born in 1894 in the back bedroom of a shabby brownstone on 103rd Street and Amsterdam Avenue in New York City. "My mother, an Anglophile (she wore a black arm band for six weeks after Queen Victoria died) and very proud of her English ancestry, named me after Sir Norman Percevel ('remember Norman Percevel,' she'd say, 'it's spelled with an *e; i* and *a* are common') who reputedly kicked Guy Fawkes down the stairs of the Tower of London after he had tried to blow up the House of Lords."

Although his namesake may have represented a splendid example of courage and virility to his mother, young Rockwell was embarrassed by the appellation. "I had a queer notion that Percevel (and especially the form Percy) was a sissy name, almost effeminate. Nobody ever called me Percy, except occasionally, but I lived in terror. I darn near died when a boy called me 'Mercy Percy'; to my relief it didn't stick. When I left home I dropped the Percevel immediately, despite my mother's earnest protestations."

Even in his childhood, Rockwell preferred the country to the city, eagerly awaiting the summer months when he would go off to a farm with his family. These months, which he described as "sheer blissfulness," formed the basis of his nostalgic recollection upon which he would draw in later years. "I actually lived the idealized version of the life of a farm boy in the late nineteenth century. I remember that, once in the country, even I changed...as much as the sun changed the color of our skins....I think that had a lot to do with what I painted later on."

Even with age, after Rockwell had come to recognize ("reluctantly") that "ugly things happen in the country as well as in the city," he continued to prefer the country. He found a

Norman
Rockwell

7. *Saturday Evening Post* cover, December 16, 1939

8. *Life* cover, November 22, 1923

quality in people that was closer to human nature, more approachable, more authentic. "Country people do fit my kind of picture better than city people," he admits. "Their faces are more open, expressive, lacking the cold veneer behind which city people seem to hide. I guess I have a bad case of the American nostalgia for the clean simple country life as opposed to the complicated world of the city."

Although the precise nature of his subject matter may not have been evident at the time, he knew he would be an artist all his life. He had a natural ability to draw ("just something I had, like a bag of lemon drops"), and was encouraged by his father, an amateur artist himself, who liked to copy drawings from magazines.

At sixteen Rockwell dropped out of high school to study art full time, first attending the rather stuffy classes at the National Academy where he found that the emphasis was on developing fine artists. He then transferred to the Art Students League, more to his liking, which prepared him for a career as an illustrator. From his afternoon classes with George Bridgman he developed his ability to depict the human figure, and from his morning classes with Thomas Fogarty, he discovered the world of illustration, and was thus introduced to his favorites—Howard Pyle and Edwin Abbey—through their reproductions. Rockwell always worked hard at his studies ("I was not a rebel"), and took whatever odd jobs he could in the evenings to help finance his art education. It was Fogarty who obtained commercial assignments for Rockwell, the first of his career. In one of these Rockwell actually earned $150 for ten or twelve drawings made for a children's book called *Tell Me Why Stories.* He was not yet eighteen years old.

Within a short period of time, Rockwell was illustrating regularly for children's publications—*St. Nicholas, American Boy, Boy's Life, Youth's Companion*—developing a great technique for depicting boys and girls that would later win him assignments for other publications he preferred. He rented Frederic Remington's former sculpture studio with his friend cartoonist Clyde Forsythe, and set himself to the serious task of becoming a professional. He wasn't particularly interested in book or magazine illustration—though this is

Norman Rockwell

THE SATURDAY EVENING POST

Vol. 191, No. 52. Published Weekly at Philadelphia. Entered as Second-Class Matter, November 18, 1879, at the Post Office at Philadelphia, under the Act of March 3, 1879.

An Illustrated Weekly
Founded A.D. 1728 by Benj. Frank.

JUNE 28, 1919

5c. THE COPY
10c in Canada

TO READER. When you finish reading this magazine, place a U. S. 1 cent stamp on this notice, mail the magazine, and it will be placed in the hands of our soldiers or sailors.
NO WRAPPING—NO ADDRESS.
A. S. Burleson, Postmaster General

Julian Street — Ben Ames Williams — William Ashley Anderson — George Kibbe Turner
Henry Watterson — Rob Wagner — Herbert Quick — Alice Duer Miller — Grace Torrey

9. *Saturday Evening Post* cover, June 28, 1919

how he made his living at the time—having instead a fixed dream in mind: a cover on the *Saturday Evening Post*. "In those days the cover of the *Post* was the greatest show window in America for an illustrator. If you did a cover for the *Post* you had arrived."

Forsythe urged his friend to apply. But Rockwell's nagging lack of self-assurance (which plagued him throughout his career) caused him to postpone and procrastinate, fearful of rejection. "Mr. George Horace Lorimer had built the *Post* from a two-bit family journal to a circulation in the millions. He was THE GREAT MR. GEORGE HORACE LORIMER, the baron of publishers. What if he didn't like my work? I'd think. Supposing he denounced me as an instance of incompetence, banished me. He's got a lot of influence. I'd go down, down, down. The kids magazines would drop me, then the dime novels and pulps would refuse to use me; I'd end up doing the wrappers for penny candies."

But Clyde Forsythe was adamant: as long as his friend Rockwell stuck to kids—not pretending to be a painter of sexy women, which was better left to other illustrators ("You're a terrible Gibson," he chided)—the *Saturday Evening Post* would most certainly find his work ideal for one of their covers.

For several weeks Rockwell prepared his portfolio for presentation to the *Post*. In order not to appear foolish at his first interview, tugging and fumbling with the strings and wrappings of his package, Rockwell had a suitcase constructed specially to carry his paintings and sketches to Philadelphia. It was a big, black, "gruesome affair," that looked a bit like a coffin, but gave him added confidence.

For the interview Rockwell had prepared two finished paintings and three sketches. The great George Horace Lorimer liked all five; he purchased the two finished paintings for $75.00 and gave Rockwell the approval to polish up the sketches for three more covers. From that time on—from 1916 to 1963—Rockwell's relationship to the *Post* was uninterrupted, even after Lorimer retired twenty years later and was succeeded by other editors and art directors. During his long career, Rockwell has painted 322 covers for this prestigious publication. (Only Leyendecker nearly equaled this number of *Post* covers.) When taken as a group, these covers chronicle his maturity. No challenge was too great as an artist. The change in graphics, for example—from figures being placed on a plain background to a fully developed painting—only helped to develop Rockwell's artistic skills even further. These covers have established Rockwell as America's greatest illustrator.

But Rockwell always worried, skeptical of his popularity, fearful of losing in the competition for the spotlight. "I worried some about being old-fashioned or the steady rise of my prosperity. I'd think about how right from the start I'd been successful and about how every other illustrator had to work in an art service or wash dishes for a while. It can't last, I'd say to myself. It's going to stop."

This frame of mind—his persistent bouts with uncertainty—served as a driving force to the artist, preventing him from becoming over-confident, repetitive, hackneyed. When, in 1942, he heard that the future of the *Post* seemed uncertain (it turned out to be only a rumor), Rockwell confesses that he felt almost relieved at the thought of no more covers for the magazine, welcoming his liberation from the self-imposed pressures: "If a cover was unpopular, I felt my work was sagging and, becoming scared, thought, I'll be dropped from the *Post*. Every new illustrator had been a threat. Perhaps he'll be better than I, I'd thought, and force me off the *Post*. So for 26 years I'd had to prove myself all over again with each cover I did." But the *Post* did not fold, and Rockwell continued to endure his bouts with uncertainty. Inexplicably, these periods of self-doubt would come upon him, out of the blue, and would pass just as inexplicably. Some periods were worse than others, but they always ended. "Each time, as I reached the point where I felt I was finished, at the end of my rope, I've managed to right myself. Always by simply sticking to it, continuing to work though everything seemed hopeless and I was scared silly."

Few artists are free of self-doubt. The creative urge is nurtured by a drive for perfection. Sensing that the finished product never lives up to exactly what the artist had in mind, he is compelled to try again. Consequently, the urge to create is frequently accompanied by a feeling of inadequacy, secret fears that are rarely known to anyone beyond the studio

Norman
Rockwell

10. *Saturday Evening Post* cover, January 17, 1920

11. *Saturday Evening Post* cover, May 26, 1928

confines. What sets Rockwell apart from so many other artists is his willingness to *confess* these inner conflicts so readily, a candor one does not expect from a public figure. This is the vulnerability that is at the core of his work, a genuine innocence we find in the man and in his art, qualities which explain—to some degree—the reason for his popularity.

Although Rockwell's work is a natural extension of his personality, his paintings for the *Post* were not executed without a great deal of thought and preparation. In spite of appearances, there was nothing casual at all about the way in which he created these covers. The biggest problem for him has always been arriving at the idea for the picture. Even now, as he looks back over his career, he finds it hard to believe how difficult it was, each and every time he began a new cover, to decide what to paint. "I never saw an idea happen or received one, whoosh, from heaven while I was washing my brushes or shaving or backing the car out of the garage. I had to beat more of them out of my head or at least maul my brain until something came out of it. It always seemed to me that it was like getting blood from a stone, except of course, that eventually something always came."

After his idea was approved by the *Post,* he would begin to paint. In the early days of his career, before he was using photography, he worked from live models. This situation presented its own problems: finding a model who was willing to take the time to pose for him was not easy. In order to paint a single figure, for example, Rockwell often worked three days, sometimes even longer, drawing the model in charcoal on the canvas, then painting over it. During these years, therefore, he used the same models over and over again, knowing only a few people who had the available time. (This was costly also, particularly when he was also obliged to pay for a chaperone accompanying a young female model!)

Although Rockwell was perfectly capable of painting from imagination, he always preferred to work directly from life, feeling that he achieved greater authenticity as a result. Frequently, however, he found himself in rather awkward circumstances as a result, such as the time he acquired a rambunctious turkey for a model. The hot-tempered bird escaped

Norman
Rockwell

12

13

12. *Saturday Evening Post* cover, September 25, 1954

13. *Saturday Evening Post* cover, August 3, 1946

14. *Saturday Evening Post* cover, December 7, 1946

15. *Saturday Evening Post* cover, September 7, 1957

14

15

POST

October 13, 1956 ~ 15¢

The Case for
The Republicans
By Minority Leader JOE MARTIN

16. *Saturday Evening Post* cover, October 13, 1956

17. *Saturday Evening Post* cover, October 6, 1956

18. *Saturday Evening Post* cover, October 29, 1960

19. *The Right to Know* (Original oil painting for *Look,* August 20, 1968). © Cowles Communications, Inc. Collection Mr. and Mrs. Irving Mitchell Felt

from the studio, ran down the street, with Rockwell running behind in hot pursuit. The artist finally managed to corner the turkey with the help of five or six boys from the neighborhood.

Children were easier to pose than the dogs, chickens, or turkeys, but he needed to devise methods to keep them put. He never asked the children to assume and hold the entire pose at one time. He would prop the child's feet into a running position with bricks or boards, making the model as comfortable as possible. Then he would pose the child's right leg and draw that, and then the left leg, right and left arms, head, and facial expression. Even so, the models would grow restless, squirm, and complain. Finally, Rockwell hit upon a system of distracting them that worked. At the beginning of the session he would stack a pile of nickles on a table alongside his easel. Every rest period he would transfer some nickles to the other side of the table, saying "now this is your pile," so that they could see just how much they were earning by holding still. The nickles made a good shiny pile for the older models; with the younger children he used pennies instead to make even bigger piles that would grow more visibly before their eyes.

The matter of authenticity has always been crucial to Rockwell's approach. His selection of models grew out of this thinking. While most artists of the time engaged professional models from agencies, Rockwell always insisted upon exactly the type required, even though this may have necessitated an extensive search. Professional models have always seemed synthetic to him; he preferred everyday people. In New Rochelle, where he lived during the early part of his career, he would sometimes wander along the streets for miles in an effort to locate the right type willing to pose. In the smaller New England communities where he lived later in his career—first Arlington, Vermont, then Stockbridge, Massachusetts—he came to know the inhabitants individually, classified them according to types, and used them over and over again for his illustrations. This explains why, walking through these communities today, you may be struck by the familiar faces. You have probably seen them many times in print.

Models aren't all he required for authenticity. If he had to do a painting in a special setting, he always tried to visit the actual location in order to get the feel of the place. And so he went to Hannibal to illustrate Mark Twain's *Tom Sawyer* and *Huckleberry Finn* and to Concord, Massachusetts, to the home of Louisa May Alcott, when he was commissioned to illustrate the writer's biography for *Woman's Home Companion.* "Sitting in the studio, I may imagine a special setting and think it real and complete, but when I search out the actual counterpart there's always some little detail that I've forgotten and that will make the illustration ring true so that the reader, whether he's ever seen such a place or not, says immediately, 'that's it; that's true.'"

In his earlier historic work, Rockwell searched out authentic antique furniture and accessories, often spending days scouring the countryside, attending auctions and poking into shops, barns, and attics for the required chairs, beds, sleighs, carriages, and even stage coaches. The costumes of the period were equally important. He enjoyed these costume pictures because they were picturesque, finding modern clothes dull by comparison. (With contemporary clothing he has always preferred the tattered and shabby ones to those that were spanking new. Once he was able to buy an old overcoat which he saw airing on a line only by purchasing with it a bag of rags and a couple of hundred pounds of old iron. The owner naturally assumed Rockwell was a junk dealer.)

It was a long time before Rockwell was willing to incorporate photography into his work. At first he used it only occasionally, "trying to hang onto at least the shreds of my self-respect," but eventually he was unable to resist the advantages that became more and more evident to him. In the beginning, he used photographs for dogs and children only, no longer forced to ask models to pose for long hours. Then came the pressure from the magazines to adopt different angles, new viewpoints into his work, as the younger artists—Stevan Dohanos and John Falter, for example—were doing. No longer limited to the simple, head-on view from his easel, Rockwell could depict a scene viewed from above, or from near the floor. Rockwell was also able to record transient effects, or subject matter located at a distance from the studio.

Characteristic of the artist, however, Rockwell would not take any shortcuts, even with photography. He never adhered closely to any one photograph in painting a picture. He used

Norman
Rockwell

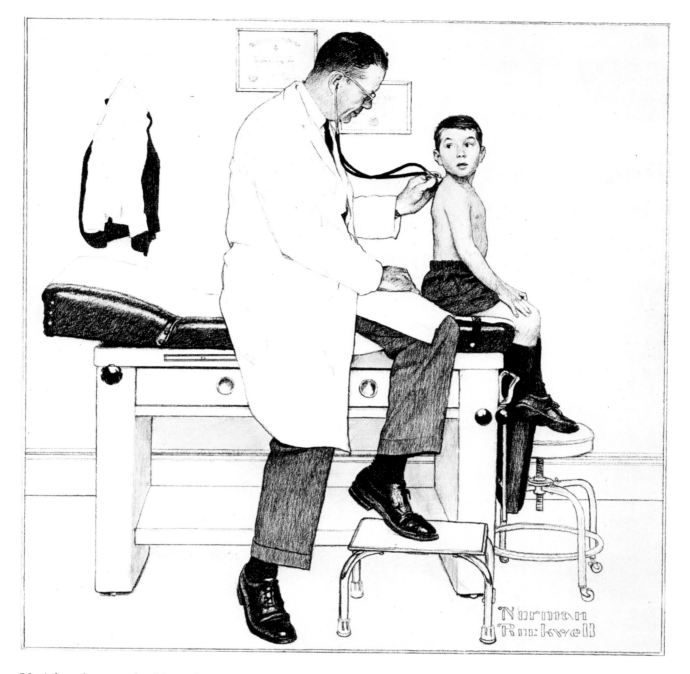

20. Advertisement for Massachusetts Mutual Life Insurance Company, Springfield

an average of seventy-five to one hundred photographs for a single *Post* cover, for example, taking details from each and incorporating them into a whole. Using a photographer (he never took the pictures himself), Rockwell created small stage productions: he would direct his models, shifting them from one position to another, changing the lighting, rearranging the setting, until every possibility was explored. Sometimes he would pose his models singly, rather than in groups. And he occasionally used the camera as a "screen test" to help him decide on the right model for the job.

The photographs relieved Rockwell of a great deal of tension in working. He no longer had to paint frantically against the clock, commanding his models to check their poses for long hours. He also found he could be less literal in painting from photographs. "Working from the model, I had found it impossible to paint a green sweater from a red sweater. It sounds silly, but I just hadn't been able to do it. So I'd had to hunt up the right sweater in green. A nuisance. When working with photographs, I seem to be able to recompose in many ways, in form, tone, and color."

During the time in which he was having his "stage production" photographed, Rockwell was constantly on the alert for anything that may have improved his original scheme. He has been known to make chance occurrences work in his favor, such as the time he converted a sunny outdoor illustration into a rainy day scene because it happened to rain while the subject was being photographed.

Norman
Rockwell

"Can't Wait!"

21. *Can't Wait!* 1972. © Brown & Bigelow, a division of Standard Packaging Corporation

22. Advertisement for Massachusetts Mutual Life Insurance Company, Springfield, 1959

23. *The Meeting* (Illustration in *Good Housekeeping*, September, 1942). Oil on canvas, 29 x 63″.
Collection Robert L. Spencer, Los Angeles

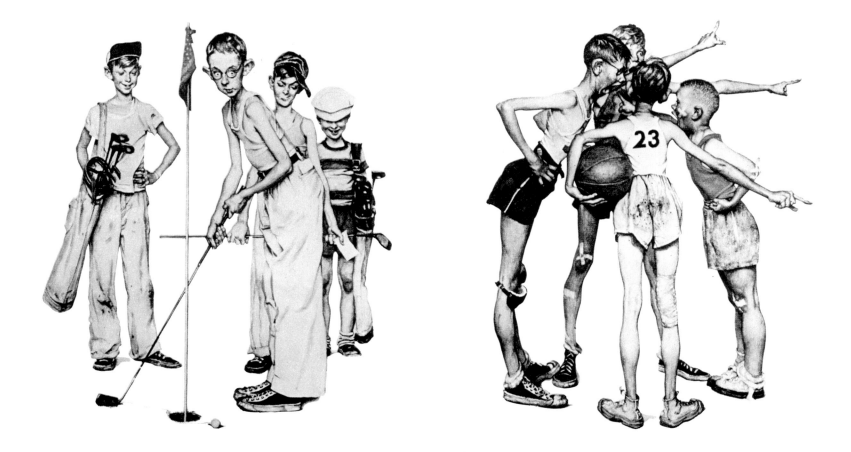

After the photography session, Rockwell had the prints developed immediately, so that he would have a complete set of 8 x 10″ prints in his hands before he started painting in the morning, usually around 8:00. Spreading them about, he would select those he could use and discard the rest. One print might have been chosen for its general composition, another for a particular figure, still another for a head or an arm, and so on. With his approved sketch and his selected photographs in hand, Rockwell then would make a study or two—sometimes more—at small scale to aid him in organizing the material. This accomplished, he would lay in the charcoal drawing onto his canvas, a procedure for which he normally used a projector.

Rockwell's current studio in Stockbridge (where he completed his last *Post* covers) is a converted barn that stands only a few feet from his house. The studio contains three rooms and a balcony: one large room for painting, a storage room, and a projection room. Between the large room in which he would paint the covers and the smaller room used for storage is a connecting chamber that was compactly designed as a projection room. Alongside the single window in the room a wooden panel hangs on tracks. By sliding this panel across the window, the room is completely blacked out. An overhead light brightens the room when the window is blocked.

Rockwell would place his linen, double-primed canvas on a built-in easel, wheel out his Balopticon (an opaque projector), and slip in the first photograph into the machine. The overhead light in the room can be dimmed by a wall switch, conveniently located to the right of the easel where the artist could have easy access to it. Rockwell would dim the light and project the image directly onto the canvas in precisely the position and scale he required. Then he would brighten the room slightly. Now able to see his own markings without losing the projection on the canvas, Rockwell would block in the outline of the first form in charcoal. Once this was in place, he would project the next photograph, taking this section from one photo, that section from another, and so on, until the entire image was outlined in charcoal on the canvas.

After spraying fixative on the charcoal drawing to prevent it from rubbing, Rockwell would return to the large room in his studio for the final stage of painting. Here Rockwell was at his best. First he would stain his canvas all over with a thin, even coating of oil paint, toning the surface in what is called an *imprimatura*. After the *imprimatura* was dry, he would create an underpainting in monochrome, generally in Mars violet, "to get a feeling of warm humanity."

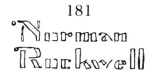

28–31. *Four Seasons* calendar: *Two Old Friends*, 1956. © Brown & Bigelow, a division of Standard Packaging Corporation

After the underpainting, Rockwell would lay in the colors, an unnerving process for him because of the persistent thoughts racing through his mind as he worked. His greatest fear was that he would kill the painting at this stage, tighten up and destroy the spontaneity of the initial drawing. He went to any extent to prevent this from occurring. "Sometimes, just as an experiment, I paint with a brick or half shingle. You can't be clever or slick with a brick or shingle. You have to paint loosely. And then I've tried painting with my left hand or half asleep or drunk. Anything so I won't tighten up, anything to break my habit of overworking a head."

As he painted, Rockwell was like a boxer in the ring: alert to danger, dodging and prancing to avoid the threatening blows, and thrusting out to assert his victory. But the process was harrowing. "It's always like this," he said about his painting. "I start a picture believing it will be a masterpiece. When I'm about half finished I decide it's no good, I'll have to start it over or, better yet, give it up. Then I discipline myself and paint it. Toward the end it improves. But it never quite fulfills the high hopes with which I began it."

While the covers for the *Saturday Evening Post* surely represent a remarkable aspect of his career, they are by no means the only work by which he is known. During his fifty-year-plus career his illustrations have appeared in every major national publication, including *Collier's, Life, Leslie's, Judge, Country Gentleman,* the *Literary Digest, Look,* naming only a few. (His last cover was a bicentennial tribute in 1976 for *American Artist.*) His advertising art has been seen frequently as well for such accounts as Massachusetts Mutual Life Insurance Company, Maxwell House Coffee, *Encyclopaedia Britannica,* and Pan American World Airways. His war posters and calendars have been circulated by the millions and his book illustrations for *Tom Sawyer* and *Huckleberry Finn* are classics.

In addition to these assignments, Rockwell also created—over a period of fifty-two years—a remarkable body of work for Brown & Bigelow, the country's largest publisher of calendars. This company had already been known for their generous contracts with other outstanding American artists (Maxfield Parrish began to work for them in 1934, for example), and they spared no expense in obtaining the best illustrations available for their calendars. The company made an arrangement with the Boy Scouts of America and with Norman Rockwell to create an annual calendar on the subject of Scouting, a series that was an immediate and enduring favorite. ("Take the number one calendar of America, the number one artist, the number one boy's organization and the number one sales force and you have a

32. *Saturday Evening Post* cover, June 10, 1922

combination that absolutely can't be beat," Brown & Bigelow proclaimed.) Each year from 1924 through 1976—with only two years missing—Rockwell created a Scouting illustration for the calendar. Rockwell enjoyed this project for Brown & Bigelow and agreed to paint another series for them as well. From 1947 to 1964 Rockwell illustrated a calendar each year on the subject of the Four Seasons, an outstanding series which was also consistently popular.

The continuity of the two series of paintings that Rockwell produced for the Brown & Bigelow calendars makes these pictures unique in his oeuvre. They are the only paintings that Rockwell ever produced that represented an ongoing effort, continuing from year to year. This no doubt contributed to their immense popularity, and it may have been a stimulus to Rockwell's creativity, for the Scouting and Four Seasons paintings are ranked by many as his most artistic productions.

The subjects of Rockwell's illustrations range from the four seasons to the four freedoms, from cheerleaders to integration, from prosperity to poverty, from Boy Scouts to veterans, from Early American settlers to astronauts, from soda jerks to presidential candidates, a panorama that narrates the growth of the United States from a colonial settlement to a major world power. His subject is—and always has been—the American Dream.

While the scope of his work is monumental in proportion, Rockwell's concepts are always basic subjects reduced simply to human scale. "I do ordinary people in everyday situations, and that's about all I can do. Whatever I want to express I have to express in those terms. I find that I can fit most anything into that frame, even fairly big ideas. Freedom of Worship is a pretty big idea. So's Freedom of Speech."

In fact, this is far more sophisticated a concept than it appears on the surface. Only an artist who is sensitive to the potential poetry in everyday scenes can draw over and over again on the simple subjects surrounding him. The richness here is in the eyes of the beholder, for he perceives what we tend to overlook: human dignity and gentleness, a poignant reminder that we never lose our innocence. In daily life he finds joy and sadness, pain and humor mingled to form a never-ending source of inspiration. He summarizes his perception in characteristically simple terms: "Early in my career I discovered that funny ideas, pure gags, were good, yes, but funny ideas with pathos were better. Not only pathos, though; just something deeper. An idea which is only humorous doesn't stay with people, but if the situation depicted has some overtones or undertones, something beyond humor, it sticks with people and they like it that much more.... It's like Dickens: tragedy and comedy, tears and laughs in the same picture to give it a greater impact."

Norman
Rockwell

33. *Saturday Evening Post* cover, October 8, 1938

34. *The Critic* (Original oil painting for *Saturday Evening Post* cover, April 16, 1955). Collection Norman Rockwell

35. *Triple Self-Portrait* (Original oil painting for *Saturday Evening Post* cover, February 13, 1960). Collection Norman Rockwell

37

36. *Girl at the Mirror* (Original oil painting for *Saturday Evening Post* cover, March 6, 1954)

37. *No Swimming* (Original oil painting for *Saturday Evening Post* cover, June 4, 1921).
Collection Norman Rockwell

38. *Fortune Teller* (Original oil painting for *Saturday Evening Post* cover, March 12, 1921). Private collection

39. *Marriage License* (Original oil painting for *Saturday Evening Post* cover, June 11, 1955). Collection Norman Rockwell

40. *After the Prom* (Original oil painting for *Saturday Evening Post* cover, May 25, 1957). Collection Mr. and Mrs. Thomas Rockwell

41. *Jester* (Original oil painting for *Saturday Evening Post* cover, February 11, 1939). Collection Mrs. G. A. Godwin

42. *100th Year of Baseball* (Original oil painting for *Saturday Evening Post* cover, July 8, 1939). National Baseball Hall of Fame and Museum, Inc., Cooperstown, New York

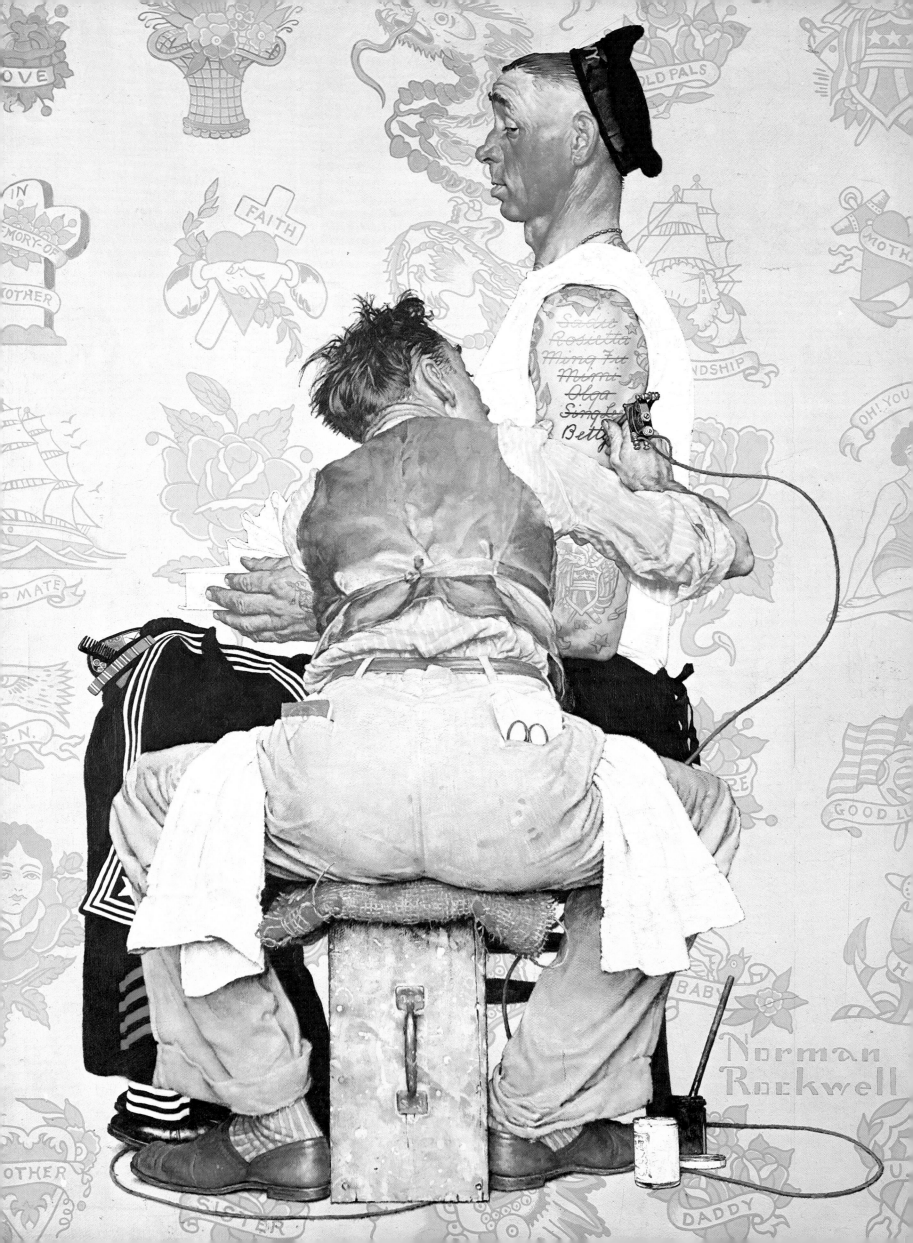

43. *The Tattoo Artist* (Original painting for *Saturday Evening Post* cover, March 4, 1944). Brooklyn Museum

44. *Weighing In* (Original oil painting for *Saturday Evening Post* cover, June 28, 1958). The New Britain Museum of American Art, Connecticut. Sanford Low Memorial Collection of American Illustration

45. Original oil painting for *Saturday Evening Post* cover, April 6, 1946. Collection Newell J. Ward Jr.

46. *The Watchmaker* (Original oil painting for The Watchmakers of Switzerland advertisement,1948, New York and Bienne, Switzerland)

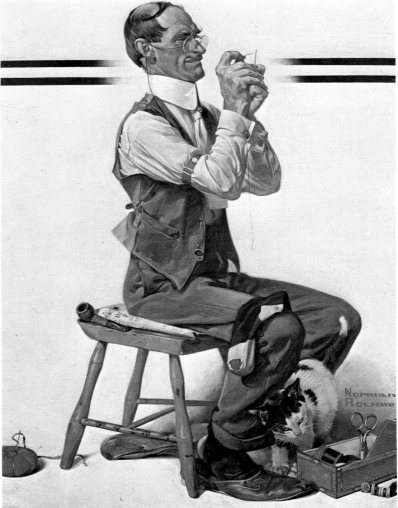

47. *Man Threading a Needle* (Original oil painting for *Saturday Evening Post* cover, April 8, 1922)

48. *Saying Grace* (Original oil painting for *Saturday Evening Post* cover, November 24, 1951). Collection Mr. and Mrs. Ken Stuart

49. *Shuffleton's Barber Shop* (Original oil painting for *Saturday Evening Post* cover, April 29, 1950). Collection Norman Rockwell

50. *Freedom from Want* (Original oil painting for poster, 1943). Collection Norman Rockwell

51. *Bing Crosby* (Part of a promotional series for 1966 movie "Stagecoach")

52. *Mongolian Man.* Collection Norman Rockwell

53. *Russian.* Collection Norman Rockwell

54. *Mary Rockwell and Erik Erikson.* Oil on canvas, 29½ x 27″

56. *Russian Woman.* 1962–64. Collection Norman Rockwell

55. *Profile of a Woman.* 1962–64. Collection Norman Rockwell

57. *Sheik* (Painting for Pan American Airways, 1957). Collection Pan American Airways

58. *Mongolian.* Collection Norman Rockwell

59. *Man with Turban*. 1962–64. Collection Norman Rockwell

60. *Celebration* (Original oil painting for *American Artist* cover, July, 1976). © 1976 Billboard Publications Inc.

1. *The Weaker Sex* (Published in *Collier's*, 1903)

Charles Dana Gibson

2. "It's an Ill Wind that Blows Nobody any Good." 1897. Life Publishing Co.

3. "The First Day Out: Every Moment of the Voyage Should be Enjoyed" (From *The Education of Mr. Pipp*, Life Publishing Co., 1898)

4. Mr. Pipp

5. *The Moon and I* (Gibson's first published drawing). 1886. Life Publishing Co.

*D*uring the Golden Age of Illustration, American publications echoed and influenced every aspect of American culture—much in the same way television does today—reflecting in their pages the aspirations of the public, the yearnings and secret dreams of a young nation still uncertain of its worth. Of all the personalities to emerge from the magazines during these years, no single creation was more expressive of its time than the Gibson Girl. An entire generation of Americans fell under the sway of her charms. In retrospect it was clear that she represented much more than a lovely face and fine carriage.

The Gibson Girl made her debut in 1890 and remained the most desirable goddess in America for nearly twenty years, her presence leaving an indelible imprint on the American character as we know it today. She arrived at a time when many Americans—with their newly acquired wealth—tended to feel embarrassed by their lack of tradition and were attempting to assert their own individuality in spite of a nagging sense of inferiority. The familiar presence of the Gibson Girl was reassuring to this audience because she demonstrated that it was possible for an American woman to be desirable and worthy, no less noble than her European rivals, and considerably more interesting. The Gibson Girl represented the independent spirit. Although she may have lacked a respectable heritage, she was also liberated from the traditions that tended to constrict her European counterparts. Without any loss of composure, she could appear equally self-assured at a cotillion, on the seat of a bicycle, or in a canoe.

The Gibson Girl was gallant, courageous, self-reliant, the symbol of an ideal. She was the flowering of the pioneer spirit that had accomplished the security and freedom making her arrival possible. She set a style in looks and dress but—even more significant—she brought about a change in social attitudes. Feminine without any emphasis on allure or sex, she was the reincarnation of her Puritan ancestors. The Gibson Girl established a new set of feminine values: by emphasizing self-reliance and gallantry as charming and legitimate feminine characteristics, she sounded the death knell to the clinging vine and to Victorian hypocrisy. Equal franchise was taken for granted in the Gibson world, and some of Gibson's most delightful drawings show women holding public office without any loss of femininity.

The Gibson Girl was equally proficient in sports as she was in politics. When golf was introduced to this country in the 1890s, she took it up immediately; she rode bicycles and wore short skirts (these so-called "golf skirts" were a daring innovation!). She occasionally committed the folly of marrying for money or for title, although she normally renounced such empty social alliances in favor of love and an American husband. She was, after all, essentially idealistic and intrinsically American. By following her example, the American woman need no longer fear that she was inferior to her European cousins; now she could hold her head high. She was undeniably irresistible in any society.

Each week Americans eagerly awaited the appearance of their ideal woman in the pages of *Life*. She was a familiar sight elsewhere in the home as well: her lovely countenance was displayed in reproductions hung on living room walls and in copies of Gibson albums on parlor tables. She was seen on ashtrays, teacups and saucers, spoons and tiles. Wallpaper patterns suitable for bachelor apartments were hung everywhere. Practitioners of pyrography—the hobby then in vogue—were urged to inscribe her image on wooden and leather surfaces throughout the home. As a result, pillow covers, shields, chair backs, table tops, whiskbroom holders, matchboxes, umbrella stands, easels, and screens were embellished by a red-hot metal point. Her face was embroidered on silk handkerchiefs, her charms set to music. "Why Do They Call Me a Gibson Girl?" a hit song of 1906 would ask. Waltzes, two-steps, and polkas were named in her honor. "A Night with Gibson" was performed by amateur groups throughout the country during the mid-nineties, and later she graduated into the professional theater. Shop windows and advertisements were filled with Gibson Girl corsets, Gibson Girl shirtwaists, skirts, shoes, hats, pompadours, and riding stocks.

The creator of the Gibson Girl—Charles Dana Gibson—could have stepped out of his own pen-and-ink illustrations. He came from the same humble roots as those of his readers and rose to a stature in society shared by the gentlemen in his pen-and-ink portrayals. Like most of his fictitious personalities, Gibson was intensely American, urbane and distinguished, very rich, and welcome in society both here and abroad. Nor was the artist any less handsome than his Gibson Man; his wife, too, was a stunning example of the Gibson Girl: they were an enviable American couple.

Born on September 14, 1867, Dana Gibson was descended from a line of New Englanders. This heritage had a marked influence on his character: he retained a Yankee practicality, stern and shrewd, coupled with an unfaltering industry that spurred him on even when the odds were against him. These character traits expressed themselves early in his boyhood when he first discovered his artistic talents. One day, his father entertained the five-year-old Dana with a pair of scissors, cutting silhouettes of animals out of paper. Fascinated with this activity, the boy continued to perform the same operation on his own. He worked at it incessantly, cutting shape after shape from these pieces of paper, retaining those that pleased him and tossing out those that failed to satisfy his high standards. It was years before he displayed any interest in drawing, so absorbing was his passion for cutting silhouettes.

Always enterprising, the boy went into partnership with his older brother Langdon and a little girl down the street, agreeing to profit by his talent by selling the cutouts to neighbors. After he created an inventory of animal silhouettes for display on the steps, the three partners launched their business in the early hours of a weekday morning, the milkman being their first and only customer. The partnership was dissolved by midday due to a lack of clients.

In spite of this discouraging first commercial effort, the boy continued to labor over his silhouettes industriously and when he was twelve, his parents sent his cutouts to an art exhibition, where they were displayed alongside many works created by considerably older hands. From this event, Gibson received his first favorable review from a critic: "Perhaps the most remarkable thing in the whole exhibition," wrote Clarence C. Cook, "are the frames that contain the silhouettes on white paper cut by Master Dana Gibson, a boy now of eleven or twelve years old, but who cut many of these figures—and many of the best of them—when he was but eight years old. In almost every case they are cut from the idea in his own mind, not copied from other pictures, and they are done without any aid whatever from teachers; the work is the product of instinct without training. The subjects are all of life in action. Whatever is done is done with a perfection that we never saw surpassed."

Despite severe financial hardships that beset the Gibson household, Dana's parents made

6. George Du Maurier

7. Paper cutouts made by Gibson when he was a boy

8. *Summer Sports.* 1904. Life Publishing Co.

9. *Marooned.* 1897. Life Publishing Co.

the necessary sacrifices to permit their son to continue in his artistic development. When he was of high school age, he entered the Art Students League, where he studied for two years. (At one point Gibson worked alongside another as-yet-unproved illustrator—Frederic Remington—who soon tired of the tedium and took off for adventure in the West after only a few weeks at the League.) Financial pressures induced the boy to strike out on his own in 1885—he was only eighteen years old—seeking commercial outlets for his work in order to assist his family in meeting their expenses.

At the time of his entrance to the market place, Gibson's ambition far exceeded his talents. His pen-and-ink efforts were still crude and unpolished, presenting little evidence of the brilliance he would display only a few years later. Rejection followed rejection as he presented his work to the awesome New York art editors, and there seemed little hope for success, in spite of better than a year's effort. Like other young illustrators, Gibson soon learned the methods of protecting what little was left of his self-esteem. After being rejected from Harper's once again, for example, Gibson learned to flee down the *back* steps of the famous publishing house in order to avoid the humiliation of encountering other illustrators who were mounting the *front* stairway of the Franklin Square building!

Years later Gibson would reflect on these days of looking for work. In his many drawings he portrayed the distressing plight nearly every young artist endures as he looks for his first jobs, painfully submitting his work before the stern eyes of an art editor. Looking back on these days, Gibson wrote, "When I got out of the art school I could draw no better, to all appearances, than when I went in—at any rate, my work wasn't a bit more salable. But I made up a portfolio of all sorts of things I had done in the school—awfully bad no doubt the greater part of them were—and started out to see what I could do. I visited every publishing house, photoengraving establishment and lithographer in the city of New York. They were all very polite; they even became pleasantly familiar with me, and some of them wanted my work. I would take a bundle of drawings to a publishing house—not skipping the biggest places—and give them to the boy without my name and address, saying I would call in a day or two. Sometimes I would go back for them—oftener I left the drawings altogether, in a desperate hope, I suppose, that they might be used if I ceased worrying about them."

It required the shrewd eye of one John Ames Mitchell, editor of *Life,* to recognize the potential of this young and timid artist. At the time, the humorous weekly was barely three years old, successfully competing against the other two humorous publications, *Puck* and *Judge.* Having been a clever illustrator and satirist himself, Mitchell possessed a keen eye for detecting talent in artists and writers and for directing the creative output of these contributors. From the start *Life* contained the work of the finest humorous illustrators working in black and white: W. Palmer Cox (with his brownies), E. W. Kemble (with his amusing black characters), Oliver Herford (cats and kings), and W. H. Hyde and Harry McVickar, who satirized high society.

At his first meeting with Gibson, Mitchell confessed later that he found the work "reasonably bad," but recognized that the young artist showed promise. He purchased a drawing to illustrate the song then so much in vogue, "The Moon and I," from Gilbert and Sullivan's *The Mikado.* The modest little drawing showed a dog tugging at a leash anchored to his dog house, straining for a better view of the moon. For this spot illustration Gibson was paid four dollars. Elated with his first triumph, the young artist lavished a full seventy-five cents on a large chicken pie to celebrate the launching of his career.

Five years later, when Gibson had already become the starring attraction of *Life,* Mitchell wrote an article on the occasion of the magazine's one thousandth number. He looked back on his first meetings with the as-yet-unknown artist and recalled: "Having myself, as a professional, done some climbing up the slippery hill of Art, I detected beneath the outer badness of these drawings, peculiarities rarely discovered in the efforts of a beginner. For the beginner, as a rule, shows far more admiration for technical cleverness than for the serious qualities of drawing and composition; and he endeavors to conceal his shortcomings by elaborate and misdirected labors. But this beginner had started out on fresher lines. His faults were good, able-bodied faults that held their heads up and looked you in the eye. No dodgings

10

11

of the difficult points, no tricks, no uncertainty, no slurring of outlines. To be sure his ladies, in consequence, were often clad in boiler iron and although he and the Almighty, at that time, were holding different views as to the effects of light and shade, there was always courage and honesty in whatever he undertook."

From the time of his first sale in the autumn of 1886, Gibson's income mounted steadily from $33.00 in that momentous month, to $49.00 the next and to $184.50 the third, precise figures recorded in a ledger by the ever-practical artist. His spot drawings during these months were produced rapidly, and he turned out as many as fifty over a period of four weeks. He sold his work to *Life, Puck,* and a miscellany of smaller accounts, but it was in the now-forgotten weekly called *Tid-Bits* that he progressed from an artist of spot drawings to an illustrator of full-page and double-page spreads. Here he developed not only a more self-assured method of attacking his subject, but a knack for meeting two-hour deadlines without faltering under pressure. Although his work for *Tid-Bits* was not remarkable, the publication provided a major showcase for his pen-and-inks and his name became more familiar to the publishing circle in New York. He continued to illustrate for *Tid-Bits* from 1886 to 1888 when it was re-named *Time* and then was combined with *Munsey's Weekly* shortly thereafter.

By then Gibson's work was already demanded by better markets. He had begun to do some advertising illustrations and was drawing regularly now for *Life,* meeting Mitchell each week for lunch to discuss new ideas for forthcoming illustrations. During these months between 1888 and 1889 Gibson satirized domestic politics, took pokes at European monarchy, gently spoofed the British, and was merciless in his attacks on Anglophiles. Gibson's work during this period was still restrained, a style currently in vogue that resembled the pen-and-ink drawings of the political satirist Thomas Nast. But it was George DuMaurier—the famed artist from England—whose series in *Punch* had the greatest influence on the young illustrator.

By 1889 Gibson was earning a sufficiently good income that he could make a pilgrimage abroad to the artists' meccas of London and Paris. In England he paid a visit to DuMaurier and in Paris he studied for two months at the Académie Julian until his funds ran out when he returned to America. He brought from this European trip a vigorous new style, more daring and assertive, demonstrating a flair and dash that would forever be associated with his pen-and-ink drawings.

With his return came new successes. He was now illustrating for all the biggest

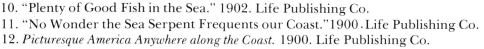

10. "Plenty of Good Fish in the Sea." 1902. Life Publishing Co.
11. "No Wonder the Sea Serpent Frequents our Coast." 1900. Life Publishing Co.
12. *Picturesque America Anywhere along the Coast.* 1900. Life Publishing Co.

magazines—*The Century; Harper's Monthly, Weekly,* and *Bazar;* and *Scribner's.* He illustrated books as well, *Mr. Van Bibber* by Richard Harding Davis, *The Luck of the Bogans* by Sarah Orne Jewett, *The Merry-Chanter* by Frank R. Stockton. And he never failed to provide a drawing each week for *Life.* By 1890 Charles Dana Gibson could enter into his ledger earnings that ranged from six to eight hundred dollars a month, three hundred of it from *Life.* He was well on his way to becoming a very successful artist, even before the debut of his Gibson Girl.

Although he had depicted women before in his drawings, the personality emerging from his pen in 1890 had taken on very unique characteristics, as forceful and contemporary as Gibson's new style. She was taller than other women currently seen in the pages of magazines (only DuMaurier's ladies were as tall), infinitely more spirited and independent, yet altogether feminine. She appeared in a stiff shirtwaist, her soft hair piled into a chignon, topped by a big plumed hat. Her flowing skirt was hiked up in back with just a hint of a bustle. She was poised and patrician. Though always well bred, there often lurked a flash of mischief in her eyes.

The Gibson Girl who soon graced the pages of *Life* each week also served to illustrate stories written by such authors as Richard Harding Davis and Charles Dudley Warner in other magazines. The Gibson Girl had become a heroine. Before long she was seen accompanied in her adventures by the so-called Gibson Man—a chivalrous suitor and squire, distinguished and debonair, yet always victim to the whim of his spirited woman.

Like the characters in his drawings, Gibson soon became a familiar face in society. His name appeared on the guest list of every important social event in New York City. On a cover for *Life* Gibson portrayed two characters in conversation: "Don't you find New York society empty and unsatisfactory?" one asked the other. "Not necessarily," the other responded. "You can take your choice in that respect. There is the Bohemian set, all brains and no style; society proper has a fair amount of each, and 'The Four Hundred,' all style and no brains." So wrote the most desirable bachelor in society at the time. Well-bred ladies yearned to pose for him, and would arrive unexpectedly in his studio (properly chaperoned, of course) to volunteer their services as model for his Gibson Girl. The most prominent socialites of the day—Helen Benedict and Rita Hone of New York, Lizzie Lynch of Flushing, Maude Bennett and Lucy Beamis of Boston, Netta Pinchot and Betty and Helen Campbell of Philadelphia were among the volunteer models who appeared incognito in Gibson drawings. Gibson's active social life ultimately brought him into touch with a desirable young debutante from Virginia, Miss Irene Langhorne, and they were married in 1895.

As Gibson enjoyed the life of high society, so did he find ample subject matter for his

14

13–14. The Gibson Girl

15. "She Looks for Relief Among Some of the Old Ones" (From *A Widow and Her Friends,* Life Publishing Co., 1900)

16. "When He Once Goes Out it is Hard to Get Him Back." 1894. Life Publishing Co.

13

16

15

17

18

21

22

19

20

23

17–23. Charles Scribner's Sons. 1899

17. *The Nursery*

18. *School Days*

19. *The Debutante*

20. *The Mother*

21. *Indian Summer*

22. *The Chaperone*

23. *The Evening*

drawings there. The stage in which his illustrations were set lay just before his eyes: the elegant Fifth Avenue chateaus; the fashionable weddings at Trinity Church and St. Bartholomew's; the balls and cotillions at Delmonico's and the Waldorf-Astoria; opera at the Metropolitan. Other chic spots favored by society were Tuxedo, Narragansett, Newport, Saratoga, and he drew them all.

While Gibson himself traveled freely in society, he never hesitated to mock the more unsavory aspects of what he witnessed. He deplored, for example, the Anglomania then so prevalent, the American frenzy for anything and everything English, the relentless hunt for titles acquired by marriage to English nobility. Gibson resented the pursuit of wealthy American girls by impoverished English dukes and belted earls, and he lamented the American haste to acquiesce to such false values. In drawing after drawing he crusaded against this fashionable trend. (He was quite surprised, indeed, when he visited London a few years later to discover that he actually liked the English, and he devoted a series of illustrations to this visit in a book entitled *London As Seen by Charles Dana Gibson.* As he commented on this trip, "I believe an American enjoys London more during his second visit. He is sure to be older for one thing, and with very little left of the prejudice he once had. He is not so apt to wear a sensitive patriotic chip on his shoulder, and for this reason he will give London a better opportunity to know him.")

From 1890 into the second decade of the twentieth century, Gibson continued to record the American social scene. Most of his drawings conveyed a satiric, romantic, or amusing idea, playing on the simplest cords—love, money, age, greed, and simple moral truths. Gibson derided those who try to climb the social ladder with wealth alone, mocking them for their ill-earned snobbery. In another favorite Gibson theme, the artist commiserated with husbands who were under the thumb of their headstrong wives. Gibson's Mr. Pipp was the character chosen to endure nearly all these.

The introduction of Mr. Pipp to the pages of *Life* was quite accidental. In 1898, on a return trip from Egypt—where Gibson had been on assignment for *McClure's*—the artist, accompanied by his wife and child, stopped in Germany. In Munich Gibson rented a studio to complete a few assignments for an English publishing firm. He continued, of course, to make his drawings for *Life* and decided upon a series of drawings that would portray the American tourist in Europe. Hearing that the famous American artist was working in his city, an aged German model wandered into the studio to ask for employment. He was an unlikely model, a type limited to only a few specialized kinds of assignments, but Gibson was immediately taken with the German's expressive face, sensing that behind this elderly, mild-mannered gentleman lurked a stern and dominating wife. In his face Gibson perceived "a ludicrousness tinged with a vague, elusive pathos, which served only to make those who laughed most heartily love him the better." Gibson decided to build an entire series around this disarming old man. "I had a definite and easily recognized type with which I was familiar, and the rest was easy. All that remained was to put him through the most likely adventures and show him as an American of his sort would appear in various situations."

Shortly thereafter, in the September 8, 1898, issue of *Life,* Mr. Pipp made his first entrance. He was depicted as the father of two beautiful daughters and married to a stout, dominating wife. In the first installment, the strong-willed women of the household command their patriarch to escort them on a trip abroad so that they can see London, Paris, Rome, Monte Carlo, and the English provinces. From this beginning evolved *The Education of Mr. Pipp,* destined to be one of Gibson's best-loved series.

While Gibson may have left an invaluable record of social history that scholars can study for years to come, he also left behind an artistic legacy that has inspired artists throughout this century, his own brand of pen-and-ink craftsmanship, widely imitated, but never duplicated. "We're not that good!" declared James Montgomery Flagg when it was suggested that he was a Gibson imitator. In fact, Gibson has always been in a class by himself. He wielded the pen with uncanny facility, accomplishing unimaginable feats in black and white. The delicacy of his penwork was never obliterated by his swift and daring strokes and he managed to convey, with

24. *Signs of Spring* (Published in *Collier's,* 1904)

25. *Never Too Old to Yearn.* 1904. Life Publishing Co.

26. *The Greatest Game in the World—His Move* (Published in *Collier's,* 1903)

27. *The Weaker Sex— I:* The First Drawing of this series gives a necessarily imperfect portrait of the hero, since he is discovered in the act of carrying on two conversations at a time. (Published in *Collier's,* 1903)

great economy, even the most complex subjects with only a few parallel lines deftly placed. Over the years his work became increasingly ambitious, yet surprisingly more relaxed as he frequently indicated subtle changes in value (a difficult feat in pen and ink), created outrageous compositions that managed to succeed in spite of all the rules he had broken on the way. Effortlessly, he could suggest the transparency of water, the mellow play of candlelight, the fading contours created by a distant fog. Without question, no American artist before or since Charles Dana Gibson could wield the pen as skillfully.

By 1900 Gibson's fame rose to unparalleled heights. His deceptively easy creations in pen and ink invited imitation from countless artists, and copyists seemed to pop up everywhere. Gibson calendars and signed proofs of Gibson drawings induced new subscribers to *Life*. Plays were written around Gibson creations: in 1905 *Mr. Pipp* ran for a full season in New York, went on the road, and was subsequently made into a motion picture. *The Gibson Play* was a two-act comedy based on another of his series, *A Widow and Her Friends*. Songs were written in honor of the Gibson Girls: "Why Do They Call Me a Gibson Girl?" appeared in *The Belle of Mayfair* in 1906, and the Ziegfeld Follies of 1907 presented "The Gibson Bathing Girl." Meanwhile, dozens of women publicly claimed to be the "Original Gibson Girl."

In addition to the large fees he received for drawings, Gibson also derived a considerable income from the publication of his fourteen albums, or "table-books," as they were then called. The first of these was named *Drawings by Charles Dana Gibson* and was published in 1894. Such albums sold for $5.00 each, some selling as many as 20,000 copies. In some cases, de luxe editions of the books were sold at $25.00 each, those of regular quality at $10.00, notably in the case of *The Education of Mr. Pipp*.

All this fanfare over Gibson's work represented a major turning point in publishing history. Never before had an illustrator so influenced American business; never before had so much money been earned from the creations of a single artist. As magazines competed for his services, the stakes grew higher and higher, culminating in the famous battle for exclusivity in 1903.

Robert Collier and his business manager Condé Nast pursued an aggressive campaign to hire the most celebrated writers and illustrators for their publication, *Collier's Weekly*. The larger format of the magazine (9 x 12″ rather than the standard 7 x 10″) attracted prominent artists and their fees were irresistible. *Collier's* had already employed Howard Pyle and Frederic Remington, and had recently signed an exclusive contract with Maxfield Parrish. It was inevitable that they would also approach Gibson, offering him staggering fees as an inducement to bring him into their fold with an exclusive contract. In spite of the tempting terms, Gibson categorically refused to desert *Life*, ever loyal to John Ames Mitchell, who had given him his start. Perceiving that they were obliged to compromise in order to win over the famous artist, *Collier's* consented to share the artist with *Life*, but with *Life* alone, agreeing to pay the artist $1,000 a drawing for one hundred drawings for *Collier's*, to be produced over a period of four years. Gibson agreed and *Collier's* began a publicity campaign to announce that publishing history had been made.

Hearing of this arrangement, *Ladies' Home Journal* suddenly published a Gibson drawing on their cover, making it appear that Gibson had ended his association with *Life* and had betrayed a contract with *Collier's*. (Actually, the *Journal's* illustration had been picked up inexpensively at a second serial right price from *The Social Ladder*, an already published Gibson series, but they managed to create quite a scandal with their Gibson cover.) *Life* published a refutation in 1903: "As a report seems to be touring the country to the effect that Mr. Gibson has departed from this *Life* and is mixed up with the *Ladies' Home Journal*, we hasten to correct a statement reflecting so injuriously upon a close personal friend of this journal. Mr. Gibson has no agreement with the *Ladies' Home Journal*. His work will appear only in *Collier's Weekly* and *Life*." Likewise, *Collier's* published a reproduction of Gibson's handwritten agreement with them and—to take full advantage of all the publicity—proceeded to reprint the same contract in daily papers for a full week. In addition, *Collier's* published a twenty-four-page booklet called *Charles Dana Gibson, The Man and His Art*, detailing the artist's career, technique, and—not secondarily—summarizing the full nature of the misunderstanding. The added

28

29

30

28. *Some Ticker Faces* (Published in *Collier's,* 1904)

29. "Mrs. Katcham prides herself on always having the latest celebrity at her house. Tonight it is no less a personage than 'Gouger.'" (From *The Social Ladder,* Life Publishing Co., 1902)

30. *The Jury of the Future—One that Might Temper Justice with Mercy* (Published in *Collier's,* 1903)

31. *The Social Ladder.* 1902. Life Publishing Co.

32. *At the National Sporting Club* (From *London*, Charles Scribner's Sons, 1897)

33. *Opening of the Racing Season* (Published in *Collier's,* 1905)

publicity effectively succeeded in embarrassing *Ladies' Home Journal* and in generating greater sales of *Collier's Weekly.*

Although numerous trips abroad had done much to increase Gibson's appreciation of Europe and had contributed greatly to the expansion of his skills as an artist, he never developed an affection for Kaiser Wilhelm II, Emperor of Germany. When the Germans invaded Belgium, Gibson urged the United States to enter the war immediately to defend Western civilization. He set aside his jokes about Germany and began an altogether serious crusade, creating a series of strong political drawings in 1916 and 1917 to arouse the public's sense of responsibility for Western Europe.

When America finally entered the war in 1917, Gibson was one of a group of artists who met in a studio to pledge themselves to contributing their efforts toward winning the war. With the newly formed Society of Illustrators as a nucleus, the artists were organized and Gibson—as President of the Society—was elected to the command post. The original group that contained, among others, James Montgomery Flagg, C. B. Falls, Jack Sheridan, and Frank De S. Casey, offered their services to the government without compensation. As a result, the Office of Public Information approved a Division of Pictorial Publicity, and Gibson was asked to direct the group. Summoning the artists each week to Keene's Chop House (and later to the Salmagundi Club) in New York, and traveling throughout the United States at his own expense, Gibson called on every American artist to serve. Flagg, Leyendecker, Falls, Christy, and dozens of other prominent illustrators created posters that were circulated widely, a pictorial campaign that urged Americans to enlist, to buy Liberty Bonds, to defend our European cousins. When victory was finally achieved, Charles Dana Gibson was one of the heroes most celebrated. James L. Fraser created a bust of Gibson to honor the artist's contribution to the war effort; France made him a chevalier of the Legion of Honor and Belgium appointed him an officer of the Crown.

World War I was a sobering experience for a young country, and the America that emerged from those embattled years was very different from what it had been prior to the war: the naive optimism that had so characterized the earlier generation was buried forever in

34. *A Box Party* (Published in *Collier's,* 1905)

the trenches. The public had become weary and more skeptical, and the publications serving this audience would have to be a good deal more sophisticated to sustain their interest. *Life* magazine faced a particularly difficult crisis after the war: not only had the taste of the American public changed dramatically, but the mainstay of the magazine—John Ames Mitchell—had died in 1918.

Returning to his drawing board after the war, Gibson agreed to work with new *Life* editor, Andrew Miller, assuming the position of art editor. The arrangement lasted for a little over a year, when the Mitchell estate put the magazine up for sale in 1920 to the highest bidder. Stunned by the prospect of a new ownership, the staff rallied behind Charles Dana Gibson, urging him to direct a syndicate backed by them and to purchase the magazine. Once again Gibson assumed a command post, and on the appointed day of the auction found himself bidding against the firm Doubleday, Page for acquisition of the magazine. The stakes rose higher and higher as the day progressed. Finally the Gibson syndicate managed to triumph in the sale, but at the overwhelming rate of $1,001 per share! Having the controlling interest in the syndicate, Gibson became the owner of the magazine that had given him his first start.

Times had changed indeed, and Gibson did not possess a great talent for the post of editor. No longer was the public interested in his Gibson Girl or in what she represented. John Held's flapper—the frisky young rebel who kicked up her heels at the Charleston and tapped her feet to the beat of jazz—had replaced her instead. Gibson was dated now, and no attempt to modernize seemed to work. The magazine went into a steady decline, its void being filled by the newer magazines, the more sophisticated humor of *The New Yorker,* and the journalistic flair of *Time* and *Fortune.* Gibson felt hopelessly ill-equipped to deal with the factions that erupted within the staff and he withdrew more and more frequently to his home in Islesboro, Maine, where he could not be easily reached. In 1932 he finally gave up altogether, selling his interest to Clair Maxwell and Henry Richter, who proceeded to transform the magazine into a monthly publication.

35. *A First Night* (From *London*, Charles Scribner's Sons, 1897)

Several years before, in 1905, Gibson had attempted to lay down his pen permanently in favor of the oil brush. With the technological advances in printing, artists were abandoning black and white and were turning to color instead. Gibson wanted very badly to join these men—Abbey, Frost, Remington, Parrish, and Smedley—and paint in oils also. Practically speaking, he had confessed earlier, "I don't paint because I have no time for it. I can't afford it." But by 1905, when he was earning $65,000 a year, he could well afford to make the change.

With his family, Gibson sailed for Europe, at the height of his career, to devote himself full-time to the study of painting. Unfortunately, his courageous plan was subverted by a financial crisis, the so-called Panic of 1907. Threatened with financial ruin, Gibson was obliged to return to his lucrative career as a pen-and-ink illustrator in America. But his desire to paint never left him, and he longed for the day when he could resume his activity at the easel.

Gibson saw such an opportunity when he resigned from *Life,* experiencing at the age of sixty-five the same determination that he had displayed at thirty-eight. Gibson immersed himself totally in his painting, experimenting constantly, painting subjects immediately surrounding him: the people and scenes of Maine, portraits of family and friends. For an artist who had worked in line for so many years, it is remarkable that he could make such a rapid adjustment to tone and color, creating rich, painterly canvases with consummate skill. In 1934 The American Academy of Arts and Letters exhibited about one hundred of these paintings, and the critic of *The New York Times,* Edward Alden Jewell, had this to say about the great pen-and-ink draftsman turned oil painter: "Make no mistake about it, Charles Dana Gibson is a painter. He proves it again and again in a way the visitor is not likely soon to forget."

Charles Dana Gibson continued to paint in oil for nearly fifteen years, working in solitude, away from the clamor of a fickle public, until he died of a heart ailment in 1944. By that time, the Gibson Girl had already become a distant memory in history.

1. *Portrait of Nancy.* 1923. Oil on canvas, 40 x 30″. Collection Judy Goffman Fine Art, Blue Bell, Pennsylvania

Howard Chandler Christy

2. "The Cunning of Lord Felixstone." Watercolor. Private collection

3. *Nancy Holding a Bouquet of Lilies.* 1916. Watercolor on paper, 42½ x 28¼". Collection Robert F. Conneen

*I*n 1892 a young artist named Howard Chandler Christy made his way to New York from Ohio for the second time; his mission was to study art and to establish a career as a painter. He had attempted to do the same nearly three years earlier—when he was sixteen—but his funds ran out before he had reached his goals. This time he was determined not to return to the Midwest until he had made his mark. In his pocket he carried some money borrowed from a wealthy relative and a letter of introduction written two years earlier by Senator John Sherman, brother of the general who had marched through Georgia. The letter stated that "Howard Christy, a young artist from Muskingum county, Ohio, is about to visit New York to continue his studies in coloring. He is a young gentleman about 17 years of age, sober and industrious, the son of a soldier and worthy of the kind assistance of any one with whom he comes in contact."

And so summarized the artistic dedication that had consumed Christy since childhood. "Smiley," as he was called then, had already exhibited those rare signs of talent at the age of three, and his parents did what they could to encourage him. Many years later the artist recalled, "I was four years old when Dad took me to Zanesville to see Charley Craig, a fine painter in his day. He went up a flight of stairs and there was Mr. Craig—a red-haired, bald-headed man—busily engaged in the painting of a river scene. The sight of that artist thrilled me like nothing I had ever before encountered in my brief life. I demanded that Dad buy me a set of paints. Mr. Craig advised him to let me learn to draw with a pencil first, but just the same I insisted on a set of watercolors. Dad broke down and bought them for me!" This marked the beginning of Christy's passion for art that remained uninterrupted for the remainder of his life.

His childhood had been like a chapter from *Huckleberry Finn* or *Tom Sawyer*. The Christy homestead overlooked a tributary of the Ohio called the Muskingum River. The side- and stern-wheelers lumbered their way on this river from Pittsburgh. "The river boats were my first fascination," he recalled in a 1929 interview. "I made friends with many of the captains

Howard Chandler Christy.

5. "The Car Come Boomin' Over the Sidewalk." 1921. Ink and wash on paper, 40 x 30". Private collection

6. *Woman with Gun and Man.* 1926. Watercolor wash on board, 37 x 35". Collection Mr. and Mrs. Joseph L. Conneen

7. *Woman and Man* (Illustration from *Cosmopolitan*, June, 1925). Charcoal on illustration board, 34 x 24". Collection Mr. and Mrs. John K. Conneen

5

6

7

and they would throw out a plank and ferry me free from the farm to Duncan Falls, a couple of miles away, where there was a grade school. The bliss of those romantic early morning rides contrasted sadly with the trudges home through the mud. Sometimes when the river was high, we kids (there were five children in my family) would be forced to walk the rail fences in many spots to avoid the mud."

On his boat trips to school, the barefooted boy would make sketches of the captain and crew. These precocious efforts received the proper amount of acclaim and he soon obtained a certain degree of local fame. "I always liked to do stuff from life. My first model was a cow. Old Bossy would hold her pose stolidly except when the flies bothered her. So I used to give my sister a penny to stand by and keep the flies away." His studio, located in the attic of the house, was where he did the majority of his work. Its location was satisfactory except for the occasional inconvenience of having to transport a live model—such as a neighbor's goat— through the house, up the stairs, and into the artist's workroom.

He received his first commission when he was ten years old: a picture for the sign of a butcher shop. He was paid ten dollars for a black-and-white bull silhouetted against a bright blue sky and painted on a wood panel with house paint. Although both artist and patron were pleased with the results, Christy received mixed reviews from the critics. "Some people objected on the grounds that a bull was not the best kind of meat, others declared that the position of the legs was wrong. As to that, I said, 'get down on all fours and walk.' That convinced them I was right."

While showing a remarkable gift for sketching and painting, the boy exhibited no talent whatsoever for schoolwork. "I always seemed to get in trouble at school. For one thing, I was left-handed, and the teacher always tried to break me of the practice." His slate was more apt to be filled with landscapes than with calculations in arithmetic. And textbooks, for him, were suitable merely as surfaces for drawing—he decorated many such books for his school chums—but they held little else of interest to Smiley Christy. As a result, he terminated his formal education at the age of twelve.

In his leisure moments, when he wasn't assisting his father with the farming, young Christy would paint and draw. A sketch he had made of a nearby historical site—the log cabin where James Garfield had taught school briefly in 1851—was published in the Toledo *Blade*. In lieu of payment, the editor of the *Blade* offered the artist a job. After consultation with a number of wiser authorities, Christy agreed to confess to the *Blade* that he was only thirteen years old, and that to accept such a promising offer might be a bit premature.

His dream was to study art in New York, and to that aim he applied himself assiduously. After he accumulated one hundred dollars in savings, his mother agreed to contribute an additional two hundred, and he ventured off to the city of his dreams and to the Art Students League. In spite of his frugality—he rented an unfurnished room, slept on the floor, and spent as little as possible—his funds ran out within a few months and he was obliged to return to Ohio.

When he returned to New York three years later, he was in a better financial situation, having agreed to borrow money from a wealthy cousin. (Typically, Christy insisted on paying back the loan with compound interest and taking out a life insurance policy to protect the loan.) This time he rented a furnished apartment and enrolled at the Art Students League and the National Academy. Within a year he displayed so much promise that his distinguished instructor at the League, William Merritt Chase, consented to tutor him privately at his famous Tenth Street studio, an honor bestowed on very few of his students.

Christy continued to study with Chase and at the Academy until 1895, when, feeling a financial pinch, he dashed off a black-and-white sketch for *Life* and sold it for six dollars. The sketch, called "After the Old Masters," pictured a bull chasing two painters over a fence, their gored canvases abandoned in the field behind them. When he realized the financial rewards he could anticipate from illustration, Christy resolved to discontinue his studies as a fine artist. "It was a question of food and shelter. I couldn't call for further sacrifice from my family, so had to give up all art or adopt a form that would provide a living." Upon hearing of his decision, however, William Merritt Chase was not quite so reasonable, and it is reported that

8. *Mr. Calvin Coolidge.* Forbes Library, Northampton, Massachusetts

9. *Mrs. Calvin Coolidge.* Forbes Library, Northampton, Massachusetts

10. *The Signing of the Constitution.* 1940. Oil on canvas, 20′ x 30′. Collection U.S. Capitol, Washington, D.C.

he refused to speak to Christy for nearly three years, so enraged was he by his student's decision to forsake fine art.

Although the prospects of earning a living from illustration were certainly more promising than his career as a fine artist, Christy barely made ends meet for the next two years. He managed to sell his sketches to *Leslie's Weekly,* to *Life,* and to other magazines, but the fees were extremely low and he frequently spent more than half his earnings on the models posing for the illustrations.

His moment arrived in 1898. When the *Maine* was sunk in Havana harbor, Christy felt the urge to contribute his efforts during the Spanish-American War. Because of the great demand for black-and-white artists, Christy secured commissions from *Harper's, Scribner's,* and *Leslie's Weekly,* and was able to venture to Cuba as a correspondent. Recalling Christy's jubilation, a New York art editor described the new recruit's last night in the city before he set out for Tampa and points south. "We found him in his studio, with all his paraphernalia spread out around him: rifle, cartridge belt, canteen—everything which had to be taken along. Christy was running excitedly about, counting his new possessions, terribly proud of them, and eager as a boy to be off. We gathered him in—a whole party of his friends—and toasted his forthcoming exploits and safe return."

As chance would have it, Christy traveled with Teddy Roosevelt's Rough Riders, and a friendship ensued between the artist and the future president. From these meetings Christy made sketches of Roosevelt and his aides, including them in a portfolio of drawings he called *Men of the Army and Navy,* which was published as a book the following year. During his stint in Cuba, Christy made numerous sketches during combat—including the famous battle of Santiago—and these dramatic drawings were widely published. By the time Christy returned to the United States he had become a well-known illustrator.

As a correspondent, Christy had also written a number of accounts which were published along with his drawings. In this capacity he joined eminent writers of the day—such as Richard Harding Davis and George Kennan—and demonstrated that he possessed a gift for words as well as pictures. In November, *Leslie's Weekly* ran a review of Christy's writing: "Among the others who have written about their experiences in the tropics, the most interesting is Howard Chandler Christy, the young artist who went to Cuba to make pictures for *Leslie's Weekly.* Mr. Christy had approved himself an artist of genius before the war, but probably no one, not even himself, suspected that he could write. But he can write; he can write in the best possible way, for he is entirely unaffected, and has told in words what he saw with the same fidelity he has employed with lines and shadows in his drawings.... It may be that in Christy we have another Remington."

Because the war brought him recognition, Christy became typed as a military artist, and the publications continued to send him war stories to illustrate after he returned to New York. First he illustrated "high adventure and deeds of valor," then he graduated to soldiers, then sailors, marines, and Rough Riders. He quickly grew tired of this "soldier stuff," and sought a way to work himself out of these restrictions. "'Surely by now I have served my apprenticeship and have earned an opportunity of just one girl—any girl,' I told the art editors, but they could not see it my way and handed me, this time, from *Scribner's* a story by Richard Harding Davis—a yarn as you can imagine, about more soldiers. But traditionally warriors must have loves and those loves must be left behind and worn on ragged sleeves whenever guns stop popping. So I portrayed this battle-scarred hero returning home, now that peace was in sight, to a girl whose features were radiantly discernible through the cloud of smoke from his pipe. She was everything my poor talent was able to make her—young, glowing, tender and infinitely sweet. Thus, out of my own dreams was fashioned the first 'Christy Girl,' whose reception turned me, almost overnight, into a painter of some of the world's most beautiful models."

The Christy Girl became the artist's emblem. She was saucy but elegant, independent but sweet. Like the Gibson Girl that preceded her, she was emancipated, and men inevitably followed her will. She had become a star. In addition to the numerous magazines that carried her lovely visage, she appeared in several of Christy's own books: *Types of the American Girl*

Howard Chandler Christy.

(1900), *Drawings by Howard Chandler Christy* (1905), *The American Girl* (1906), *The Christy Girl* (1906), *Our Girls* (1907), *The Christy Book of Drawings* (1908), *Liberty Belles* (1912).

Inevitably, of course, the question would be posed, who is the Christy Girl? "She started out as an idea, turned into a dream, and eventually, because in those days I couldn't afford an exclusive model, became a composite of the girls who were posing for Gibson, Wenzell and Church. As one of them said facetiously at the time, 'She should have been good; she combined the best features of all of them.'"

The Christy Girl didn't remain a composite for long, however. Fame came so rapidly to Christy as a result of the addition to his repertoire that he was able to afford exclusive models. He married one of these models, Maybelle Thompson, the daughter of an Army officer. She had long ropes of dark curly hair and luminous brown eyes. Their relationship was tumultuous—even after their separation ten years later—the subject of frequent newspaper headlines and gossip columns. Beset with many emotional problems, Christy actively set about to restore his mental health: he abstained from alcohol, became a Christian Scientist in 1908, and returned to a quiet life in Ohio with his only daughter, Natalie.

Christy went back to his family's farm in Duncan Falls, near Zanesville, Ohio. During the seven years he lived there, he reestablished his roots in the Buckeye State, renewing his associations with his boyhood friends and farming his land as he did when he was a youth. His status as a celebrity of Muskingum County has endured to the present, and he is still the subject of local exhibitions and historical studies. One such study, by local historian Norris Schneider, represents the only written information we have of this period in Christy's life.

Christy built a low, rambling bungalow, containing a colonial fireplace and many unusually large rooms, including numerous bedrooms on the second floor where he could place guests and models. Because of his affection for his time spent in the military, Christy dubbed this home "The Barracks." Each morning he would hoist the American flag up the pole in front of the house and lower it each evening. A cannon standing alongside the flagpole was set off every Fourth of July in a patriotic salute.

In spite of his physical removal from New York City, Christy never interrupted his assignments for the New York publications during this period. He continued to receive regular shipments of novels and serials by mail. Although occasionally Christy would hire local men or boys as models, he preferred to import professional female models to "The Barracks," housing them in the rooms allocated for them on the second floor. According to Schneider, "Christy received $150 in payment for each illustration and could paint four a week." Schneider quotes Christy as saying, "In one month I had four serials, either ending or beginning, and I had to paint twenty-seven pictures in twenty-eight days. And I got 'em all in on time, too. Nobody ever beat that record." In fact, Christy did some of the best illustrations of his career in the years he lived in Ohio, as he worked in his studio each day from 9:00 to 4:00.

Ultimately the city lured him back into its fold, and he decided to return to New York in 1915, becoming one of the first tenants to reside at the Hotel des Artistes on Sixty-seventh Street just after its construction. Christy remained in these quarters for the duration of his life, and the elegant studio currently remains intact. In fact, Christy was so identified with the famous building that the restaurant downstairs—called the Café des Artistes—dedicated a room to him in the thirties. The eminent painter executed several murals for this "Christy Room," and they still decorate the walls of the restaurant.

Christy was a New York celebrity, joining a circle of prominent artists, actors, and writers in their boisterous gatherings at the Players Club, the Aldine Club, and the Lambs Club, where he and James Montgomery Flagg were always the life of the party. The newspapers and magazines would follow his whereabouts incessantly. One week Christy broke into print three times with his escapades: he rode a trick pony at the Circus Ball; drew Miss Motor Corps of America while seated on an old beer case; and ventured to declare to the entire American public that he considered the Venus de Milo poorly proportioned, particularly at the lower extremities.

Howard Chandler Christy.

11. *I Want You for the Navy.* 1917. Library of Congress

12. *If You Want to Fight!* 1915. Library of Congress

13. *Patriotic League.* 1918. Library of Congress

As creator of the Christy Girl, his observations on female pulchritude were of continual interest to the public, and interviews with the artist on this subject appeared frequently in print for many, many years. One such headline reads: "Not The 'V' But The Wearer Determines Its Modesty, Says Illustrator Christy." Another reads: "Great Artist Pooh-Poohs Idea There are No Beautiful Women." The ideal American woman adheres to certain standards, he would declare: "One of the standards of beauty is health. We love pink cheeks, clear eyes, white teeth, firm slenderness, glossy hair, animation—all meaning health or imitating it. Health and pep are American ideals. An American who doesn't have them is out of balance, and therefore not up to American beauty standards...as an artist I personally admire grace and proportion above all, plus animation."

Because of his expertise on the subject, he was invited to judge the first Miss America Beauty Contest in Atlantic City in 1921. He was the only judge that year, but the following year he was joined by James Montgomery Flagg, Norman Rockwell, Coles Phillips, and Charles Chambers. In his autobiography Norman Rockwell described this occasion, indicating that Christy dominated the entire affair much to the annoyance of the other judges. The opening banquet and ball, for example, "looked like a reception for Christy." Throughout the week of the competition, Christy continued to capture the limelight. "At the right moment," reported Rockwell, "when the photographers were clustering around trying to get a good picture and shouting at us to smile, move in, move out, stand up, sit down, Christy would appear in a white suit and broad-brimmed Stetson with a beautiful contestant on each arm, and the photographers would leave us milling about and run to take his picture." In spite of the antagonism the other judges felt toward Christy, they would have all agreed with Rockwell's final estimation: "We couldn't dislike Christy for it. He had such a warm, jovial personality: flamboyantly good-natured, boomingly cheerful. And if he liked publicity so much and was so good at getting it, well, I couldn't hate him for it. It seemed to go with his

Howard Chandler Christy.

character. It fed him and he fed it. Publicity and he were right for each other. Like pearls and duchesses or cole slaw and church suppers."

Fashions and fads may come and go, but Christy's evaluation of the American female remained consistent throughout the years to come. Even in 1948, when interviewed again on the same subject, Christy observed the following about American women: "Take it from me, women have not changed much. It is only superficialities that have altered. The girl who went down to the railroad station to wave good-by to the boy on his way to Cuba, to avenge the sinking of the Maine, did not have rouge on her face and her nails were the color God made them. If she was daring, perhaps a tiny speck of black court plaster on her cheek made her look paler. She wore long skirts and the curves of her figure were accentuated in a big way. But at heart she was the same as the slim girls, whose carmine-tipped fingers twisted radio dials, trying to find out about the 'boy friend' who was fighting for his country in Europe or the Pacific. Oh, yes, the young people nowadays think that they are much more sophisticated than their grandmothers whom I drew. Take it from one who knows, they are not. Sure, they know all about inhibitions, neuroses, and stuff like that. They are more outspoken, too, and delight in calling spades shovels. In some ways they are more honest. But believe me, grandma's charm or allure was not any different from granddaughter's 'it' or 'oomph.' Necking was an unknown word in the old days, but sparking wasn't and a crushed leg-of-mutton sleeve was as much of a give-away then as lipstick on the party of the second part is now. Summer breezes blew as soft, moonlight was just as romantic and human hearts responded with the same kind of throbs."

Christy required that his subjects conform to his image of the ideal American female, and he employed the most desirable models of his day to pose for him. None, however, was lovelier than Nancy Palmer. Bearing a letter of introduction, this attractive young woman from upstate New York came first to see Charles Dana Gibson for a position as a model. Unable to use her services, Gibson thought immediately of Howard Chandler Christy and sent her to his friend, certain that her lovely countenance would be ideal for the Christy Girl. Nancy Palmer's jewel-like blue eyes were soft and full, framed by long lashes, and she had a healthy pink-and-white complexion, and an open, irresistible smile. Seeing her, Christy was enchanted immediately and used her exclusively for his illustrations for several years. They married in 1919, as soon as he was able to make the final divorce settlements with his former wife.

Rockwell described Nancy Palmer Christy as "a big, handsome, blonde woman who always reminded me of an 1890s burlesque queen," but the American public must have formed a very different impression from the hundreds of illustrations that burst forth from Christy's studio over the next five years. Her face was seen everywhere between 1916 and 1921, but no single example of her charm is more familiar today than that appearing in Christy's famous poster of World War I, "Gee I Wish I Were a Man." Receiving his assignment from the Division of Pictorial Publicity (of which Charles Dana Gibson was director), Christy devised a poster that would effectively lure young men into the recruitment centers (conscription had not yet been introduced). The poster was an overwhelming success, becoming to the Navy what James Montgomery Flagg's "I Want You" was to the Army, and thousands of citizens enlisted in the Navy as a result of its appeal. (The many posters Christy painted during World War I were his first public service efforts, but were by no means his last. He was a fervent patriot, and over the following years, without receiving any remuneration, devoted himself to a variety of other causes as well, including the Police Athletic League, Red Cross, Salvation Army, and the Children's Humane Army.) In recognition of his public service, the United States Naval Academy elected him an honorary member of the academy's class of 1921 (the only civilian ever to receive this honor), and he proudly wore their class ring all his life.

Indeed, Christy was a man of many dimensions, and he had the wife to encourage him. Since leaving school to become an illustrator, Christy had dreamed of the day when he would paint in the same tradition of those he admired—William Merritt Chase and John Singer Sargent, for example—returning to the easel as a fine artist. The landscapes he had painted in Ohio had pleased him greatly and, by contrast, he had grown weary of dishing up the Christy Girl each time the demand called for her. In 1921, while he was at the peak of his career, he

Howard Chandler Christy.

14. *Gee!! I Wish I Were a Man.* 1917. Library of Congress

15. *Americans All!* 1917. Library of Congress

16. *Fight or Buy Bonds.* 1917. Liberty Loan poster. Library of Congress

17. *The Spirit of America.* 1919. Library of Congress

18. *Your Angel of Mercy.* Red Cross poster. Oil on canvas, 49½ x 33½". Collection Judy Goffman Fine Art

19. *Meadow Wee River, Connecticut.* 50 x 37½″. Collection Robert F. Conneen

20. Folding screen. Oil on fabric, approx. 7′ x 10′. Collection Robert F. Conneen

announced that he was retiring from magazine illustration to devote himself entirely to the painting of portraits. He did very few illustrations after 1921.

The same enthusiasm Christy had applied to illustration was now poured into his portraits. In the first year of his new career he had completed thirty canvases, including portraits of Mrs. William Randolph Hearst and President Warren G. Harding. But this was only the beginning. Christy was destined to become the most fashionable portrait painter of his day and the list of luminaries to sit for him is impressive: Will Rogers, Herbert Hoover, Mary Baker Eddy, Norman Vincent Peale, Fritz Kreisler, the Prince of Wales, the Crown Prince of Italy, Amelia Earhart, Captain Eddie Rickenbacker, to name only a few.

Painting portraits was ideal for Christy, not only because he could finally apply himself to ambitious canvases, but because of the social life that was attached to these activities as well. Christy was an outgoing, gregarious fellow, delighting in the company of interesting people. When he was commissioned to do the portrait of President Coolidge, Christy and his wife spent several weeks as guests of the President before the painting began. For the following three weeks the President posed for Christy four hours a day before the painting was completed. Christy was also selected to paint Benito Mussolini in 1927, and as a result made a trip to Europe as guest of Il Duce, residing in Mussolini's palace for several weeks while painting the portrait.

Christy seemed to be on a first-name basis with nearly every important figure in public life. His name appeared in society columns and occasional items in the gossip columns would suggest a scandal now and then, just enough to keep the tongues wagging in New York.

Despite his status as social celebrity, Christy's schedule deviated little over the years. He would rise each morning about 8:00, stroll through Central Park ("to get the feeling of people," he claimed) and return to his studio for six full hours of painting. He padded around the studio in tattered house slippers and was apt to be wearing a perky carnation tucked into the pocket of his smock. He smoked a pipe constantly. As he painted, he swayed back and forth to get the proper perspective. Holding the brush in his left hand, he would dip it into the tin cup containing the turpentine, then wipe the utensil with a rag, and deposit the rag into the pie plate nearby, before dabbing the color on his specially designed palette.

Even when she wasn't in the room, the presence of Christy's wife was always sensed. Throughout the studio stood fresh flowers in tall silver vases, and birds chirped gingerly from their cages along the windows. Mrs. Christy would enter when necessary to entertain a nervous sitter, helping to relax the subject with casual conversation as Christy scrutinized over her shoulder. She performed as Christy's press agent and social secretary, keeping his engagements in order, preparing his outfits, and entertaining the steady stream of guests who stopped by the studio. At these gatherings Christy remained the life of the party (he would do a hand spring at a moment's notice!), ever robust, his striking white hair and bushy white eyebrows topping the sparkling blue eyes.

The most dramatic event in Christy's career came at the end of the thirties when he was commissioned to paint the Signing of the Constitution for the Capitol. Receiving $30,000 for the assignment, Christy devoted more than two years to research, scouring libraries and picture collections for likenesses and descriptions of the Constitution's thirty-nine signers. Every detail was considered, from the buckles on the shoes to the architectural ornamentation of the room's interior. The canvas was huge—twenty feet by thirty feet—so large, in fact, that Christy was unable to locate any room in Washington large enough for a studio, until he landed upon the sail loft at the Navy Yard. He worked here every day from 9:00 to 3:00 for eight months. When the painting was complete, twenty men were required to lug the 1,700-pound painting from the Navy Yard to the Capitol. It was unveiled in 1940, then transferred to its final location above the east Grand Stairway in the Capitol the following year. It still hangs there.

Christy's career remained active until his eightieth year. With characteristic enthusiasm, he continued to paint portraits, historical paintings, and landscapes (very reminiscent of William Merritt Chase, his instructor from so many years before). He passed away in his apartment at the Hotel des Artistes in 1952. An unfinished painting stood waiting at his easel.

247

Howard Chandler Christy.

21

23

21. *Portrait of Nancy.* 1928. Oil on canvas, 94 x 58″.
Collection Robert F. Conneen

22. *Mrs. Calvin Coolidge.* Oil on canvas, life size.
Collection The White House, Washington, D.C.

23. Portrait sketch of Jo Davidson. March 29, 1936. Oil
on canvas, 42 x 30″. Collection Robert F. Conneen

25

27

24. *Indian and Christy Girl.* 1913. Gouache on illustration board, 50 x 34″. Collection Phyllis Jacobson

25–26. Illustrations from *The Christy Girl*, 1906

27. *The Cleansing of a Lie* (Published in *Harper's Monthly*, 1901). Pastel on illustration board, 37½ x 20″. Collection Judy Goffman Fine Art, Blue Bell, Pennsylvania

26

28

29

30

28–31. Café des Artistes, New York, with murals by Howard Chandler Christy

32

33

34

32. *Self-Portrait with Model.* c. 1935. Oil on canvas,
50 x 40″. Collection Judy Goffman Fine Art, Blue Bell,
Pennsylvania

33. Mural from the Café des Artistes, New York

34. *Two Nudes.* 1939. Oil on canvas, approx. 83 x 59″. Collection
Robert F. Conneen

35. *Odalisque.* 1933. Oil on canvas, 40 x 50″. Collection Judy Goffman
Fine Art, Blue Bell, Pennsylvania

35

1. *I Want You*, 1917. Collection Susan E. Meyer. Courtesy Watson-Guptill

James Montgomery Flagg

2. Original watercolor drawing of Uncle Sam (*Leslie's Weekly* cover, 1917).
Collection Smithsonian Institution, Washington, D.C.

3. "Nobody saw us but the squirrel" (Original illustration for *Harper's*, 1919). Watercolor on illustration board, 29½ x 21½". Collection Susan E. Meyer

4. *John Barrymore*. 1941. Charcoal. Courtesy Everett Raymond Kinstler

JACK BARRYMORE

James Montgomery Flagg

*J*ames Montgomery Flagg was not only an artist of his time, but a thoroughly active participant in the life he depicted. He was one of America's most popular illustrators, one of its most conspicuous bohemians.

The world Flagg painted and drew, the world in which he lived, was the urban America of the early twentieth century. Unlike some others of his contemporaries whose illustrations appeared in several of the same publications—such as N. C. Wyeth, J. C. Leyendecker, Norman Rockwell, and Maxfield Parrish—James Montgomery Flagg was an urban illustrator. He cared not a hoot for designs that pictured a world of dream-like fantasy. He was bored by rural America, by small-town sweetness, and he never developed a taste for the dramatic American landscape of the West. Whereas some of his contemporaries relished their life in the countryside—in Pennsylvania or in New Hampshire, for example—Flagg never lived far from the city, the whirlwind movement of a growing urban culture. He traveled in the orbit of "the well-knowns," the celebrities in the theatrical, literary, artistic, and political milieu of a country struggling to establish its identity. When the theater was in full swing in New York City, Flagg was drawing and painting the portraits of the notable performers and was writing plays himself. When Hollywood films burst forth, there was Flagg, portraying the new stars. (There was Flagg, in fact, writing twenty-four of his own films!) When war erupted, Flagg was illustrating posters for the military. The movement of America was recorded by Flagg in his countless illustrations that appeared in every prominent magazine in the country.

James Montgomery Flagg was an impatient creature, even at birth. While his mother was visiting her parents in Pelham Manor, New York, Jimmy rushed onto the scene two months ahead of schedule and was born on June 18, 1877. This impertinence characterized his activities from then on, and he claimed that he was *born* a rebel.

Flagg's intimacy with New York City dates from his boyhood; he grew up in the cosmopolitan atmosphere of a city enjoying its greatest period. His father, Elisha, and his mother, Anna, lived at various times in Brooklyn and Manhattan, and he recalls his childhood simply: "All happy."

Flagg's entry into the publishing world had begun in 1889 when he was twelve years old, the year in which he sold his first illustration to *St. Nicholas* for ten dollars. When he was fourteen, Flagg sold his first illustration to the humor magazine *Life* (for eight dollars) and

James Montgomery Flagg

5. *Two Arrivals* (Original illustration for *Harper's Weekly,* March, 1907). Pen and ink on illustration board, 19½ x 27¾". Courtesy Berry-Hill Galleries, New York

6. *Her Departure* (Illustration for *The Adventures of Kitty Cobb*, George H. Doran Company, 1912)

became a regular member of the staff, an association that was to last for twenty years. He worked rapidly, even in his teens, selling about five drawings a week. By the time Flagg was sixteen he was also firmly established on the staff of *Life*'s rival magazine, *Judge.*

When he was sixteen, Flagg submitted his drawings for admission to the National Academy School and was turned down, so he went to study at the Art Students League. If Flagg developed remarkably as an artist, he was not inclined to attribute this to his formal art education. Years later, in a letter to the New York *Herald Tribune,* he wrote, "There are no art teachers. Art cannot be taught. Artists are born that way. They educate themselves, or else they do not become educated....I happen to have been born an artist. Ask anyone who doesn't know. I wasted six years of my young life in art schools. As far as any benefit accruing to me from them—I was working on the outside all the time, anyway. Nothing but total disability or death could have stopped me. I had to be an artist—I was born that way....You can't breed an artist. You can only breed mediocrity."

Flagg traveled frequently to Europe, even after his marriage in 1899 to Nellie McCormick. But New York City was his home, and it was here that his career blossomed. Every week some publication carried a Flagg illustration. In addition to the highly esteemed *Scribner's,* Flagg also continued to work regularly for all the major publications, including *Judge, Life, Cosmopolitan, Good Housekeeping, Liberty,* and *Harper's Weekly.* (His humorous pen and inks appeared on the center spread of *Harper's Weekly* for several years, and a group of them were reissued in a book titled *City People,* published by Charles Scribner's Sons in 1909.) His name became as familiar as the writers whose stories and books he illustrated: P. G. Wodehouse (whose character Jeeves the Butler entertained *Cosmopolitan* readers for months on end), Sinclair Lewis, W. J. Locke, and Booth Tarkington. He received so many assignments that he claimed to have averaged an illustration a day for years—and the quantity of his work reproduced between 1904 and 1950 (as well as his earnings) substantiates the accuracy of this estimate.

Flagg was not only a productive illustrator, he was also enormously versatile. The growth and variation in his work developed as the technical capabilities of printing increased. Line engravings demanded a linear treatment, and no artist—save perhaps Charles Dana Gibson—was so expert in pen and ink as Flagg. As halftone reproduction became more prevalent, Flagg displayed his prowess in opaque and transparent watercolor and oils. He worked in monochrome for halftone reproduction, with a full palette for color reproduction. He was equally skilled in charcoal and pencil. He was even a consummate sculptor. No medium was too difficult for him and, except for pastel (which he disliked), he used them all with ease.

If Flagg's cockiness in person was at times an annoying trait, in his work it was his great virtue. His uncanny skill as a draftsman and his overwhelming self-assurance enabled him to attack any assignment with vigor. He avoided trickery in his work, convinced that technical

JAMES MONTGOMERY FLAGG

7. *Music* (Illustration for *City People*, Charles Scribner's Sons, 1909)   8. *The Art Class* (Illustration for *City People*, Charles Scribner's Sons, 1909)
9. Detail from *Selling Slogans* (Original illustration for *Life*). 26¾ x 21¼". Courtesy Berry-Hill Galleries, New York

stunts were merely efforts to disguise the shortcomings of an artist lacking a true foundation or real ability. He considered mechanical shortcuts shameful, sneering at illustrators who used cameras, Balopticons, pantographs, and Lucies. In an interview with Everett Raymond Kinstler, Flagg had this to say of skill: "I would say to you who have a talent for drawing and a love of creating that you will find the greatest benefit in continually drawing from life—or even sketching; any place any time. I can draw but I cannot teach drawing. It cannot be taught. Not drawing from life. Mechanical drawing can be taught—that I know nothing about." ("Artists of Note" by Everett Raymond Kinstler, *Artist,* July, 1958)

When asked if he had to read the stories he illustrated, Flagg retorted, "I'm going to have a flock of little cards printed, telling the real facts as to how vital it is for an illustrator to enter into the spirit of the story and actually know each character before he can picture what that character looks like. Good illustrating is far more than depicting a bit of action as described by the author."

Flagg's greatest output was in pen and ink, the medium he considered most difficult. (Actually, he used the term "penanink" loosely, because his illustrations also included a good deal of brushwork.) Working on large sheets of illustration board (approximately 22 x 30"), he began by dashing in a pencil drawing to block out his ink, rarely making corrections and seldom abandoning the drawing entirely. (He considered the casual pencil tones integral to the drawing and forbade any unknowing art editor from erasing the lines.) Although the drawing would be reduced to a small fraction of the size (five inches, perhaps), Flagg felt more comfortable working large, with space to move about freely. He anticipated the ultimate reduction by spacing the lines appropriately so that they would tighten without filling in when the drawing was reduced. Yet examination of these drawings full scale reveals his expert handling of a difficult medium, effects that are dazzling in their energy. He rarely used any form of cross-hatching, a common procedure for the pen artist, but rather achieved a full range of effects with simple parallel lines, placed with decisive economy. Solid blacks, brushed in swiftly, could indicate a volume beneath by mere suggestion. Scratching into the black tones, he obtained reversal—white on black rather than black on white—so that he could suggest details in shadow. He worked in full control of the medium, yet the work appears effortlessly executed, spontaneous and assured.

Flagg had his favorite models. His wife appeared in numerous illustrations; his friend John Barrymore appeared in several; Barrymore's first wife, Katharine Harris, was also a familiar figure in many Flagg illustrations. The majority of his models, however, were professional. These were the saucy women characterized as "Flagg girls," working their way into all the major publications and at least one (Norma Shearer) into Hollywood fame. A few of these models also worked their way into Flagg's heart: "Many of those girls were *so* beautiful; and artists are *such* fools! If I had this side of life to live over again, I'd again be just such a fool as I was!"

GOOD TO THE LAST DROP

9

The Flagg girl was always the artist's ideal, regardless of the current fashions. In the 1920s, when women were fashionably flat-chested, Flagg girls were always shapely. Every beauty Flagg depicted, every woman he ever loved, met his definition of that ideal, and she never changed through the years: "She should be tall, with wide shoulders; a face as symmetrical as a Greek vase; thick, wavy hair, either dark or light; thick, long lashes; straight short nose tipped up a bit at the end, her eyes so full of feminine allure that your heart skips a beat when you gaze into them. But physical beauty isn't enough. To be really beautiful a woman must have certain fundamental qualities of spirit—serenity, kindness, courage, humor, and passion."

This was the Flagg girl.

Just as his women formed the prototype of all that was beautiful, so his young men represented the ultimate in masculine good looks and charm. If these men in Flagg illustrations appear to resemble the artist, this is no illusion. In fact, Flagg posed for a number of the illustrations himself, and he corresponded to the male ideal as well as any of his models. He was obviously aware of his own good features, and his satanic, carefully cultivated eyebrows became his distinctive physical trademark.

Fortunately, Flagg was already too old to fight by the time World War I erupted, because he did not have the proper attitude for battle: he was convinced that men went to war for excitement, not for noble ideals. Actually, the United States profited more from Flagg the Artist than they would have from Flagg the Warrior. In 1917 New York Governor Whitman appointed Flagg "State Military Artist."

Today Flagg is remembered more for his poster "I Want You" than for any other achievement of his career. Strange as it may seem, this artist, whose work was exhibited every week in all the major publications, was made immortal by this single poster, a minute fraction of his total output. Yet if he is to be remembered for any one thing, this poster is the most obvious selection. Originally drawn for the cover of *Leslie's Weekly,* "I Want You" was to become the most famous poster of both world wars, an estimated four million copies issued in the first World War and about 400,000 in the second.

The idea for "I Want You" probably derived from Alfred Leete's British poster depicting Lord Kitchener, "Your Country Needs You." Flagg did not deny or admit to the similarity, but felt the question was irrelevant. For an artist who freely dispensed ideas, he did not hesitate to borrow either. How well the idea was handled was far more interesting to him than its origin. Formerly a benign old man in stars and stripes, Uncle Sam was transformed by Flagg into a compelling leader who meant business. Never again would Uncle Sam be regarded in quite the old manner.

Posters for recruitment required an official body of artists. The voluntary organization responsible for producing these posters was the Division of Pictorial Publicity launched by a group of artists, with Charles Dana Gibson as chairman. During the entire course of the war the group met once a week at Keene's Chop House in New York City to discuss the government's requests. A "captain" was appointed to expedite the desired posters: he would select an appropriate artist for the assignment, approve the sketch made by the artist, then pass the sketch along to Committee Headquarters in Washington. Upon approval, the poster would be completed by the artist.

Flagg's Uncle Sam poster was so successful that he stopped attending the weekly meetings: "I became horribly bored with rising toasts." Although he continued to be a member of the group, he worked alone, and during the course of the war he designed forty-six posters.

The New York Public Library on Forty-second Street became the forum for publicity campaigns during World War I. A crowd would gather on the steps to watch the artists paint recruitment posters; entertainers came to perform on the steps; thousand-dollar Liberty Bonds were sold in exchange for portrait drawings. The illustrator Arthur William Brown recalled his collaboration with Flagg on the Library steps: "Flagg did the figures and I smeared in the background. We used live models and, with a girl wrapped in stars and stripes, we did one on a scaffold high up in Times Square. The wind was strong; the street below looked safe and inviting."

JAMES MONTGOMERY FLAGG

YOUR BEST GIRL NUMBER

Life

PRICE 10 CENTS
Vol. 60, No. 1550. July 11, 1912

HAS THIS EVER HAPPENED TO YOU?

JAMES MONTGOMERY FLAGG

11

Life

JAMES MONTGOMERY FLAGG

12

Life

FEBRUARY 1, 1923

"God helps them that help themselves"
Benjamin Franklin

PRICE 15 CENTS

JAMES MONTGOMERY FLAGG

13

10. Drawing for limerick from *Tomfoolery*. Life Publishing Company, 1904

11. *Life* cover, July 11, 1912

12. Original design for *Life* cover, c. 1910. Ink and wash on illustration board, 15 x 12½″. Courtesy Berry-Hill Galleries, New York

13. *Life* cover, February 1, 1923

14. Detail from *Selling Slogans* (Original illustration for *Life*). Pen and ink on illustration board, 26¾ x 21¼″. Courtesy Berry-Hill Galleries, New York

14

"THE SUPER-SIX"

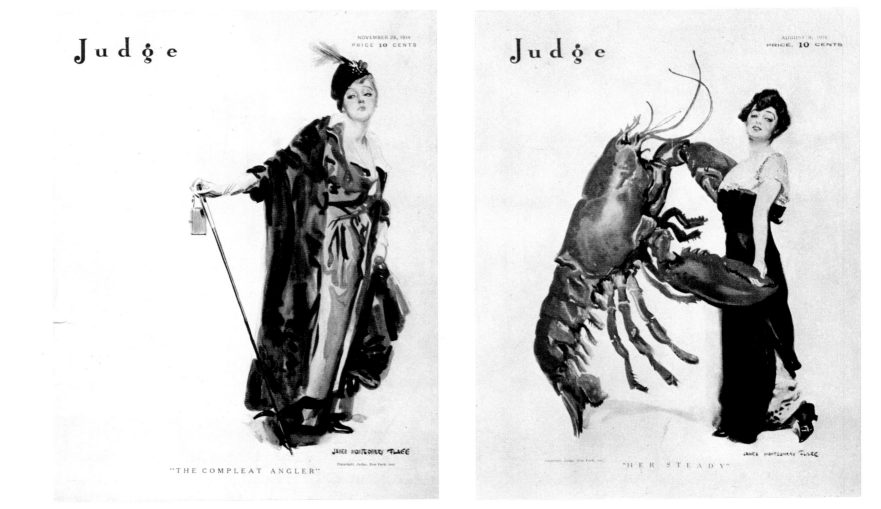

15. *Judge* cover, November 28, 1914   16. *Judge* cover, August 8, 1914

17–18. Details from *Selling Slogans* (Original illustration for *Life*). 26¾ x 21¼″. Courtesy Berry-Hill Galleries, New York

17

Flagg's ink-and-wash posters of World War I were widely circulated. Cloaked in white robes or in stars and stripes, the Flagg girls now represented America itself: seductive and courageous, proud and hopeful. Flagg girls continued to carry the message loud and clear to millions of Americans throughout the war.

Although Flagg was a proficient easel painter, he never claimed to be a fine artist. He was frequently quoted as saying, "The only difference between a fine artist and an illustrator is that the latter can draw, eats three square meals a day, and can afford to pay for them." Flagg's distaste for modern art was legendary, the most contemptible artist being Picasso: "His work is kin to the nasty scrawls chalked on an alley wall by underprivileged monster boys." Flagg was equally vitriolic against Renoir ("His banalities were apparently painted with pillow feathers and lipstick"), and he dismissed Manet, Cézanne, and Van Gogh as charlatans. (Oddly enough, Flagg felt that Monet was the greatest landscapist in history. If this seems inconsistent with his view on modern art, he did not think so: "It's silly to speak of 'modern art.' There's no such thing. Art is good or bad, time has nothing to do with it.")

It is not surprising that Flagg's great hero was John Singer Sargent, an artist who displayed the vigor and facility Flagg desired in his own work. He admired Sargent's draftsmanship, a gift he also found in the work of Velázquez but not in that of Whistler. In spite of Flagg's respect for the artist's talents, Flagg did not like Sargent when they met in London: "Sargent was more English than the English; in fact, not to be too refined about it, his manner was snotty." Nevertheless, he never lost his high regard for Sargent's gifts.

In boasting that he "made friends and enemies lavishly," James Montgomery Flagg did not exaggerate. He was detestably candid and would have been proud to acknowledge that he won enemies more easily than friends. He valued honesty above all: "As a rule the world tries to squash, with pragmatic and worldly-wise apothegms, anyone who says what he thinks…so we live in a world of Near-Freedoms, especially the Near-Freedom of Speech."

264

18

19. *Judge* cover, January 23, 1915. Courtesy Everett Raymond Kinstler

20. *Judge* cover, March 27, 1909. Courtesy Everett Raymond Kinstler

21. *Judge* cover, October 3, 1914. Courtesy Everett Raymond Kinstler

22. *Judge* cover, July 12, 1924. Courtesy Watson-Guptill

23. Original design for *Life* cover, 1909. Watercolor, 25 x 20".
Courtesy Everett Raymond Kinstler

24–25. Designs for *Life* covers, c. 1910. Courtesy Everett
Raymond Kinstler

26. *Life* cover, December 8, 1910

27. Original design for *Life* cover, c. 1910. Ink and wash on illustration board. Courtesy Everett Raymond Kinstler

28. *Judge* cover, June 13, 1914. Courtesy Everett Raymond Kinstler

29. *Leslie's Weekly* cover, July 12, 1917. Courtesy New York Public Library

30

30. "In mourning? Bobbie asked, eyeing the trouserings" (Original illustration for *Cosmopolitan*, January, 1930). Pen and ink on illustration board, 23 x 29". Courtesy Everett Raymond Kinstler

31. "And the world moved on, forgotten" (Original illustration for *Liberty*). Pen and ink on illustration board, 29 x 23". Reprinted by permission of Liberty Library Corp. Courtesy Everett Raymond Kinstler

32. "In short, my dear, I love you" (Original illustration for *Cosmopolitan*, May, 1916). Pen and ink on illustration board, 23½ x 16½". Collection Susan E. Meyer

31

32

33. *Nervy Nat*

34. Detail from *Selling Slogans* (Original illustration for *Life*). 26¾ x 21¼". Courtesy Berry-Hill Galleries, New York

Flagg exercised his freedom of speech freely and chose his friends accordingly. He preferred the company of individualists, of talented, creative men who also mocked the conventional world.

Flagg was identified with the Roaring Twenties, the frenzied whirlwind of decadent urban life. In fact, he was in the limelight for thirty-five years, an intimate associate of the most notable entertainers, writers, and artists of the era. The carefree, bohemian camaraderie of the hard-working, heavy-drinking, stunt-making circle of friends is gone now. Yet when it was in full motion, Flagg was at its core: James Montgomery Flagg was never far from the action.

Out of the spirit of conviviality emerged the notorious New York clubs, the institutions that characterized the spirit of the city in the decades between 1910 and 1930. "One of the most pathetic impulses of Americans is their urge to form clubs," Flagg observed years later. "I think it's a form of infantilism springing from an inferiority complex; a fear of loneliness and a desire to expand the little ego." Yet Flagg himself was an avid club member, and his escapades with his cronies continued to amuse him for many years.

John Barrymore's friendship with Flagg was notorious. At the time Barrymore was married to his first wife, Katharine Harris, the couple saw a great deal of the Flaggs. As an actor, Barrymore was a genius ("In whatever role Jack played he was great"), but Flagg also loved the man: "A great scholar, a great actor, a great occultist, a great drinker, a great swordsman, a great conversationalist, a great companion, a great wit and a great gent.... I want to underline the fact that in spite of Jack's drinking, he had something that transcended this obvious weakness, that shone through the unhappy fumes like a sunrise through mist. People who loved him know that."

Those who knew Flagg were convinced that a life without actors would have been a lonely world for him. He thrived on the excitement of the theater. When the focus of the entertainment world shifted from the legitimate theater in New York City to the gala films in Hollywood, James Montgomery Flagg was not far behind. His portfolio included the portraits of every notable actor or actress of the times. Until the fifties Flagg's charcoal portraits of these film dignitaries appeared in each issue of *Photoplay.* A portrait by Flagg meant an actor had arrived.

Flagg made his first trip to Hollywood in 1903 and returned several times through the years. He raised his glass at countless parties, enjoyed the company of beautiful women, and made many friends (and enemies), as usual.

Finding discretion an unnecessary bore, Flagg never hesitated to declare his opinions of the celebrities he drew and painted. Like the drawings, his commentaries were forthright, bluntness being a virtue he valued highly. The list of actresses he considered most beautiful included Hedy Lamarr ("It would be only a blind and deaf man who wouldn't fall in love with her. She would be the only living woman I would forgive for not having full breasts"), Joan Fontaine ("She has everything"), Greta Garbo ("I can think of no woman I would prefer to draw and paint"), Merle Oberon ("Much more beautiful to meet than to see, even on the screen"), Rosalind Russell ("There's a grand gal"). He had his favorite actors as well: W. C. Fields ("The greatest and subtlest low comedian of his era"), William Powell ("A special favorite of mine, intelligent, witty, sensitive to others, and a gentleman. I'm sure he wouldn't mind my saying I classed him with Barrymore"), Victor Mature ("Almost too good looking, but no swish about him"), Bob Hope ("World famous for his giving joyous laughter to millions. Maybe he *is* funny!").

Even when the joke was played on him—rather than the reverse—he didn't mind repeating it. For example, he loved to tell the story of drawing Jane Russell ("Perhaps the last word in sultritude") at her swimming pool. As they left the pool, she took his arm seductively and told Flagg that she liked him. Enormously pleased with himself, Flagg asked what she liked about him. "You remind me of my grandfather," she replied. He had no comment.

Even in his final years, Flagg never lost the spikey public image he had worked so long to perfect. Newspaper interviews with Flagg appearing periodically continued to portray him as the sassy personality he had always been. His witty commentaries on modern art and beautiful women still appeared in journals: "Physically attractive women are the most plentiful thing

36

35   JAMES MONTGOMERY FLAGG

37

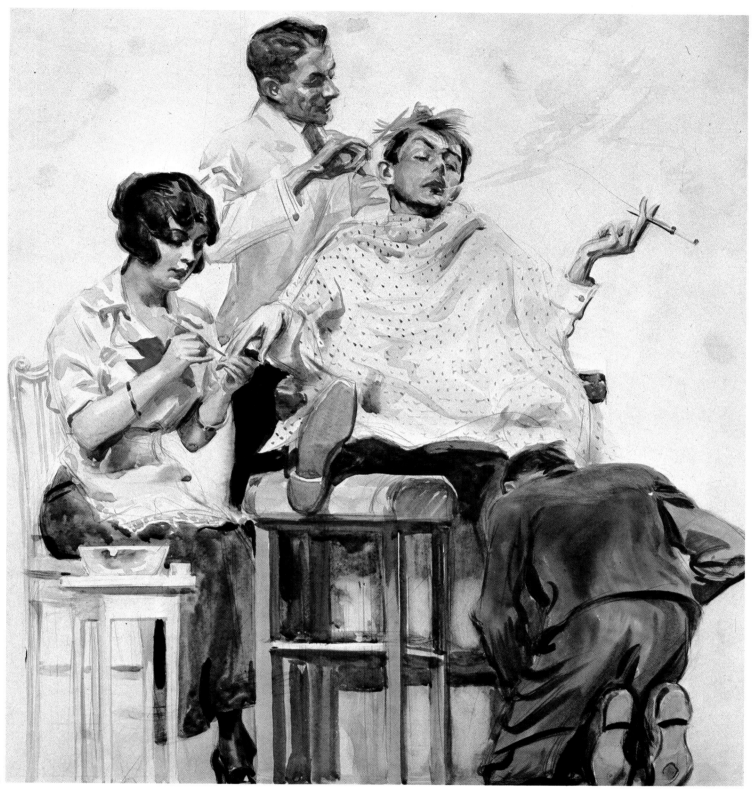

38

35. *Home Victorious* (Original magazine illustration). Watercolor on illustration board, 25½ x 17½". Private collection

36. Design for *Life* cover, c. 1910. Courtesy Everett Raymond Kinstler

37. Design for *Life* cover, c. 1910. Courtesy Everett Raymond Kinstler

38. *A Man of Affairs* (Illustration for *Judge*, 1913). Watercolor, 23 x 21". Collection Sheldon Swope Art Gallery, Terre Haute, Indiana

39. Design for *Life* cover, c. 1910. Courtesy Everett Raymond Kinstler

39

40. *Portrait of Ilse Hoffmann.* Oil on canvas, 50 x 40″. Private collection

41. Detail from *Selling Slogans* (Original illustration for *Life*). Pen and ink on illustration board, 26¾ x 21¼″. Courtesy Berry-Hill Galleries, New York

produced in America. My only regret is that (with failing eyesight) I miss seeing the new beauties."

Flagg was repelled by the values of the new generation. Refusing to withdraw into the serenity of old age, he struck out at the new values, alienating a generation that no longer needed him. For a man who had—from his teens—been in the spotlight, these final years in his studio on Fifty-seventh Street, his failing eyesight and the aftereffects of two heart attacks preventing him from working any longer, were unbearable for him. "I can't stand the look of my present age. All my life I have been a worshipper of that beauty of human form you see in some men and women. All my life I have associated with the clever and witty, the brains you find in some people. Is it any wonder I don't like to look at the physical mess and mental dullness that has set in for me? As far back as I can remember, I've been in the limelight; now I'd rather be dead than be passed by, ignored."

Unlike many of his contemporaries, Flagg lived to see himself drift into obscurity, a painful process for one who never cared about the future. He may have been proud of his youthful abandon ("I've always been more interested in battling life today than in trying to build a dead tomorrow"), but he paid a price for it. In his younger years he made many friends, but the friendships were neither lasting nor profound. His closest friends in the final years were much younger than himself: "I rarely see most of my best friends nowadays. Some I don't see because they're dead; others are practically dead. I'm old enough to be the father of most of my pals, because I don't enjoy people my own age, they're shot and worn out."

James Montgomery Flagg died on May 27, 1960, three weeks before his eighty-third birthday. Appropriately, for Flagg had always been headline copy, his obituary appeared on the front page of New York papers. He was buried at Woodlawn Cemetery in New York, and only twenty people came to pay their last respects to a man who was once "sitting on top of the world."

"THAT SCHOOL-GIRL COMPLEXION" 41

JAMES MONTGOMERY FLAGG

42

42. *Standing Nude.* Oil on canvas, 47½ x 23½". Collection Lotos Club, New York

43. *The Fencer.* Oil on canvas, 47½ x 23½". Collection Lotos Club, New York

44. Design for *Life* cover, c. 1910. Courtesy Everett Raymond Kinstler

43

44

45

46

48

45. *Portrait of Mark Twain.* Oil on canvas, 27½ x 22″. Collection Lotos Club, New York

46. *John Barrymore as Hamlet.* Oil on canvas, 43¾ x 53″. Collection The Museum of the City of New York

47. *Ethel Barrymore.* Oil on canvas, 48½ x 37½″. Collection The Museum of the City of New York

48. *John Drew.* Oil on canvas, 50 x 40″. Collection Guild Hall, East Hampton, New York

47

49. *Wake up, America!* 1918. Collection Susan E. Meyer

Will you have a part in Victory?

WRITE TO THE NATIONAL WAR GARDEN COMMISSION ~ WASHINGTON, D.C. for free books on gardening, canning & drying.

"Every Garden a Munition Plant"

Charles Lathrop Pack, President

50. *Will You Have a Part in Victory?* 1918.
Library of Congress

STAGE WOMEN'S WAR RELIEF

51. *Stage Women's War Relief.* 1918 Collection
Susan E. Meyer

SIDE BY SIDE~ BRITANNIA!

Britain's Day Dec. 7th 1918
MASS MEETING

52. *Side by Side–Britannia!* 1918. Collection Susan E. Meyer

ALL FOR ONE AND ONE FOR ALL!
VIVE LA FRANCE!

Allied Tribute to France: July 14, at 5 p.m.
MASS MEETING on the French National Holiday
to show we all stand together till we win Peace by Victory

53. *Vive La France!* c. 1918. Collection Susan E. Meyer

54. *First in the Fight, Always Faithful.* c. 1918. Collection Susan E. Meyer

55. *The Navy Needs You!* 1918. Collection Naval Historical Center, Washington, D.C.

56. *Together We Win.* c. 1918. Library of Congress

57. *Travel? Adventure?* c. 1918. Library of Congress

58. *Tell That to the Marines!* 1918. Library of Congress

1. "Milkman, Good Morning" (Original painting for *Life*). 9½ x 8″. Courtesy Mrs. John Held Jr.

John Held Jr.

2. *Flapper* (From *Held's Angels* by John Held Jr. and Frank B. Gilbreth Jr. New York: Thomas Y. Crowell Company, 1952)

3. *She Left Home Under a Cloud* (From *Held's Angels* by John Held Jr. and Frank B. Gilbreth Jr. New York: Thomas Y. Crowell Company, 1952)

4. "We Used to Wear Colors on our Arm, Too" (From *Grim Youth* by John Held Jr. New York: Vanguard Press, 1930)

A s John Held Jr. made his ascent into the limelight, joining the other eminent New York illustrators of the day, an era was drawing to a close. More than any other artist of his time, John Held Jr. represented the new generation, the spirit and character of the 1920s. His name became synonymous with that of the so-called Flapper Generation. Although the work of older artists—such as Flagg, Leyendecker, and Parrish—continued to be widely reproduced in all the major publications, the differences between these men and Held were far greater than the ten or twenty years in age that separated them. Even Norman Rockwell—who was actually five years *younger* than Held—continued in the tradition of those older artists whose work he admired. But John Held Jr. knew no such predecessors.

In fact, Held is somewhat of an odd-ball in American illustration. His work was idiosyncratic, bearing no stylistic resemblance to that of any other artist before him. His comic point of view was equally unique. Born and raised in Salt Lake City, far from the capital of the art world, Held knew no formal art education, except for a brief stint with the sculptor Mahonri Young. He did not stamp the well-trodden path to the Art Students League, to the Brandywine, or to Paris. Without any artistic heritage to speak of, his view of life and the way he conveyed that view was entirely eccentric, yet it echoed in a singular way a truthful and altogether authentic picture of the time in which he lived. Therefore, while he may have been an artistic maverick, he was also the prototype of an age.

John Held Jr. was descended from a line of eccentrics. His father, John Held Sr., had been adopted at the age of nine by Dr. John R. Park, a Mormon educator, who imported the boy to Salt Lake City from Switzerland because of the child's evident talent in penwork. Dr. Park had hoped that sound instruction in art and music would one day lead the boy to become an art teacher at what is now the University of Utah, but John Sr. had other ideas: at the age of nineteen he left Dr. Park to start his own career independently. He made copperplate engravings (including in his work an edition of the *Book of Mormon*), and manufactured fountain pens in his own stationery shop. Shortly afterward, he adapted his childhood education with the flügelhorn by acquiring a cornet, on which he practiced diligently for five

John Held Jr.

years before forming a company of fifty musicians. The so-called Held's Band, organized the year John Jr. was born, continued to perform every Saturday night in Salt Lake City's Liberty Park, and played in public at every important occasion for nearly fifty years.

On his mother's side was the Evans family. Grandfather Evans was a Mormon who had migrated from England to settle in Salt Lake City, crossing the American plains only three years after Brigham Young's famous westward journey. While he was employed as a stage carpenter at the Salt Lake Theater, his daughter (John Jr.'s mother) joined the company as an actress. Later she became known as Salt Lake City's first "Bloomer Girl" after she shocked the town by riding a bicycle in public, wearing bloomers.

Born in 1889, the eldest of six children, John Jr. benefited greatly from his parentage. From his father he learned the art of engraving—a skill he used in a rather unorthodox manner throughout his life—and from his mother he gained a great affection for the theater, continuing his involvement there in later years. From both parents he received encouragement to pursue his artistic interest in whatever way he chose. (The Mormon religion, incidentally, had a less marked influence: "To me as a boy," he recalled many years later, "religion was not important other than it was a part of life as we lived it.")

John Jr. drew and painted continually throughout his childhood, working in a studio above his father's shop or in the theater where his mother was performing, and earning a small revenue from these efforts whenever he could. "Mother conceded that my drawing was a distant relative of the Arts," Held wrote, "but in it she saw a living for me, perhaps in a garret. Yet even at that time I was making small money with my cartoons and I was engraving initials on the popular fad of the day, Friendship Hearts. These were small silver or gold bangles that the younger female set collected. The donor always had his initials engraved on the gift. I got to be pretty expert at engraving these at two and one-half cents a letter, after school in Dad's shop."

The prospects for earning a living from his creations became still more promising when he sold his first cartoon to a local newspaper for nine dollars. He was nine years old. By the time he was fifteen he was already a professional illustrator, having sold his first cartoon (a woodcut) to *Life,* and he joined the staff of the *Salt Lake City Tribune* as a sports illustrator and cartoonist when he was sixteen.

As chance would have it, a boyhood chum of Held's also joined the staff of the *Tribune* as a cub reporter, and their friendship at the paper formed the basis for future collaborations. This was Harold Ross, who would—twenty years later—launch a magazine called *The New Yorker* and employ Held as one of his chief contributors right from the start. While they worked side by side at the *Tribune,* Held would entertain his pal with his woodcuts (a technique learned from his father), amusing scenes that satirized in an antiquated style what Held described as "a wild, free existence in an inter-Rocky Mountain settlement with my friends the whores, the pimps, the gamblers, the hopheads and the lenient police who used to know [me] as The Mormon Kid."

In 1912 John Held Jr. took the great plunge: he left Salt Lake City for New York to make his fortune, arriving in the great metropolis with four dollars in his pocket and a wife (Myrtle) in hand. He found employment with the Colliers Street Railway Advertising Company, making streetcar posters, and later with the advertising department of Wanamaker's department store. At night he experimented with a variety of drawing styles and with his sculpture whenever his funds permitted. He continued to work at his blockprints, adapting the style and content of other periods to his own particular sagas. The "Frankie and Johnny" series of linocuts emerged from these nighttime experiments.

Hard work and persistent submissions to the humor magazines finally began to pay off, and by 1915 his illustrations were beginning to appear in several publications, including *Vanity Fair, Life,* and *Judge.* (Oddly, these were frequently published under the name Myrtle Held, although just why he substituted his wife's name is not known.) He managed to make ends meet—though he was by no means yet living in the lap of luxury—until his career was interrupted by the war. In 1917 he was attached to the United States Naval Intelligence agency as an artist and cartographer, assigned to create maps and to sketch military installations on an

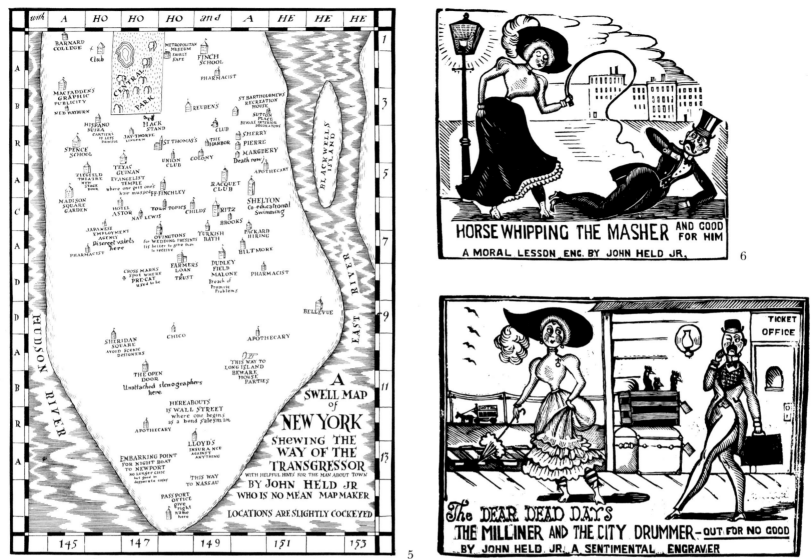

5. *A Swell Map of New York* (Published in *The New Yorker*, December 31, 1927). Pen and ink, 12⅞ x 18¼″. Collection of Mrs. John Held Jr.
6. *Horse Whipping the Masher* (© *The New Yorker* Magazine Inc., 1928, 1956). 13⅝ x 11⅝″. Collection Mrs. John Held Jr.
7. *The Milliner and the City Drummer* (© *The New Yorker* Magazine, Inc., 1928, 1956). 11⅞ x 10³/₁₆″. Collection Mrs. John Held Jr.

expedition to Central America. In addition to these assignments, Held drew incessantly, so that by the end of the war his portfolio was filled with new material. This period in his career turned out not to be an interruption after all: he returned from the war with added gusto and an even more eccentric sense of humor, now expressed in a style all his own.

The sophisticated wit of John Held Jr. appealed immediately to the war-weary public. Held conveyed the absurdity of his generation, capturing the spirit of the new age, and endowing it with a brazen directness that characterized the period. Gone were the days of the patrician dignity embodied in the Gibson Girl. Enter now the swinging, bouncing, jabbering, and altogether outrageous Flapper Girl. No longer was the ideal American female a full-breasted and majestic woman; she had become—born from Held's pen—a long-legged, flat-chested, skinny angel of a girl, nervous and restless, shameless and irreverent. She was a vamp, a co-ed, and her boyfriend—equally irresistible—wore a coonskin coat, bell-bottomed trousers, and a dashing polka-dotted tie. Here was Betty Co-ed; her date for the Midwestern U game (and the frat party following the game) was none other than Joe College himself.

With these pictures, Held depicted the new morals and mores of the Roaring Twenties as his two engaging sweethearts spooned, mooned, and swooned to Jazz. The Victorian age had passed, and a new vocabulary was introduced.

Held on Parking: "Parking is a delightful evening's study. The student and female companion drive out to some lonely place on a little-used road. There the car is stopped and the lights turned out. If the young lady is adept at parking, there is no difficulty. But, if she is one that the student isn't very well acquainted with, it is always convenient to run out of gas at

285

John Held Jr

8. "I'm Very Fond of the Gothic Because of the Lovely Places to Roost" (From *The Flesh is Weak* by John Held Jr. New York: Vanguard Press, 1931)

9. "He Would Keep Us in the Air for Hours" (From *The Flesh is Weak* by John Held Jr. New York: Vanguard Press, 1931). Pen and ink, 6¼ x 9¾"

some dark spot. At this point, the young lady either walks back, or she doesn't. If a closed car is used, there is more room if one door is opened."

Held on Bushing: "Bushing is, in some respects, the same as Parking. A car is not necessary for Bushing. A heavy dew is disastrous to really good Bushing. But on a dry moonlit night, with the windows of the club house sparkling with light, and the faint strain of a waltz floating out over the ornamental shrubbery, Bushing is very intriguing. If a bench is convenient, so much the better. If you do your Bushing at the country club, don't let the lady walk on the eighteenth green in French-heeled shoes."

All through the 1920s Held's work was to be seen everywhere—in newspapers, in advertisements, in comic strips ("Margie" and "Rah Rah Roselie"), in travel posters, in books and magazines *(Life, Judge, Vanity Fair, Collier's, College Humor, Harper's Bazaar),* on refreshment carts, and on the backs of the slickers worn by nearly every American youth. Looking back on those days many years later, Held was sober in his appraisal of all this: "In those years when I started to caricature the time and foibles of the younger generation, I had no idea that it would ever be called 'The Flapper Period'; I was merely commenting on what I saw going on around me. I must confess that I was mainly bent on making a living. Then due to the vicissitudes of the day and the subjects that I drew, my drawings hit upon what was—I say this in all modesty—a popular note. I made so many drawings that I grew to loathe the little characters. But time has dimmed that loathing, so I look back now with amusement, and not a little amazement, to think in this day and age, that a young girl smoking or drinking or necking—and 'parking' as it was called—or cutting her hair short were subjects for editorial comment, and the nation cried, 'what is going to become of the younger generation?' Time has also answered that question."

John Held Jr

Nineteen twenty-five was a big year for Held. While riding on horseback, he was thrown and kicked by the horse. Later Held would say, "I didn't do my best work till I got kicked in the head by a horse." But 1925 was also the year his old school chum Harold Ross launched the magazine *The New Yorker,* and invited Held to contribute. Wary of repeating Held's familiar flappers—already identified with other magazines—Ross suggested a return to the blockprints he had found so entertaining during the time they had worked on the *Tribune* together. Held was delighted with the change of pace and plunged into a fresh series of linocuts (and scratchboard drawings that resembled the blockprints), developing an altogether different style of material for *The New Yorker* for the next several years. Now he had two very diverse artistic sides to his illustration, and to this he added a third: a series of decorative maps (an interest that probably dated back to his wartime experience as a cartographer), providing detailed information on such desirable locations as "A Swell Map of New York Shewing the Way of the Transgressor, with Helpful Hints for the Man About Town," or a "Map of Saratoga Springs, which contains many things that should be left out, and many that should be put in." As if his drawing and painting didn't keep him busy enough, Held also designed costumes and scenery for a number of Broadway musical revues.

With the incredible popularity of his work came sudden wealth. "It doesn't make any sense," Held commented in retrospect. "I used to work all day, days and nights. Nobody believes me now, when I tell this, but people used to send me blank checks to make drawings for them. I could write in my own price....What could I do? I came to New York from Salt Lake with just four dollars in my pocket. I was looking for success and I found it...I guess I knew then it didn't make any sense. But I couldn't let go. I had a tiger by the tail."

Unlike F. Scott Fitzgerald, the writer to whom Held has often been compared, or James Montgomery Flagg—the notorious bohemian of the Roaring Twenties—John Held preferred a rather quiet life to that of his wanton, bootlegging colleagues hobnobbing around New York. In 1919, with his second wife, he purchased a small farm, called Grindstone Hill Farm, near Weston, Connecticut. Before long the house and grounds were overrun with guests, animals, and a Chinese cook named Chung Wi. He remedied this in 1924 by buying a second Grindstone Hill Farm nearer Westport, one hundred sixty-three acres on which he could expand the menagerie with the addition of geese, pigs, pure-bred dogs, horses, servants, a golf pro, and a team of mules he named Abercrombie and Fitch. From a forge on the farm were constructed designs in wrought iron. He rode horseback regularly, was a gentleman farmer, a horsebreeder, avid tap dancer and singer of cowboy songs. Without ever leaving his home or making a speech, he ran for Congress in 1927 and, to everyone's relief (especially his own), lost the election by a wide margin. As the family expanded (he adopted three children), so did the house, until it had become quite a mansion, worthy of an article in the January 1929 issue of *House and Garden.*

All this was too good to last, and with the Depression John Held Jr. was brought sharply down to earth. He lost a great deal of money on the stock market and had his savings, along with those of countless others, swindled away by the Swedish "Match King," Ivar Kreuger. With all that, the flapper had gone and long skirts had entered. In 1931 Held had a nervous breakdown and divorced his second wife. Ironically, what proceeded from this point represented one of the most productive periods of his life.

In the thirties, Held remarried for a third time, and turned to writing and sculpture. He spun out ten books on modern youth, six of which were written and illustrated in a three-year period: *Grim Youth* (1931), *Women Are Necessary* (1931), *The Flesh Is Weak* (1932), *The Works of John Held, Jr.* (1932), *A Bowl of Cherries* (1933), and *Crosstown* (1934). In 1937 he produced "Tops Variety Show," which promoted collegiate talent. As master of ceremonies for the network radio program, he traveled around the country, broadcasting from the leading colleges and universities. Finally, he designed the sets for "Hellzapoppin," the comedy that opened on Broadway in 1938.

10. *Cowboy Tightening Girth.* Bronze, 9½″ high. Collection Mrs. John Held Jr.

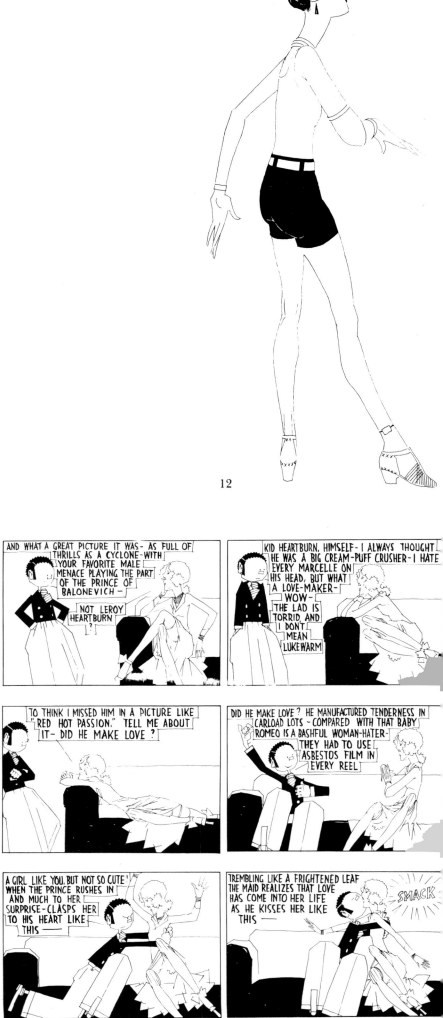

12

11

11. "Okay, Meet Me at the Corner" (From *The Flesh is Weak* by John Held Jr. New York: Vanguard Press, 1931). Pen and ink, 6⅝ x 9³/₁₆″. Collection Mrs. John Held Jr.

12. "May I Save You?" (From *Held's Angels* by John Held Jr. and Frank B. Gilbreth, Jr. New York: Thomas Y. Crowell Company, 1952). Pen and ink, 9¹¹/₁₆ x 9¾″. Collection Mrs. John Held Jr.

13

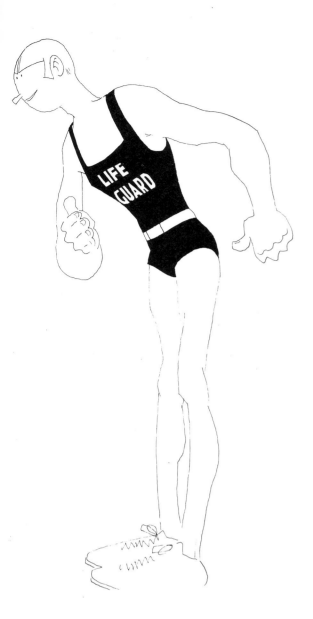

14

13. "And What a Great Picture it Was." Pen and ink, 21½ x 20³/₁₆″. © 1930 King Features Syndicate, Inc. Collection Mrs. John Held Jr.

14. "Go on, Talk To Me Some More, Spug" (From *Grim Youth* by John Held Jr. New York: Vanguard Press, 1930)

16

17

18

15. *Cello Player* (*Vanity Fair* cover). Opaque watercolor, 11 x 9½". Collection Mrs. John Held Jr.

16. *Jugglers* (*Vanity Fair* cover). Opaque watercolor, 11 x 9½". Collection Mr. Walt Reed

17. *Croquet Players* (*Vanity Fair* cover). Opaque watercolor, 11 x 9½". Collection Mrs. John Held Jr.

18. *Skier* (*Vanity Fair* cover). Opaque watercolor, 11 x 9½". Collection Mrs. John Held Jr.

19. "Five Minutes More"(From *The Dublin Letters*, 1931). Pen and ink, 6⁹/₁₆ x 10⅜". Collection Mrs. John Held Jr.

20. "I Figure a Little Wrestling Was the Least I could Do For Her" (From *The Flesh is Weak* by John Held Jr. New York: Vanguard Press, 1931). Pen and ink, 10¾ x 14¾". Collection Mrs. John Held Jr.

21. "What is Sauce for the Gander is Apple Sauce for the Goose" (From *Held's Angels* by John Held Jr. and Frank B. Gilbreth Jr. New York: Thomas Y. Crowell Company, 1952)

22. "Walter Wasn't a Very Good Saxophone Player" (From *Grim Youth* by John Held Jr. New York: Vanguard Press, 1930)

During the same decade, Held turned more and more to sculpture as well (in 1939 he had a successful one-man exhibition in New York), and concentrated on his favorite subject—horses. Many of these were modeled from his own stock and from those he saw later when he became the first Artist-in-Residence at Harvard and shortly thereafter at the University of Georgia. He also turned to landscapes in watercolor, painting scenes of New York and of his neighboring countryside, and to children's books and animal fantasies.

In 1942 Held married Margaret Janes, his fourth wife, and they worked in Belmar, New Jersey, as civilians in the Signal Corps during the war. Near Belmar he purchased a farm where he lived quietly with his wife until his death in 1958.

Although Held is remembered today primarily for his bubble-headed flappers and sheiks of the twenties, and for recreating—through their escapades—the spirit of their decade, it would be an error to appraise his contribution exclusively in terms of this aspect of his work. Distracted by the comic nature of his characterizations, it is only too tempting to overlook Held's brilliance as an artist, a gift that transcends the content of his illustrations. As a draftsman and as a designer, Held was supreme. Held himself deliberately avoided any self-conscious display of artistic pyrotechnics—though he could have performed them all.

Held was unique in a number of ways. His pen-and-ink drawings were constructed with a confident sense of space—like jigsaw puzzles—revealing an astute comprehension of how far he could extend the components of his drawing without danger of fragmentation. For example, his uncanny sense of contour enabled him to abandon a border altogether without disrupting the unity of the drawing. Even when he felt the design called for a border, he integrated the straight lines into the drawing itself, so that they might appear as architectural details perhaps, or a natural continuation of some other lines in the drawing. In other instances, when the drawings were entirely framed by a border, he interrupted the lines here and there to admit some part of the drawing into its construction—balloons floating up into the ceiling perhaps, or a high-heeled shoe penetrating it.

Within the drawing itself, Held was extraordinarily versatile in his use of line. Every detail of the drawing was another design element. He would frequently butt herringbone slashes into sweeping curves, or interrupt diagonal lines with an opposing diagonal. (Held dressed like his drawings, incidentally. He was familiarly seen in a tweed jacket, dark trousers, and patterned tie, not one of which seemed to belong together, yet, worn in this way, the strange components appeared as a deliberate ensemble.)

293

John Held Jr

23. *Argument over Score* (Unpublished illustration). Opaque watercolor, 15¼ x 11″. © Mrs. John Held Jr.

24. *Breaking A Garter* (Unpublished illustration). Opaque watercolor, 15¼ x 11″. © Mrs. John Held Jr.

25. *Golf Bootlegger* (Unpublished illustration). Opaque watercolor, 15½ x 11″. © Mrs. John Held Jr.

26. *Hornet's Nest* (Unpublished illustration). Opaque watercolor, 15½ x 11″. © Mrs. John Held Jr.

23

24

25

With the crazy disarray of lines zigging and zagging this way and that, Held was conscious of the play of shapes that were adjacent to each other, and he distributed patterns of black and white in unusual relationships. By squinting at the drawings, the viewer can obliterate the pen lines and focus only on the placement of black areas within the page. What becomes evident instantly is Held's ability to abstract shapes and to place them in a daring and unorthodox relation to one another. Yet in spite of his unfaltering sense of line and shape as they appear placed on a two-dimensional surface, he could adjust his perceptions easily to three-dimensional space, creating bold and sensitive sculptures very different from his drawings.

If his gift for design was great, Held's draftsmanship was equally proficient. With an economy of strokes he could suggest value, volume, texture, perspective; yet he adhered to none of the traditional rules of drawing. His subjects, twisted about into some of the most unlikely poses, were convincingly portrayed in contour, elastic bodies shaped by Held's will. He could draw anything well, especially animals, for which he had a special fondness (and which, oddly enough, were more individualized in their depiction than his humans).

Held carried his particular talent for black and white into his blockprints and scratchboards with ease. Here he used massive line—very different from the delicate strokes of his pen and inks—and tended to work in reverse, from black to white, rather than from white to black. In these he adopted not only a different technique, but an altogether different approach as well, an almost crude style, reminiscent of the woodcuts from an earlier time, and narrating stories from the Gay Nineties rather than from the Roaring Twenties.

Held was not restricted to black and white, however, for he was a most unusual colorist as well. He had a whimsical palette—if such a word can be applied to color—heightening the humor of his comic work with an array of pinks, yellows, and browns placed in the most bizarre relationship! In his landscapes, painted later, Held continued to experiment further with unusual techniques in handling watercolor. Here he freely used sediment washes, pointillism, and even flat, opaque applications of color when it suited him, never falling back on the time-honored, traditional rules dictating the handling of the medium.

Held's creative mind knew no bounds and he explored every outlet for its expression: writing, painting, sculpture, costume and set design. In the end, he had lived according to the credo put forth in his own book *Crosstown:* "Don't ever begin to believe that when you get to a certain point you're there. Don't ever put a limit to what you want to be, because when you get to that place you're nowhere. Don't ever set yourself a stopping place, because maybe that's just the beginning."

John Held Jr

28. *Sitting Pretty* (*Life* cover). Watercolor, 14½ x 11¼″. Collection Mrs. John Held Jr.

29. *Spring Blossoms* (Unpublished calendar). Opaque watercolor, 10 x 20″. © Mrs. John Held Jr.

30. *Haying* (Unpublished calendar). Opaque watercolor, 10¼ x 18″. © Mrs. John Held Jr.

31. *Harvest and Gulls* (Unpublished calendar). Opaque watercolor, 10½ x 20″. © Mrs. John Held Jr.

32. *Gulls Following Plow* (Unpublished calendar). Opaque watercolor, 10¼ x 18″. © Mrs. John Held Jr.

33. *Cows Watching Plane* (Unpublished calendar). Opaque watercolor, 10 x 20″. © Mrs. John Held Jr.

35

36

34. *Indian Satyr and Goats* (Unpublished calendar). Opaque watercolor, 20 x 15¼". © Mrs. John Held Jr.

35. *Cowboy St. Francis* (Unpublished calendar). Opaque watercolor, 20 x 15". © Mrs. John Held Jr.

36. *Satyr Cowboys* (Unpublished calendar). Opaque watercolor, 20 x15". © Mrs. John Held Jr.

37. *Cowboy's Grave* (Unpublished calendar). Opaque watercolor, 9½ x 19½". © Mrs. John Held Jr.

37

Selected Bibliography

Allen, Douglas (ed.). *Frederic Remington's Own Outdoors.* New York: The Dial Press, 1964.

———— and Allen, Douglas, Jr. *N. C. Wyeth.* New York: Crown Publishers, 1971.

Buechner, Thomas. *Norman Rockwell: Artist and Illustrator.* New York: Harry N. Abrams, 1970.

Downey, Fairfax. *Portrait of an Era as Drawn by C. D. Gibson.* New York: Charles Scribner's Sons, 1936.

Elzea, Rowland. *Howard Pyle.* New York: A Peacock Press/Bantam Book, 1975.

Exman, Eugene. *The Brothers Harper.* New York: Harper & Row, Publishers, 1965.

————. *The House of Harper.* New York: Harper & Row, Publishers, 1967.

Flagg, James Montgomery. *Roses and Buckshot.* New York: G. P. Putnam's Sons, 1946.

Guptill, Arthur. *Norman Rockwell, Illustrator.* New York: Watson-Guptill Publications, 1946 and 1970.

Hassrick, Peter. *Frederic Remington.* New York: Harry N. Abrams, 1973.

Kramer, Dale. *Ross and the New Yorker.* New York: Doubleday and Co., 1951.

Ludwig, Coy. *Maxfield Parrish.* New York: Watson-Guptill Publications, 1973.

McLanathan, Richard. *The Brandywine Heritage.* Greenwich: New York Graphic Society, 1971.

McClure, S. S. *My Autobiography.* New York: Frederick Ungar Publishing Co., 1963.

McCracken, Harold (ed.). *Frederick Remington's Own West.* New York: The Dial Press, 1960.

————. *The Frederic Remington Book.* New York: Doubleday & Co., 1966.

Meyer, Susan E. *James Montgomery Flagg.* New York: Watson-Guptill Publications, 1974.

————. "Three Generations of the Wyeth Family," *American Artist,* February, 1975.

Mott, Frank Luther. *A History of American Magazines,* Vol. III. Cambridge, Mass.: Harvard University Press, 1957.

Murrell, William. *A History of American Graphic Humor, 1865–1938.* New York: The Macmillan Company, 1938.

Pitz, Henry C. *Howard Pyle.* New York: Clarkson N. Potter, Inc., 1975.

————. *The Brandywine Tradition.* Boston: Houghton Mifflin Company, 1969.

————. *The Gibson Girl and her America.* New York: Dover Publications, 1969.

Reed, Walt. *The Illustrator in America.* New York: Reinhold Publishing Corp., 1966.

Rockwell, Norman. *My Adventures as an Illustrator.* New York: Doubleday & Co., 1960.

Schau, Michael. *J. C. Leyendecker.* New York: Watson-Guptill Publications, 1974.

Schneider, Norris. *Howard Chandler Christy.* Zanesville, Ohio: private publication, 1975.

Tebbel, John. *A History of Book Publishing in the United States,* Vol. II. New York: R. R. Bowker, 1975.

————. *The American Magazine: A Compact History.* New York: Hawthorn Books, 1969.

Wyeth, Betsy James. *The Wyeths: The Intimate Correspondence of N. C. Wyeth.* Boston: Gambit, 1971.

Index

309

Photo Credits

Numbers refer to the illustration
number within each chapter.